Managing Two Worlds

DATE DUE

NOV 0 2 2005	OCT 2 8 2005
NOV 20 2007	NOV 0 7 2007
OCT 1 5 2008	OCT 2 7 2008
MAR 2 3 2009	MAR 1 3 2009
FEB 1 0 2014	MAR 1 0 201
APR 0 7 2014	APR 1 5 2014
OCT 1 4 2015	NOV 1 8 2015

CARR McLEAN. TORONTO FORM #38-297

Managing Two Worlds

The Experiences and Concerns
of Immigrant Youth in Ontario

160201

EDITED BY

PAUL ANISEF AND KENISE MURPHY KILBRIDE

Canadian Scholars' Press Inc.
Toronto

Managing Two Worlds: The Experiences and Concerns of Immigrant Youth in Ontario
edited by Paul Anisef and Kenise Murphy Kilbride

First published in 2003 by
Canadian Scholars' Press Inc.
180 Bloor Street West, Suite 801
Toronto, Ontario
M5S 2V6

www.cspi.org

CSPI gratefully acknowledges financial support for our publishing activities from the Government of Canada through the Book Publishing Industry Development Program (BPIDP) and the Government of Ontario through the Ontario Book Publishing Tax Credit Program.

National Library of Canada Cataloguing in Publication

Managing two worlds : the experiences and concerns of immigrant youth in Ontario / edited by Paul Anisef and Kenise Murphy Kilbride.

ISBN 1-55130-217-9

1. Immigrant children—Ontario—Social conditions. 2. Teenage immigrants—Ontario—Social conditions. I. Anisef, Paul, 1942- II. Kilbride, Kenise Murphy

HV4013.C2M35 2003   305.9'06912'09713   C2003-903914-5

Cover design by HotHouse Canada
Text design and layout by Susan Thomas/Digital Zone

03   04   05   06   07   08   7   6   5   4   3   2   1

Printed and bound in Canada by AGMV Marquis Imprimeur Inc.

Canadä

Table of Contents

Acknowledgements

In response to a call issued by the Ontario Region Settlement Directorate of Citizenship and Immigration Canada, six organizations explored different aspects of the immigrant settlement process for youth in Ontario. The editors acknowledge with gratitude the collaboration of the five research partners, which made the work of this book so much easier and more enjoyable: the Centre for Research and Education in Human Services (Kitchener), the Coalition of Visible Minority Women (Toronto), the Council of Agencies Serving South Asians and the South Asian Women's Centre (Toronto), the Family Services Association (Toronto), and Pinecrest-Queensway Health and Community Services (Ottawa).

We also thank the Ontario Administration of Settlement and Integration Services (OASIS) of the Ministry of Citizenship and Immigration Canada, not only for its funding but for their identification of immigrant youth as particularly in need of research; the findings more than support their conviction. Particular thanks are extended to Elizabeth Gryte and Elisete Bettencourt at OASIS, who have provided sound advice and warm encouragement throughout this project.

The ongoing support of Dr. Morton Beiser, Ted Richmond, and Fidelia Torres of the Joint Centre for Excellence for Research on Immigration and Settlement, Toronto (CERIS), as well as of Dr. Carl Amrhein, then Dean of Arts and Science at the University of Toronto, and currently Vice-President (Academic) and Provost of the University of Alberta, has been greatly appreciated.

We also extend our gratitude for the invaluable contributions of Etta Baichman-Anisef and Rhanda Khattar in producing an amalgamated report from the research. The work of Jadranka Bacic in creating a comprehensive overview of the research literature in the area and the efforts of Siobhan Kilbride in editing down the original CERIS report are gratefully acknowledged. We would also like to thank Susan Keeble for helping us assemble and type parts of the original report, and our debt for the invaluable assistance of Melodie Mayson with the editing and proofreading of the manuscript is considerable and gladly proclaimed.

INTRODUCTION

PAUL ANISEF AND KENISE MURPHY KILBRIDE
*Joint Centre of Excellence for Research on Immigration
and Settlement, Toronto*

Of the approximately 200,000 individuals—both immigrants and refugees—who settle in Canada each year, about half eventually relocate somewhere in Ontario. Over 70,000 of these people arrive in Toronto every year. Data from the 1996 census show that 77.2 per cent of all immigrants to Canada between 1991 and 1996 came from Asia, the Middle East, Africa, Central and South America, and the Caribbean (Statistics Canada, 1996). Today, the immigrant population in Toronto constitutes 48 per cent of the population of the entire city and it is likely that this influx will continue to escalate as the annual target rate for immigrants and refugees has been set at over 225,000.

With this volume and diversity of immigration, it is both obvious and critical that service providers and policy-makers must improve settlement service practices for their growing number of immigrant and refugee clients. Such improvements must be initiated not only to accommodate the needs of the sheer magnitude of newcomers to Ontario but also to facilitate their adaptation in ways that will respect their languages, cultural traditions, and lifestyles, and help to support new types of Canadian identity formation. As Ontario had earlier moved from a predominantly Anglo identity to embrace Italian-Canadian, Greco-Canadian, and many other types of Euro-Canadian identities, so now its challenge has been to become more broadly inclusive. The post-World War II challenge to embrace other European identities has become a global reach to be more inclusive, and the youth in this study offered many suggestions for meeting this challenge.

RATIONALE FOR RESEARCH ON YOUTH

A significant area of concern for service providers and policy-makers is the country's newcomer youth population. As today's growth in immigrant settlement continues to rise, many youth under the age of twenty-four also settle in the Toronto area with their families. According to a 1998 report by the Canadian Council on Social Development (CCSD) on the progress of Canada's children, there is a notable growth in the number of newcomer youth residing in Canada, especially in urban centres (Canadian Council on Social Development, 1998b). For example, between 1991 and 1996, the number of immigrant youth in Canada escalated by 26 per cent. In addition, 30 per cent of the youth population in Toronto is composed of immigrants.

As this population group is growing and the federal government is committed to increasing its current level of immigrant intake, it is important to ensure that the needs and concerns of newcomer youth are addressed effectively. This requires obtaining relevant and current information about immigrant youth issues, conducting research that specifically targets newcomer youth, and providing adequate settlement services that can meet the diverse needs of this group. Finding ways to integrate cultural diversity and to help individuals retain and express their own uniqueness is one of the major challenges that service providers and policy-makers face. Consequently, a more holistic perspective in understanding the unique experiences of newcomer youth is needed (McDonnell & Hill, 1993, pp. 101–111). In the past, research has focused predominantly on the general needs and concerns of immigrant adults and children of elementary school ages. There is, however, a lack of research that explores the intersection of youth issues and immigrant issues. *Managing Two Worlds* identifies and examines a range of challenges and needs encountered by immigrant youth as they make the transition to life in Canada, exploring issues that include personal adaptation to a new culture; coping with a new and often different school environment; adjusting to changed family dynamics that accompany immigration; and finding employment in a new country. In order to determine the types of programs and services that are beneficial to immigrant youth in responding to these types of issues, it is important to identify and catalogue the diverse needs among youth of different ethnocultural backgrounds.

RESEARCH OBJECTIVES OF THE SIX PARTNERS

In view of the paucity of existing information about the issues of immigrant youth and of the growing need to respond to them effectively, the Ontario Administration of Settlement and Integration Services of the Department of Citizenship and Immigration Canada issued a call for proposals on immigrant youth needs to explore the different aspects of the youth immigrant settlement process in terms of "best practices" for youth. Six organizations were awarded the commission. They are: the Joint Centre of Excellence for Research on Immigration and Settlement, Toronto (CERIS); the Family Service Association of Toronto (FSA); the Centre for Research and Education in Health Services, Kitchener/Waterloo (CREHS); the Council of Agencies Serving South Asians (CASSA) working as a partner agency to the South Asian Women's Centre (SAWC); Pinecrest-Queensway Health and Community Services, Ottawa/Carlton (PQHCS); and the Coalition of Visible Minority Women (CVMW). The project's objectives were to identify the needs, experiences, and concerns of immigrant youth from different cultural and racial backgrounds and to ascertain the gaps between their perceived needs and existing services.

The six organizations that conducted this research into the needs of immigrant youth all have extensive previous experience dealing with issues of settlement, immigration, and youth concerns. Based on their previous experience and work, moreover, each brought a unique perspective to the project by focusing on different contexts and aspects of the youth experience and settlement process. Methods included extensive literature reviews; key informant interviews; focus groups of youth, family members, and service providers; psychological tests; and surveys.

Emphasis was on integrating the concerns of parents, community members, and service providers, as these concerns tend to describe more clearly the issues that immigrant families and youth confront. The specific objectives of the organizations reflect these aims, while also focusing on areas that concern the particular work of each organization. The unique voice of each group is therefore clearly heard in its report, as it speaks to what is central to its experience with youth.

(1) The Centre for Research and Education in Health Services, Kitchener/Waterloo (CREHS)

CREHS's work has been to understand and examine the challenges faced by immigrant youth and their families in the Kitchener/Waterloo area throughout the settlement process and to identify gaps between youth's expectations and the existing service programs and facilities. It also sought to identify concrete strategies and practices for supporting the integration of newcomer youth from diverse cultural and racial backgrounds into the region. The process of carrying out research in this manner became an indirect way of enhancing services for immigrant youth, as it focused on the lives of youth within the family, school, and community, and it allowed youth to voice their concerns and problems so that they could take ownership of the knowledge created and act on it. The participatory action research method that CREHS uses in this and its many other projects reflects its commitment to empowering those with whom it works, and its practice of publicly reporting back to its research participants is a unique contribution to their communities. This commitment to empowerment will be clearly seen in their chapter.

(2) The Council of Agencies Serving South Asians working as a partner agency to the South Asian Women's Centre (CASSA/SAWC)

The focus CASSA/SAWC took reflects both organizations' long commitment to "exploring, deciphering and decoding the lived realities of South Asian youth living in Toronto." In terms of their collaborative study, the partnering agencies hoped to understand how cultural and racial differences affect youth's identity formation, how coping mechanisms are utilized to facilitate settlement, and how the competing needs of both conforming to and resisting the host culture influence the process of settlement for youth. The research identified the issues faced by South Asian youth and their families in settling into life in the Greater Toronto area (GTA) and illuminates the diversity within the group, with differences arising from nationality, ethnicity, religion, social class, and gender. The authors' focus on racism articulates their own reflections on the findings of their research, and offers a unique perspective on the experience of young immigrants who find themselves "visible minorities" in Canada. In addition, the voices of the young people they cite paint a revealing portrait of youth who struggle with conflicting expectations of family members and peers, and diverse experiences, both helpful and alienating, with education and employment in Canada.

(3) Family Service Association of Toronto (FSA)

FSA's approach reflects its unique expertise in psychology and the considerable counselling experience of its team. The findings from this study are therefore a solid counterpart to the more sociological studies conducted by other groups. FSA's goal was to explore some of the psychological factors that affect the settlement, adaptation, and integration process of youth. Its research sought to uncover the knowledge and skills required for better adjustment and integration. The study targeted external factors that affect the settlement process of youth groups in general, such as interpersonal demands (e.g., new school, teachers, peers), as well as factors influencing the settlement process that are specific to individual personality traits, such as personality determinants (individual adaptation responses to different experiences), personal satisfaction (with oneself, parents, guardians, classmates, school, and teachers), and attitudes toward Canadian society (how one conceptualizes mainstream culture and values). In this way, it addressed the adaptation mechanisms that individual youth utilize in their settlement process. These factors, according to the FSA, not only affect youth settlement but also play a large role in their future in Canada in terms of their mental health, academic success, and integration into Canadian society.

(4) Pinecrest-Queensway Health and Community Services, Ottawa/Carleton (PQHCS)

Through a series of initiatives producing anecdotal evidence, PQHCS identified the barriers to employment that are a key component in the issues facing newcomer youth in the Ottawa/Carleton region. Its objective, therefore, was to explore youth settlement issues in terms of employment in particular as well as overall integration and adaptation in general. By defining some of the issues that immigrant youth face in the labour force, PQHCS hopes that existing services and programs may become more sensitive to the needs of youth in the community and new strategies may be implemented to help youth acquire and maintain good employment. This is consistent with PQHCS's focus on programs to connect youth with the larger employment market, and to forge connections among the youth themselves to enhance their networking and reflection skills. The newspaper produced by and for youth in the course of their project gives testimony to a proactive approach in working with youth, one from which the youth themselves derived immediate benefit.

(5) The Coalition of Visible Minority Women, Ontario (CVMW)

CVMW's approach was based on the observation that existing services, such as English as a second language (ESL) programs, do not successfully address many of the issues arising from language and communication barriers that hinder the settlement process of English-speaking African and Caribbean immigrants in Canada. By singling out these two groups for particular, much needed attention, the organization identified relationships among level of language proficiency and barriers in education, training, the law, and career attainment. To identify these obstacles more clearly, one of the agency's objectives was to identify gaps in services for youth seeking employment and to explore some of the chronic unemployment issues facing newcomer youth because of language, communication, and other barriers related to integration. The unique experience of an immigrant group who arrive with no language other than English, or whose entire education has been in English, yet who find themselves not understood in English-speaking Canada, offers a special challenge that the researchers do well to highlight. Their sympathy with these young people enables them to depict a compelling image of what this challenge involves.

(6) Joint Centre of Excellence for Research on Immigration and Settlement, Toronto (CERIS)

CERIS's research focused on the needs and concerns of newcomer youth and the "emerging best practices" employed by service providers who attempt to meet those needs and thus support the integration of immigrant youth into Canadian society. To identify "best practices" for providing and maintaining effective settlement programs and service delivery, CERIS examined the effects of settlement on newcomer youth from different cultural and racial backgrounds by identifying the needs of immigrant youth as they and their parents see them, and by surveying 145 service providers who provide education, employment, health, and social services to newcomer youth. Research conducted by CERIS indicated strong agreement among service providers across all sectors that newcomer youth needs vary by cultural and racial background and gender, and that there is not nearly enough support for these youth, particularly in the educational settings where they can most easily be reached. The purpose of CERIS as a research centre focused on the settlement issues of immigrants is reflected in the report's coverage of issues and areas affecting these youth.

METHODOLOGY

The methods used in this project reflect both the common goals of accurately reflecting the lives of immigrant youth and the unique perspectives adopted by each organization. Thus, while the organizations all conducted their work in ways that included the actual stories that newcomer youth shared about their experiences, each also applied methods that were consistent with and informed by its different research assumptions. Some organizations designed methods simply as techniques for gathering information, while others designed methods specifically related to their purpose as organizations. For example, while CERIS and FSA designed their research methods simply to acquire information for analysis, CREHS used an action-oriented, participatory approach, and CASSA/SAWC employed a theoretical framework of marginalization to inform the methods they employed.

It is also worth noting that the youth and their parents involved in the various studies that comprised this project include both immigrants and refugees from a wide variety of ethno-racial groups; as well, in two cases (CASSA/SAWC and CERIS) the research included newcomer youth who could be considered vulnerable or "at risk" (Kilbride & Anisef, 2001). When the different studies comprising this collaborative project are amalgamated, therefore, they present a deeper perspective that takes into account the multi-faceted nature of youth immigration, adaptation, and settlement. They provide a better understanding of the many challenges faced by newcomer youth today and yield insight into ways to overcome the barriers to their successful integration into Canadian society.

In order to gather this information and arrive at a more complete understanding of the issues, qualitative research methods were predominantly used and quantitative methods supplemented the process. Methodological tools employed included focus group discussions, in-depth interviews, surveys, and psychological tests. The ages of the newcomer youth ranged from sixteen to twenty-four in order to bring to light the issues faced by adolescents who are not quite adults as well as those just out of childhood. To highlight the challenges confronted by newcomer youth because of immigration and to involve participants who could adequately reflect on their settlement experiences, the youth had to have arrived in Canada after the age of six.

Youth and parents held either immigrant or refugee status and came from the following countries and geographical areas: Africa (Somalia, Eritrea, Ethiopia, Uganda, Ghana, Zambia, Nigeria,

Kenya); Europe (former USSR, especially Russia and Bosnia; the former Yugoslavia, particularly Croatia and Serbia; Finland, Hungary, and Portugal); the Caribbean (Jamaica, Trinidad and Tobago, Grenada, and Barbados); Asia (Afghanistan, China and Hong Kong, Vietnam, Cambodia, Sri Lanka, Pakistan, India, Bangladesh, Saudi Arabia, Kuwait, Philippines, Korea, and Iran); and Latin America (Chile and Nicaragua).

Since the researchers believed that gender, class, and ethnicity are among the most important factors that affect the settlement of youth, most of the organizations set up their research in ways that could reflect these factors. For example, the majority consistently divided focus group sessions along gender and ethnic lines; a few, however, included culturally heterogeneous and mixed gender groups. Finally, since there are large immigrant populations concentrated in the Greater Toronto area, the Kitchener/Waterloo area, and the Ottawa/Carleton area, these three areas were targeted as research sites, i.e., CVMW, CERIS, FSA, and CASSA/SAWC focused on the GTA; CREHS focused on the Kitchener/Waterloo area; and PQHCS focused on the Ottawa/Carleton area. The methodological approaches of the groups follow.

Specific Methods

(1) The Centre for Research and Education in Health Services, Kitchener/Waterloo (CREHS)

CREHS's predominantly qualitative approach, based on facilitated focus group interviews, was directed by a stakeholder steering committee composed of immigrant youth, family members, and service providers. The steering committee guided the research in all its five stages. The first stage, understanding the context, involved gathering demographic information about immigrants who reside in the Waterloo region and contacting service providers in the area. The second stage, conducting focus group interviews, involved carrying out eleven focus group interviews: six were composed of youth participants; three of parents; and two of service providers. The third stage, holding a community forum, was a facilitated gathering where focus group participants and all interested community were able to share, discuss, and prioritize research findings. The fourth stage, developing action steps, involved the development and implementation of recommendations to enhance youth services. The final stage, dissemination of products, was accomplished through a variety of mediums including a community forum, the media, workshop presentations, meetings with government officials, and a presentation at the Fifth International Metropolis Conference held in Vancouver in November 2000.

(2) The Council of Agencies Serving South Asians in partnership with the South Asian Women's Centre (CASSA/SAWC)

CASSA/SAWC engaged in a qualitative study that used focus group discussions to facilitate the youth's exploration of the relationship between their South Asian culture and the dominant mainstream culture. The partners created an advisory committee to provide guidance and direction in all stages of the research process. The advisory committee attended committee meetings, identified outreach strategies for recruiting participants, helped with organizing focus groups, acted as interpreters, and provided feedback on the draft report. The focus groups were divided primarily across gender lines and then in terms of particular factors like their pre-immigration situation and religion. Tamils were placed in a separate group because of their unique pre-immigration experience of civil war. Muslims and Sikhs were placed in separate groups because religion plays a major role in their settlement process. A few multi-ethnic focus groups were held to reflect Toronto's cultural and ethno-linguistic diversity.

(3) Family Service Association of Toronto (FSA)

The FSA study utilized both quantitative and qualitative methods. For its highly psychological quantitative portion, FSA used several research instruments including a demographic questionnaire, adaptation response scale, personal satisfaction scale, satisfaction with parents/guardians scale, satisfaction with classmates scale, satisfaction with school/teachers scale, attitude toward Canadian society scale, settlement and adaptation outcome scale, youth self-report, and "draw a human figure" test. For its qualitative portion, FSA held focus group interviews with both youth and parents to ascertain the thoughts, experiences, and concerns of those involved.

(4) Pinecrest-Queensway Health and Community Services, Ottawa/Carleton (PQHCS)

PQHCS used both qualitative and quantitative methods. The former were used in the interviews and focus group interviews, while the latter were used to provide a profile of the population that participated in the study. The organization also engaged in a study of the available resources and information about immigrant youth in the Ottawa/Carleton region. In the early stages of the research PQHCS set up an Advisory Committee to provide input and resources into the design of the study and to identify research materials and possible participants and locations for the focus groups. The PQHCS study included two major components. In the first component an innovative youth-oriented newspaper entitled "DYG (Diverse Youth Workers)" was created, which allowed youth to engage in innovative leadership training methods in order to identify barriers to their integration. The second component, entitled "Work for Youth Research Project," explored issues of unemployment in terms of immigrant youth opportunities. The interviews and focus groups provided insights into the challenges confronted by youth in accessing the labour force in the Ottawa/Carleton region and in the west end of Ottawa.

(5) The Coalition of Visible Minority Women, Ontario (CVMW)

To obtain a more accurate understanding of the issues facing immigrant youth from Africa and the Caribbean, CVMW conducted focus group interviews with newcomer youth and parents. The interviews were divided into two components. In the first part, youth were asked to comment on general issues such as differences in values, beliefs, and behaviour between Canada and their countries of origin and also on available services in Toronto. In the second part of the interviews youth commented specifically on issues of language and communication. Additional information about place of birth, level of education completed, occupation, and languages spoken at home was gathered through a questionnaire completed by each participant. In addition to language and communication issues, the focus group yielded rich data covering the social, psychological, and cultural aspects of youth migration and settlement.

(6) Joint Centre of Excellence for Research on Immigration and Settlement, Toronto (CERIS)

To identify "best practices" for supporting the integration and adaptation of newcomer youth into Canadian society, CERIS conducted an in-depth exploration of newcomer youth issues using both quantitative and qualitative methods. The research included an extensive literature review on the needs of newcomer youth and the services available to them; in-depth personal interviews with fifteen key informants representing a cross-section of agencies in education, employment, mental health, social and health services areas; a telephone survey of 145 service providers; and focus group interviews with newcomer youth and mothers. The research focused on five sectors of society: education, health, social services, employment, and mental health.

REVIEW OF THE LITERATURE

At the outset of the project, extensive literature searches were carried out by each of the six organizations in order to determine the extent of existing research about immigrant youth issues in their areas of interest, and to design new research that would not duplicate what had already been conducted.

The review of the literature confirmed the prior experience of the researchers: there is no real attention being given to newcomer youth aged sixteen to twenty-four. Their needs, whether the youth came as very young children or as adolescents, have not been systematically documented, nor have services for them been systematically identified anywhere. The review contributed a sense of the major issues confronting this age group:

- identity development confounded by dual sources of identity, when home and peer groups come from different cultures

- language issues that arise particularly in school
- lack of recognition, for older youth, of prior learning experience
- conflicts in values beyond those characteristic of many adolescents, namely those between home and peer group, as these conflicts are between values of institutions: those of the family and those of the school as representative of the larger community
- differences in issues for male and female youth that are not necessarily found in all youth's experiences but are characteristic of some cultures in particular

The review of the literature also identified some programs that are being offered to youth in various locations in Canada. The most relevant information from the general literature review was in the areas of health including mental health, education, employment, and social services.

Health and Mental Health

The literature review found a number of significant sources in this area. A federal-provincial study, *Toward a Healthy Future*, reports that "Canadians are among the healthiest people in the world; however this good health is not enjoyed equally by everyone".[1] The country's youth population is suffering from stress that is evident in the increased rates of unhealthy practices such as smoking, having unprotected sex, and dropping out of school, as well as feeling depressed and suicidal. It is argued that stress-related problems among young people are linked to high unemployment and pressure to perform well in school. The same source quotes Shaun Peck, a doctor at the British Columbia Health Department, that dropping out of school early is very damaging to youngsters' future well-being because their chances for secure employment are lower, and they will probably be less healthy in the future, given the link shown between income and health. The report points out that the persistent gap in health status between people of high income and low income is most apparent among youth and Aboriginal groups.

The healthy development and integration of newcomer youth

into all spheres of Canadian society is dependent on numerous and often interrelated factors. A primary determinant of physical, social, and emotional well-being is the family, but several other components characteristic of the newcomer experience can influence the future health status of immigrant youth. The literature review confirmed the fundamental importance for these youth of being part of a strong and loving family. In addition, studies showed that a stable family income improves the likelihood of living in safe neighbourhoods and attending good schools. The absence of some or all of these elements in newcomer households often makes it difficult for parents to create a supportive environment that enhances the future well-being of their children.

The settlement, adaptation, and integration process of newcomer immigrant and refugee youth into Canadian society is a multifaceted experience involving numerous different factors. Also, the process itself in many cases can be extraordinarily intense and stressful. A number of recent studies with immigrant and refugee youth samples have revealed significant adaptive and integration problems previously eclipsed by the stereotype that these youth are problem-free and have high rates of academic success (Chiu & Ring, 1998; Goodenow & Espin, 1993; Huang, 1989; Rivera-Sinclair, 1997; Rousseau, Drapeau, & Corin, 1997; Pawiluk et al., 1996; Seat, 1997).

For immigrant and refugee youth the experience of migration occasions significant life changes in their physical environment, socio-cultural community, and interpersonal affiliations. Reviews of literature on this topic point to long lists of variables to consider such as language fluency, age at migration, sex, financial resources, degree of identification with the host culture, amount of social interactions with the host society, etc. (Berry et al. 1987; Church, 1982; Furnham & Bochner, 1986). In Canada, in addition to facing the usual and highly intensive developmental issues specific for adolescence at a time typically associated with the difficult process of growth and independence, immigrant and refugee newcomer youth must start a new socialization process. They must meet new academic challenges; learn new expectations from their schools, teachers, and parents; gain acceptance into new peer groups; and develop new kinds of social competence (Seat and Richards, 1998).

A recent analysis of data obtained from a longitudinal study of children and youth indicates that "30 per cent of all immigrant children live in families whose total income falls below the official poverty line" (Beiser, Shik, & Curyk, 1999). The researchers note that immigrant children with unstable families are "less likely to prosper scholastically and are more likely to become delinquent" (Beiser, Shik, & Curyk, 1999). Family stability and ethnic resilience have a considerable impact on the behaviour of immigrant and refugee children. This form of social capital is an essential component of well-being and may help foster personal achievement; however, data obtained from community-based samples, according to Beiser, suggest that some newcomer children experience greater risk for alcohol abuse, drug addiction, delinquency, depression, and posttraumatic stress disorder.

The socio-economic environment of newcomer children and adolescents is a determinant of their health and well-being. In his book, *Strangers at the Gate: The "Boat People's" First Ten Years in Canada*, Beiser (1999) evaluates the existence of a link between employment and mental health through the analysis of community surveys of refugees and Canadian residents in Vancouver. Beiser found that newcomer youth were twice as likely to suffer from depression than individuals aged thirty-five and older, adding that "statistics on suicide are also consistent in portraying the young as highly distressed and vulnerable" (pp. 81–82). He argues that it is essential to alleviate job discrimination and economic disparity in order to curb increasing rates of depression among newcomer youth and facilitate their successful integration into Canadian life (p. 162).

It is apparent from this review of the literature on newcomer youth that socio-economic status has a serious impact on the healthy emotional and social development of children and adolescents. Most researchers agree that very little is known about the psychosocial and mental health problems of immigrant children. Both the Canadian Ethnocultural Council (CEC) and the Canadian Council for Refugees (CCR) agree that the mental health of immigrants and refugees remains an important priority for service providers (Beiser, 1999, p. 162).

The problems facing newcomer children and youth are numerous and threatening to both their physical and social development. The risk associated with maladaptive experiences is high among children from disadvantaged populations. Most researchers consider the socio-economic disparity between mainstream and newcomer groups as the primary determinant of negative development (Beiser, Shik, & Curyk, 1999; Bertrand, 1998; Fralick & Hyndman, 1998; James, 1997; Steinhauer, 1998). Adjusting to a new culture and language, as well as to new surroundings and peer expectations, is difficult to achieve without family stability and economic security. The inability to adapt successfully to the norms of society often results in problems at school and creates a greater risk for substance abuse, delinquency, and depression.

By way of illustration, Wadhwani's (1999) study focuses on the specific issue of suicide ideation among South Asian youth in Canada and was prompted by the recent notable increase in suicides among South Asian youth (p. 4). The study reveals a number of disturbing and distressing trends among South Asian youth:

- 30 per cent of the 104 participants indicated that they had considered suicide
- of those who considered suicide, 50 per cent thought that "family pressures" were the number one cause or reason for thinking about suicide as an option
- 60 per cent of participants cited school as the main source of stress
- 80 per cent of those who had admitted to having engaged in suicidal thoughts were female
- 60 per cent of the participants who indicated that they were "always depressed" had considered suicide (Wadhwani, 1999, p. 77)

Much of the literature on the health and well-being of newcomer youth is informed by the theory of ethnic resiliency. Steinhauer (1998) defines resiliency as the ability to achieve "unusually good adaptation in the face of severe stress and/or the ability of the stressed person to rebound to the pre-stress level of adaptation" (p. 51). The ability to identify with and respect one's cultural origin can help foster personal resilience and improve the likelihood for healthy development and integration (Beiser, Shik, & Curyk, 1999).

James (1997) reports that newcomer children and adolescents in the United States experience a variety of cognitive and emotional changes through the absence of their familiar language, culture, and community. The subsequent adjustments to life in a new country often result in the increased risk of trauma or psychosocial problems, school failure, and drug abuse, as well as other delinquent behaviour. James (1997) suggests that "the early identification of immigrant children at risk for these problems can help school personnel and health care providers plan culturally appropriate and effective interventions" (p. 98). It is believed that many newcomers suffer from anxiety over the loss of all things familiar and experience a culture shock that can cause emotional maladjustment (James, 1997, p. 99). Difficulties with language acquisition and the lack of peer acceptance can impede the academic performance of a newcomer and be a source of stress.

The support of family, friends, and the community can provide a healthy intervention into negative behaviour by allowing children and adolescents to develop ethnic resilience and foster strong social networks (Fralick & Hyndman, 1998, p. 319). Other researchers also cite the need for intervention programs in order to curtail the risk associated with newcomer adaptation (Beiser, Shik, & Curyk, 1999; Bertrand, 1998; James, 1997; Steinhauer, 1998). Both James and Bertrand stress that children "at risk" must be identified early in order to help service providers plan effective interventions that are culturally appropriate to the unique social and emotional needs of newcomer youth.

Early intervention in the education of children is critical for the successful integration of newcomer youth because the experiences of early childhood tend to define social and behavioural patterns. Bertrand (1998) considers ways to enrich the preschool experiences of children from disadvantaged backgrounds and evaluates several initiatives designed to improve their physical, social, and mental health. "A child's socio-economic status, determined by family income, parental occupations, and parental education levels, strongly influences the development of the child" (Bertrand, 1998, p. 8). Bertrand suggests programs that focus on children at increased risk for negative social and emotional development. It is essential that children identified as "at risk" be provided with tools to improve their chances at successful adaptation.

For those immigrant children and adolescents with psychosocial problems, James makes several recommendations aimed at improving the delivery of services. Pointing out that such children have unique social and emotional needs, she recommends that course work and in-service training programs be developed to equip counsellors, nurses, teachers, and health educators with the knowledge and experience to deal with children suffering from migration-linked psychosocial problems. She suggests that culturally appropriate counselling and social services in schools be developed and made widely accessible. James also proposes that suitable diagnostic and assessment tools be tailored to immigrant children and their families, and that a preventative or early intervention program be created to identify initial "culture shock" (James 1997, p. 102)

Educational Attainment

The literature confirms that social, economic, and demographic changes in Canadian society have placed a tremendous amount of pressure on educational systems to respond to the accompanying growth in the diversity of student enrolment. The public school system in Toronto serves an extraordinarily diverse student body. Close to half of the students within the jurisdiction of the Toronto District School Board (TDSB)[2] are from non-English-speaking families and represent over seventy-six language groups (Cheng & Yau, 1997). Between 1992 and 1996, one-third of students attending schools in Toronto came from over 170 countries, and 59 per cent of recent arrivals were considered to be "high need." With such a large number of culturally diverse youth, there is a greater demand for services from the local board of education, as well as from settlement and ethnocultural organizations. Some of the needs identified by researchers include academic support, parental involvement in the education of children, the recognition of the unique circumstances and experiences of newcomer youth, as well as training for teachers, school staff, and settlement workers.

In the introduction to *Learning and Sociological Profiles of Canadian High School Students*, Anisef and Bunch (1994) report that some visible minority youth may encounter significant challenges in coping with the school system. They perform poorly in class, suffer from behavioural problems, or drop out of school altogether. Some of the principal factors underlying these problems include school policies, the discriminatory attitudes of teachers, and the organizational structure of schools where achievement or success among minority youth is not encouraged (Anisef & Bunch 1994, pp. 8–10). This environment has often proven hostile for some immigrant students. It has led to poor attendance, fostered feelings of hostility toward school, and produced an increase in delinquent behaviour. Although many schools now recognize ethnocultural diversity and make efforts to prevent discrimination, Anisef and Bunch assert that visible minority youth "will continue to be at risk unless the system as a whole is actively working to accommodate their differences and needs" (Anisef & Bunch 1994, pp. 9–10).

Lam (1994) maintains that education is considered a liberating force toward the equalization of opportunities in an ethnically stratified society; however, many studies have found that equal educational opportunities in Canada are limited for some ethnic groups (Anisef & Okihiro, 1982; Li, 1999). A student's ethnocultural background and socio-economic status are important factors influencing his or her educational progress. Numerous elements, such as teacher biases, economic inequality, and institutional or systemic discrimination, act as barriers for immigrant youth in the attainment of equal educational opportunities. Anisef and Bunch (1994) also note the high correlation between socio-economic status and academic performance. Low-income households often cannot provide an environment conducive to learning since many of these children consume less nutritional foods, have less access to private space for homework, are less likely to own computers, and have parents with lower educational levels. Students from low-income backgrounds also face discriminatory treatment and lower teacher expectations. These elements work together to produce low self-esteem and poor motivation to learn among minority students (Anisef & Bunch, 1994, p. 10)

Lam (1994) believes that the negative employment experiences of parents may have an adverse effect on their children's decision to leave the school system (p. 124). Parents' marginalized position may pressure youth to drop out of school to work and help support their families. These individuals feel it is more important to enter the labour market and contribute to the family income than to continue studying. They may also learn from their parents' experience that educational success cannot provide them with the means to achieve social status in a high-profile occupational category (Lam, 1994, p. 125). A study carried out by the Canadian Youth Foundation (CYF) indicates that youth in Canada are generally losing confidence in the public school system and post-secondary education. It reports that most youngsters have serious doubts about the value of their education and the ability of schools to prepare them for the job market (Canadian Youth Foundation, 1995, p. 20). They remain concerned that schools cannot provide adequate skills or direction to help them in the transition from school to work.

While various programs, such as special education classes and ESL courses, assist children with their educational progress, Lam (1994) stresses that the school system needs to clarify its objectives: "Are we concerned primarily with ways to assist immigrant youth to "fit into" the existing educational system or are we concerned with why and how the education system fails to meet their needs?" (p. 129). The problems facing youth are rooted in socio-economic inequality and different forms of institutional and systemic discrimination. ESL programs may only temporarily deal with limitations to educational progress, and special education classes may only further stigmatize newcomer students in society.

Johnson and Peters (1994) report that the diverse needs of Ontario students are often overlooked. Accordingly, they are convinced that there is a need for a more student-based, participatory educational program aimed at accommodating diversity and change. Four principal themes are underscored in their report:
- the need to address and eliminate race, ethnic, gender, and class bias from the school system
- the need for a fully integrated educational system to accommodate the diverse needs of all young adult learners
- the need to build strong linkages between schools and various sectors of the community
- the need for greater parental involvement (Johnson & Peters, 1994, pp. 441–455)

Like Lam, Johnson and Peters believe that programs such as heritage language (HL) and English as a second language (ESL) are not sufficient to cope with the problem of alienation that causes some immigrant or visible minority students to perform poorly or to leave the education system prematurely. Johnson and Peters state that the problems facing marginalized youth are rooted in institutional and systemic discrimination. An understanding of such issues may be gained by examining the literature on Caribbean youth. Caribbean youth face pressure in school from their parents, teachers, and peers. Teachers' expectations significantly affect students' progress in school, but in the case of Caribbean students, the expectations are often based on a perceived stereotype: poor language and communication skills, low levels of participation, and (in the case of the males) higher levels of aggression (Anderson & Grant, 1987; Foster, 1996). Furthermore, Caribbean youth themselves are confused by the Canadian education system when they are assessed as not speaking English. A disproportionate number are put back several grades, assigned to special education classes, or placed in ESL programs. The teachers' low expectations of these students and misunderstanding of their culture all compound communication problems for Caribbean youth (Edwards, 1986).

Parents assume that schools operate the same way in Canada as in the Caribbean. They do not always understand the dilemmas that their children face in school. Caribbean parents are more likely to be concerned with the discipline problems in school and the limited amount of homework assigned. They have high confidence that the school as an institution is meeting the needs of their children (James & Brathwaite, 1996).

However, Caribbean youth may find themselves failing in school, isolated, and increasingly frustrated. Their parents do not understand their dilemma and are more likely to blame the children for their failing, while the youth recognize that their teachers expect little from them, and there is little in the curriculum with which they can identify. In addition, the Caribbean way of socializing is seen as negative. All of these factors contribute to underachievement and a high dropout rate for Caribbean students (Dei et al., 1997).

The school system must accommodate the growing diversity of the student population and offer curricula and programs that are relevant to their experiences, learning needs, and aspirations (Anisef & Bunch, 1994, p. 7). It is essential to understand the traditions, learning aptitudes, family structures, and moral values of immigrant and refugee youth in order to develop programs designed to meet their educational needs (Lam, 1994, p. 127). Such an approach could provide much needed support for newcomer youth as they attempt to adapt to the new society.

Zhou and Bankston (1998) explore how aspects of an immigrant culture work as social capital to affect the adaptation experiences of immigrant youth. Their argument is based upon a case study of Vietnamese youth in the United States. They assert that Vietnamese students who possess a stronger association with traditional values, including a commitment to a work ethic, and are significantly involved in the ethnic community, tend to perform remarkably well in school. These values are consistent with the expectations of the ethnic community and reflect a "high level of social integration among Vietnamese youth" (Zhou & Bankston, 1998, p. 821). Zhou and Bankston also report that some studies of Indo-Chinese refugees (Caplan, Whitmore, & Choy, 1989; Gold, 1992) show that culture, family, and the sense of belonging to an ethnic community have promoted the need for academic attainment and excellence among Indo-Chinese students. Their research and conclusions, and those of others, indicate that ethnic resources, seen as social capital, can provide disadvantaged offspring with an adaptive advantage (Kilbride, 1999; Zhou & Bankston, 1998, p. 821).

In a recent literature review on newcomer children and youth in Canada, Beiser, Shik, and Curyk (1999) similarly note that immigrant children of parents who are conscious of the worth of what their own tradition has to offer as well as what Canada offers them are more likely to perform well in school than the children of immigrants who attempt a total assimilation into Canadian society. They report that researchers have underscored "the respect for education embedded in some cultural traditions, parental ambition and enterprise, and the insecurity over minority status" as important factors contributing to the academic success achieved by some newcomer students (Beiser, Shik, & Curyk, 1999). Deyhle (1995) also reports that students who achieve academic success are those who feel securely embedded in their traditional culture, while those at highest risk for failure in school are those "who feel disenfranchised from their own culture and at the same time experience racial conflict" (pp. 419–420).

Gibson (1997) writes that "minority youth do better in school when they feel strongly anchored in the identities of their families, communities and peers, and when they feel supported in pursuing a strategy of selective or additive acculturation" (pp. 445–446). Cummins (1997) is similarly concerned with newcomer students' ability to negotiate their cultural identities in a new society. He believes that a more flexible and inclusive framework is needed to account for the variability of academic outcomes and to plan educational interventions to school failure.

The focus group statements of mainly Asian immigrants in Vancouver led Hiebert (1998) to note that immigrant families often equate their hope for the future with their children's education. Many cited the standard of education and opportunities for children as the main reasons for choosing to come to Canada; however, "the disjunction between hopes and actual experiences in schooling and employment often meant a fragile sense of the future and of family settlement in Canada" (Hiebert, 1998, pp. 18–19). When questioned about the adjustment of young people to Canadian society, many participants suggested that while immigrant parents struggle in adapting, "[immigrant] children adjust quickly." Children learn new languages and adapt to cultural expectations more easily than adults, and their locally attained educational qualifications are more readily accepted by Canadian employers (Hiebert, 1998, p. 15).

It is important to note that not all researchers agree that children adapt easily. A study conducted by the Canadian Youth Foundation focuses on the problems experienced by immigrant youth who possess educational qualifications from outside Canada. They face considerable difficulty in getting recognition for their educational qualifications. The report provides insight into the discontent of newcomer youth, and how systemic problems and economic difficulties may prevent individuals from reaching their goals (Canadian Youth Foundation, 1995, p. 21).

The problems facing newcomer youth may be more complex than first imagined. More research is needed not only to examine how newcomer youth fare in school, but also to register their views, feelings, and sentiments in order to identify the reasons visible minority youth in particular show poor academic performance or drop out of school. An American study by McDonnell and Hill (1993) indicates that older students experience difficulty adapting because they are unprepared for the level of instruction offered in school. The researchers also point out that pressure from family often forces older students out of school in order to find work and provide for the family. A study of newcomer youth on a community college campus in Toronto showed that educational and financial concerns affected the majority of immigrant students, yet the college provided very little assistance in helping students meet those needs (Kilbride & D'Arcangelo, 2000). In the United States McDonnell and Hill (1993) blame local governments for not taking seriously the responsibility for the welfare of immigrant students and for not assisting parents in adjusting to economic and civil life (pp. 85–86).

It is evident from this review of the literature on newcomer youth that academic progress is a significant component of healthy integration. Schools can act as agents of academic and social growth if they adopt appropriate practices designed to help children at risk. Newcomer youth need academic support, parental and community involvement, and cross-cultural understanding of their unique circumstances and experiences. Many of the researchers cited in this chapter believe that intervention measures are necessary when unmet challenges arising from the migration and settlement process risk students' education progress.

Lam, like Johnson and Peters, suggests a number of specific programs that he believes will foster a positive school environment and help facilitate the integration process for immigrant youth. The research findings indicate that "a more responsive and flexible approach to classroom instruction, to the school as a community institution with open boundaries, and to the diversity of learning needs, backgrounds and expectations in our changing population" is needed (Anisef & Bunch, 1994, p. 13). The recommendations made by Lam and Johnson and Peters appear to consider the importance of accommodating ethnocultural diversity in the school system, but fail to appreciate the immediate and unique needs of newcomer youth.

The proposed programs understand poor academic performance and school absenteeism to be mainly the result of school-related problems, such as teacher biases, inadequate testing methods, or the lack of a diverse perspective in the curriculum. Anisef (1998) is concerned that they fail to address adequately other factors, such as economic insecurity, unemployment, poor mental health, stress, or depression (p. 279). It is important to note, therefore, that the underlying reasons behind dropping out of school may involve more than those factors that have a direct association with the operation of the school system (Anisef, 1998, p. 286). Anisef stresses that dropping out of school is not a single act or an event that happens independently of any other factors. It is a process in which different but interrelated factors—ranging from the individual and family to school, community, the job market, and government policy—are involved (Anisef, 1998, pp. 289–303). Treating the matter as a process rather than an independent event makes better sense from both a research and "best practice" perspective, but only if an analysis of all those interrelated factors is made vis-à-vis the aspirations, goals, choices, opportunities, and constraints of the individual actors. A process analysis approach may provide researchers with better analytical tools to examine problems associated with why visible minority youth of certain ethnocultural backgrounds perform poorly in school or choose to drop out.

It is essential that more research be conducted on the relation between educational attainment and the positive adaptation experiences of newcomer youth. The conclusions and recommendations made by most researchers clearly point to the school system's important role in promoting settlement and integration. It is apparent that a collaborative and integrative effort must be made to meet the needs of newcomer youth most effectively.

Access to Employment and Economic Mobility

The literature indicates that the youth unemployment rate in Canada is reaching critical proportions, and the greatest casualties appear to be newcomer youth, a phenomenon that is discussed in Chapter 3. The ability to obtain gainful employment is hampered by their aptitude for learning in the host society. There are numerous factors that inhibit academic progress for newcomer children. Their socio-economic experiences and ethnocultural background make them particularly susceptible to negative influences and discrimination. This has made it increasingly difficult for children and adolescents to acquire the level of skills and training needed to compete in the labour market.

The Canadian Council on Social Development (CCSD) reports that there are about two million youth between the ages of fifteen and nineteen in Canada. The high unemployment rate is something that affects all youth in Canada, but an analysis of statistical data reveals that newcomer youth face greater obstacles to employment and are far less likely than Canadian-born youth to have had any kind of work experience. In 1996, there were twice as many immigrants between the ages of seventeen and nineteen with no previous work-related experience. A correlation was found between socio-economic background and access to employment opportunities. Youth from low-income families face greater challenges in acquiring job experience than do those living in high- or middle-income families. The same pattern holds true for immigrant youth compared to Canadian-born youth. "Immigrant youth may be at a disadvantage in finding work due to their lack of family contacts in business, their efforts to learn one of Canada's official languages, their responsibilities at home, or their families' expectations that they focus solely on school work" (CCSD, 1998b, p. 8).

The CCSD report exposes some of the realities facing newcomer youth when searching for employment. It is obvious that the barriers adolescents cross warrant further attention, but the report does not provide enough data on the needs and concerns specific to immigrant youth, such as family expectations, responsibilities at home, or a negative school environment. The study further examines the impact of work opportunities on students' health habits, such as alcohol use, smoking, stress, and aggressive behaviour.

Not to be underestimated in importance among some groups of newcomer youth groups is the role of language with regard to employment and employability. Thus, in a study conducted by Kasozi (1986), 60 per cent of the research subjects stated that their accent was an obstacle in integrating into society and finding employment. Some 28 per cent lost or left their former employment because of language problems.

In *Youth Unemployment: Canada's Rite of Passage,* the Canadian Youth Foundation used focus groups to document the experiences of Canadian youth between the ages of fifteen and twenty-nine. The study sample included disparate groups of middle-class, Aboriginal, immigrant, and street youth. The report reveals that most youth see themselves as "occupationally challenged despite their best efforts to the contrary." They characterize themselves as "demoralized job seekers with rapidly diminishing expectations" (Canadian Youth Foundation 1995, pp. 1, 7). Many feel dependent on their parents and are forced to delay leading independent lives and starting their own families.

Although the CYF's investigation has primarily explored the attitudinal trends of middle-class youth, it has provided some information on immigrant youth through comparisons with the other cohorts. Researchers for the CYF note that both immigrant and street youth lack personal networks and support systems to assist them in their search for employment. Middle-class youth have devised individual coping strategies through self-employment and contract work, while immigrant and street youth are completely reliant on government agencies to prepare them for the job market. Participants cited the need for more apprenticeships and practicums, and claimed that schools do not provide youth with enough information and counselling at ages early enough to move them toward the labour market effectively. In the case of immigrant youth, the report shows that the participants feel "completely vulnerable to the government's policies and regulations" (Canadian Youth Foundation, 1995, p. 34). Furthermore, as many immigrant participants are reported to have no family to turn to, "they often rely almost exclusively on counseling" (Canadian Youth Foundation, 1995, p. 34) that they receive through community organizations. The CYF's study does not, however, explore the nature of such counselling in order to assess its efficacy in assisting newcomer and immigrant youth. It does succeed in identifying a set of factors underlying the joblessness of immigrant, Aboriginal, and street youth, which include "the lack of socioeconomic-economic opportunities, social and cultural barriers, or an unwillingness to accept low-paying work" (Canadian Youth Foundation, 1995, p. 34).

Anisef (1998) investigates the important transition from school to employment as a primary determinant of socio-economic advancement or stagnation for newcomer youth. He argues that Canadian schools are failing to prepare adequately adolescents for the job market. His research warns of the particular vulnerability to marginalization experienced by minority and disadvantaged youth during the transition to adulthood (Anisef, 1998, p. 275). Anisef examines two intervention programs, Change Your Future and the Ontario Youth Apprenticeship Program (OYAP), which were designed to facilitate the transition from school to work for Canadian youth. Change Your Future targets visible minority youth considered to be at risk for dropping out of school and features individual and group counselling, mentoring, and alternative schooling. The program has been moderately successful in its attempt to understand the transition from school to work as a process that requires support and follow-up (Anisef, 1998, pp. 294–296). OYAP is similar to co-operative education. It helps students obtain job placements to ease the school-to-work transition. The student who participates in OYAP is allowed to develop work-related skills, and earn wages, class credits, and apprenticeship hours simultaneously. Despite the well-strategized intentions of OYAP, Anisef is critical of the program because it has not succeeded in overcoming employers' reluctance to hire "at risk" adolescents (Anisef, 1998, pp. 297–300).

Johnson and Peters also consider the correlation between positive employment experiences and the healthy social and economic development of newcomer youth. The nature of employment obtained can have an impact on the chances for economic mobility. Johnson and Peters (1994) therefore argue for a strengthened relationship between education and employment (pp. 444–445). They see opportunities for learning and socio-economic growth for students outside the school and accordingly stress the importance of building links between the school and community. A community initiative, Community-Based Education for Work, Career and Life (CWCL), is discussed because it involves a coordination of efforts among schools, labour, industry, and government. The authors also mention co-operative education, training and apprenticeship programs, and community mentoring as ways to promote learning opportunities for students outside the school (Johnson & Peters, 1994, p. 445).

The relationship between educational attainment and access to employment is accepted by most researchers. Johnson and Peters suggest that schools need to be flexible and adaptable in order to accommodate the unique needs of immigrant youth. Researchers examining the economic opportunities for immigrant youth clearly point to the need for more flexibility in the system in order to respond to the needs, concerns, and experiences specific to newcomer youth. It is evident from this review of the literature that newcomer youth need assistance with the transition from school to work. The research revealed that immigrant youth might be at a disadvantage in finding work because of their ethnic background, language deficiencies, family responsibilities, economic insecurity, and difficulties with school. It is essential that more research be conducted to find ways to facilitate newcomer youth in their transition to adulthood and their search for suitable employment.

Social Services

The acclimatization, adaptation, and integration of immigrants require a significant commitment to assistance from the various organizations serving these newcomers. The early stages of acclimatization and adaptation can be referred to as the period of settlement when newcomers make initial adjustments to life in a new country as they find suitable and affordable housing, learn the language, and search for employment. Integration is the longer-term process that newcomers experience as they endeavour to become full and equal participants in all the various dimensions of society (Canadian Council for Refugees, 1998, p. 14). A greater proportion of the programs offered by service providers has tended to focus on adult newcomers; however, it has become increasingly important for these organizations to respond to the needs and concerns of newcomer children and youth as well. Younger immigrants need assistance to adjust successfully and participate fully in Canadian economic, social, and political life.

There have been very few research studies or needs assessments targeted specifically at newcomer youth, but those that have been conducted recognize the value of refugee- and immigrant-serving organizations. The strength of these organizations lies both in the potential they have for the adoption of a diversity of approaches to program development and in their roots in the community. They are committed to cost-effective programs that work, are account-able to the community they serve, and take a holistic approach to meeting the needs of their clients (Canadian Council for Refugees, 1998, p. 33). The Canadian Council for Refugees identifies four spheres of settlement and integration where service providers should focus their efforts:

- *Economic integration:* includes acquiring skills, entering the job market, and achieving financial independence
- *Social integration:* includes establishing social networks and accessing institutions
- *Cultural integration:* includes adapting various aspects of lifestyle and engaging in efforts to redefine cultural identity
- *Political integration:* includes citizenship, voting, and civic participation (Canadian Council for Refugees, 1998, p. 18)

It is essential that service providers direct their program delivery to these areas of integration. Newcomer youth need assistance with language acquisition, cultural orientation and acceptance, building community networks, and accessing employment in order to achieve full participation in Canadian society (Canadian Council for Refugees, 1998, p. 10).

A study of socio-economic and demographic trends in Ottawa-Carleton reveals that the level of education achieved remains a significant barrier to employment and socio-economic advance-ment (Social Planning Council of Ottawa-Carleton and United Way/Centraide Ottawa-Carleton, 1999, p. 12). Beiser, Shik, and Curyk (1999) propose a model for the adoption of an integrated approach to service provision that relates migration stresses to a variety of outcomes. They emphasize the importance of self-esteem as a component of well-being and as a predictor of achievement. Other researchers have also noted the importance of supporting the culture and first language of newcomer youth groups in order to facilitate their cognitive development and self-esteem (North York Board of Education, 1988; Toronto Board of Education, 1997).

It is commonly accepted that the ability to speak and understand the language of the host society is the key to participation in the economic, social, cultural, and political spheres of that society (Canadian Council for Refugees, 1998, p. 23). The most prevalent of services provided is language classes; however, upon completion of such classes youth typically acquire only a superficial oral fluency (North York Board of Education, 1988). This may not be adequate for their academic achievement or for their social and emotional integration into Canadian society. Researchers have made several suggestions to improve services and assist with the integration of newcomer youth. They include peer mentoring, social groups for youth, after-school recreational and academic assistance programs, better monitoring of students once they leave ESL classes, better access to services, and greater sensitivity from mainstream society to the needs and experiences of newcomers.

The increase in poverty and the need for emergency social support has come at a time when the voluntary sector has been struggling to maintain its standard of operations in the face of government cutbacks to the social safety net. Several programs have been developed as a response to the needs of children from disadvantaged populations. Research on children and nutrition indicates that malnutrition can alter intellectual development by interfering with a child's overall health, energy level, rate of motor development, and rate of growth. In October 1998, the Ministry of Education provided a $500,000 grant to Ottawa's Carleton School Board for programs that would provide students with breakfast before classes. The school breakfast program, with extra funding from organizations and local businesses, has spread to thirty-eight elementary schools in Ottawa-Carleton (Clifford, 1999).

Meneses (1999) suggests that, in addition to the collective efforts of community agencies, schools, and government departments, an attempt must be made to provide innovative ways to meet newcomer needs and provide services. The Canadian Institute for Advanced Research (CIAR) and the Centre for Studies of Children at Risk (CSCR) describe one such method in their 1995 report. A west end Toronto shopping mall was experiencing a decrease in business because of loitering youth and a subsequent increase in criminal activity. The mall management recognized the extent of the problems and challenges confronting these youth. In collaboration with them, as well as their parents, local schools, police, and other community resources, a youth services office was opened in the mall. It provided many services, including culturally sensitive counselling and community support services to youth and their families; the municipal government hired a youth counsellor; and the local board of education offered alternative educational opportunities on site.

Lack of information is a serious problem for many newcomers. The majority of respondents to a survey in Halton (Meneses, 1999) had little or no knowledge about the critical issues that they would have to deal with in their settlement process. Other than receiving the Ontario Health Insurance Plan (OHIP) and making an appointment with a doctor, few knew how to access other health care services (e.g., for mental health, drug and alcohol problems, and nutrition). Respondents to the Halton survey (Meneses, 1999) indicated that one of their concerns was the lack of information. It is clear from the literature that it is essential that newcomers understand more than just how to access services. Respondents in this study requested information about a multitude of topics, such as Canadian culture, parental roles, the expectations of the education system, and the roles of teachers, as well as acceptable behaviour and mainstream values.

A report by Yau (1995) proposed the development of a public information office in schools in collaboration with community, government, and ethnocultural groups. The offices would provide, in a variety of languages, comprehensive packages that could include information on legal, health care, housing, citizenship, the school system, community services, and other pertinent concerns. In addition, the office could act as a referral service for students and families. It is apparent that a collaborative effort must be made in order to meet the needs of newcomer youth most effectively. The recommendations made by several researchers allude to the school system's important role in promoting settlement and integration. It can be used as a forum for disseminating information, gaining access to families and consequently inviting greater participation in their children's education, referring newcomers to services, and assisting mainstream society to become more culturally sensitive to the needs and experiences of newcomers.

The literature reviewed remarks on the lack of understanding about the specific needs and cultural backgrounds of newcomer youth. These individuals are struggling to reconcile two separate cultural existences as they attempt to adjust to the social norms of the host society while maintaining their own heritage. They also face linguistic and cultural barriers when accessing services, as well as racism and discrimination in daily life (Spigelblatt, 1999).

CONCLUSION

The remainder of this book explores in greater detail the issues outlined in this introduction. Chapters 2 through 7 provide details of the research themes, methodologies, and findings of each partner organization's projects, with each chapter providing rich detail and unique insights with respect to a particular portion of the major issues for the settlement of newcomer youth identified in our general literature review. In the Conclusion we present an integrated summary of the key findings, discuss the policy implications of the research, and explore the future directions of research in this field.

In these following chapters, therefore, the reader will find much that has been learned, more again about what remains to be further explored, and still more concerning what needs to be done. We trust that this book will be explored with a sensitivity to the key perspectives that motivated this collaborative project: a willingness to listen to the voices of immigrant and refugee youth, as well as their families and service providers, and a concern for the practical policy implications of the research in order to improve the settlement outcomes for newcomer youth in Canada.

NOTES

[1] The results of the federal-provincial study were reported in William Walker, "Canadians Healthier But Stress Hits Young," in *The Toronto Star* (September 17, 1999), 1.

2   In January 1997, when the City of Toronto and the five other municipalities were amalgamated into one city, the six school boards in Metropolitan Toronto were similarly amalgamated into the Toronto District School Board, resulting in a lack of comparability in data across Metropolitan Toronto.

TABLE ONE: COMPOSITION OF FOCUS GROUPS

	FSA		CERIS	CREHS	CASSA/SAWC	PQHCS	CVMW
	Qualitative	Quantitative					
Format	Focus groups		Focus groups, interviews, & surveys	Focus groups	Focus groups	Focus groups & interviews	Focus groups
# of groups	6 youth	12 youth	18 youth	6 youth	13 youth	6 youth	4 youth
		2 parents (Chinese & Serbian)	7 mothers	3 parents	1 (15 mothers & 1 father)	3 community members	2 parents (African & Caribbean)
			150 organizations	2 service providers		2 service providers	
			15 key informants				
Details: # of participants or groups	170 female youth; 130 male youth		8 female & 8 male culturally homogeneous youth; 1 female & 1 male mixed North African youth	61 people were interviewed	32 female youth; 31 male youth	57 youth; 31 community members; 26 service proiders (in both focus groups & interviews)	2 African youth (female/male); 2 Caribbean youth (female/male); 1 African parent & 1 Caribbean parent
Participants per group	50 youth	Max. of 8 youth		3–9	8–10 youth		
Age range of Youth	16–19		16–20	16–20	16–24	16–24	16–24

TABLE ONE: COMPOSITION OF FOCUS GROUPS (*continued*)

	FSA		CERIS	CREHS	CASSA/SAWC	PQHCS	CVMW
	Qualitative	Quantitative					
Requirements	Came to Canada at or after age of 7; have been in Canada at last a year		Arrived in Canada after age of 6	Arrival to Canada (1990s)	Arrived in Canada at or after age of 8	Not in school full-time; born outside Canada; employment status: unemployed/underemployed	Length of stay in Canada: Africans (5 years or more), Caribbean (10 years or fewer)
Countries/ continent of origin or ethnic makeup or languages spoken	Africa, Caribbean, Central & South America, China, Eastern Europe, South East Asia	Youth groups: Somalia, Former USSR, Afghanistan, Bosnia/Croatia Seribia, China & Hong Kong, Vietnam, Finland, Cambodia	Portugal, Philippines, Korea, Africa, Iran, Russia, Northeast Africa (Eritria, Ethiopia & Somalia), Jamaica	Asia, Europe, Africa, Latin America	Sri Lanka, Pakistan, India, Kenya, Bangladesh, Saudi Arabia, Kuwait	Languages: Somali, Arabic, Spanish, Farsi, Serbo-Croatian, Russian	Languages: African (English, Twi, Fanti, Akan, Beni, Edo) Caribbean (English)
Groups divisions (cultural, gender)			Always divided by gender; divided by ethnic lines (except 2 North African groups)	Groups have a mix of gender, but also included 1 male group & 1 female group	Divided by gender first, then along ethnic grounds; finally along religious lines		Divided by gender and area of origin
Target area	Toronto	Toronto	Toronto	Waterloo/ Kitchener	Toronto	Ottawa/ Carleton region	Toronto

CHAPTER 1

Immigrant Youth in Waterloo Region

RICK JANZEN AND JOANNA OCHOCKA
Centre for Research and Education in Human Services

INTRODUCTION

The research discussed in this chapter is based on a qualitative study of immigrant youth in Waterloo region, an urban and rural community in southwestern Ontario, Canada. This study applied an exploratory and inductive research approach to document the issues confronting immigrant youth in their first years in Canada. The research was carried out by the Centre for Research and Education in Human Services, an independent, non-profit research organization located in Kitchener, Ontario. Having a community-based research centre with its twenty-year history of using qualitative and participatory action research created a safe link for all involved. Staff from the Centre for Research and Education have extensive experience in community partnerships and provided leadership by building bridges among various stakeholder groups involved in this study.

The purpose of this research study was twofold: (1) to understand the diverse settlement issues of immigrant youth (aged sixteen to twenty) within Waterloo region, and (2) to develop specific and concrete strategies for supporting youth in addressing their issues. There were three main factors that motivated this study:

- relatively little research on issues immigrant youth face in Canada
- large and diverse immigrant population in Waterloo region
- gaps in supports for immigrant youth in Waterloo region identified by local service providers

CONTEXT

With over 400,000 people, Waterloo region includes the three cities of Kitchener, Waterloo, and Cambridge; is rich in Mennonite history; and is surrounded by small towns and some of the best farmland in Ontario. The economy of Waterloo region has shifted in recent years from manufacturing (textile and furniture) to the new high-tech sector and industries. Both universities (University of Waterloo and Wilfrid Laurier University) and Conestoga College are key players in the expansion of education, training, and jobs in the information and technology sector. Despite strong population growth, a relatively flourishing economy, and high-income earnings, not everyone shares in the region's wealth. The region has a larger gap between its rich and poor citizens than the national average. Many of those in poverty are recent immigrants (Urban Poverty Consortium of Waterloo Region, 2000).

Diverse Immigration Population

Waterloo region is a large immigrant destination in Canada, with a relatively large, diverse, and growing immigrant youth population. For example, in 1996, 21 per cent of residents in the region were immigrants, and of all immigrants, 42 per cent were under the age of twenty (1996 census). Kitchener (the largest city of the region) has proportionally the fourth-largest immigrant population of all cities in Canada, with approximately one-quarter (24.5 per cent) of all residents being immigrants (1996 census). The largest group of recent immigrants to Waterloo region came from Eastern Europe (24 per cent), mainly Poland, Romania, and former Yugoslavia. The next largest groups originated from India, Vietnam, El Salvador, United Kingdom, China, United States, Guyana, and Somalia.

Since 1996, the trend of immigrants originating from Yugoslavia and Romania has continued, but the number of immigrants from Poland dropped significantly after 1993 (Citizenship and Immigration Canada, 1998). The top languages of recent immigrant youth (under the age of twenty) include Serbo-Croatian, English, Spanish, Romanian, Somalian, Arabic, and Vietnamese.

There are two striking characteristics about the immigrants and immigrant youth coming to Waterloo region. First, many of them are *refugees*. In fact, the cities of Kitchener and Waterloo receive a much higher proportion of refugees than Ontario as a whole. Thirty-three per cent of immigrants destined for Kitchener-Waterloo in 1995 were refugees, compared to 14 per cent for Ontario as a whole (Citizenship and Immigration Canada, 1998).

Waterloo region also attracts many *secondary migrants* (immigrants moving to the region from other provinces and cities in Canada). This implies that the region is receiving more recent immigrants than traditional data sources (such as Citizenship and Immigration Canada [CIC] data) would lead us to believe. Local service providers estimate that several hundred new immigrants (up to an additional one-third of total new arrivals) come to the region each year by way of secondary migration. These immigrants had originally declared another region as their destination (mainly Quebec), but have since moved into our region.

The best indicator of secondary migration is the number of registrations in elementary English as a Second Language (ESL) programs at the Waterloo Region District School Board. ESL registration had increased from 1,437 in 1994 to 3,107 in 1998. Meanwhile, during the same time period CIC data showed a slight decrease in children and youth destined for the region.

Services and Supports for Immigrant Youth

Although the region's demographics show an increasingly large and diverse immigrant youth population, services and supports for immigrant youth remain limited. Settlement services tend to focus largely on providing support for adult immigrants. Support for immigrant youth tend to be ad hoc and in small pockets across the region.

There are three major agencies providing formal settlement services: YMCA Settlement and Integration Services, Kitchener-Waterloo YMCA Cross-Cultural and Community Services, and Kitchener-Waterloo Multicultural Centre. All three organizations focus on provision of supports for families, but mainly to adults. Children and youth are supported indirectly through their families. Most of the services for youth deal with assistance in accessing educational institutions and health providers, as well as some crisis intervention.

In addition to the three main settlement services mentioned above, there are four employment support programs for immigrants. These four programs are offered under the umbrella of the New Canadian Employment Services and have a central intake. In addition, a number of ethnic clubs, associations, and faith communities offer complementary settlement services and support in helping people sponsor family members and other individuals from overseas.

Unlike the Greater Toronto area, very few ethno-specific organizations provide formal settlement services in Waterloo region. Immigrants typically go to organizations that serve people from multiple ethnic backgrounds. We will notice later in the chapter that when suggesting future supports, immigrant youth, their parents, and service providers also emphasize solutions that are multicultural in focus.

Services and supports specifically for immigrant youth in Waterloo region are not that common. Where they do exist, they tend to be less formal in nature. Examples of these informal support initiatives include:

- The School Host Program (through the YMCA Settlement and Integration Services) offers support for immigrant youth by matching them with their Canadian friends from the same school. Recently, the program also provided support for children who are survivors of war trauma through a play therapy program based on group work.
- Several ESL programs throughout the Waterloo Region District School Board also offer peer supports for immigrant youth on an occasional basis.
- The Somali Association, in partnership with Big Sisters of Kitchener-Waterloo and Area, offer a homework club for Somali children who need school work support.
- K-W Multicultural Centre recently offered an orientation program to newly arrived youth (grades 7 and 8) from Kosovo.

Despite a rapid and diverse growth of immigration since the 1960s, there has been relatively little research on immigrant youth carried out in Waterloo region and elsewhere in Canada. In fact, there has been substantially more research carried out on the adjustment of immigrant adults than on immigrant youth (Hicks, Lalonde, & Pepler, 1993). Immigrant youth's needs and issues, whether they are very young children or adolescents, are not documented or understood, especially during their first years in Canada. Also, there are gaps in understanding in any comprehensive way the various services and supports available to these youth (Anisef & Kilbride, 2001). Our research study helped to fill this gap by investigating the challenges faced by a specific age group of immigrant youth (aged sixteen to twenty) in adapting to Canada.

METHODOLOGY
Qualitative Methods and Ecological Framework

Because the knowledge about immigrant youth has been very limited, a qualitative approach with an emphasis on inductive analysis was the method of choice for studying these phenomena. At this point it was more important to develop an understanding of the issues and people's experiences than to generate hypotheses or test these hypotheses.

This research relied primarily on qualitative methods. Qualitative approaches allowed for rich and in-depth description of issues and experiences (Patton, 1990) and for examination of multiple levels of social context (Bronfenbrenner, 1979). We used focus group interviews to gather information (Fern, 2001; Greenbaun, 1999). The use of focus groups with people who have historically not had a voice is becoming more common. Furthermore, focus groups reduce the potentially intimidating nature of face-to-face interviews (Madriz, 2000).

We believe that understanding and addressing challenges faced by immigrant youth cannot be done in isolation from those areas that have an influence on their lives (see Table 1.1 on page 64). In other words, immigrant youth issues were placed in the context of their families, schools, friends, and broader community. For this reason, we involved family members, schools, service providers, and other community members—in addition to youth—in identifying the issues and in developing the solutions.

Research Approach

Our research approach was based on values of participatory action research (Nelson, Ochocka, Griffin, & Lord, 1998) and the assumptions of social constructivism (Lincoln & Guba, 1985). The authors had previous experience with participatory action research and a strong belief in multiple constructions of the nature of social reality. This approach to field research involves the maximum participation of all stakeholders, including those whose lives are affected by the problem under study, in the systematic collection and analysis of information for the purpose of taking action and making change (Nelson, Ochocka, et al., 1998, p. 885).

Our research process involved a high degree of co-operation between researchers and stakeholders, with constant feedback loops and a commitment to using the findings and raising all participants' consciousness about the problem in its social context (Borkman & Schubert, 1994; Chesler, 1991; Gaventa, 1993; Lewin, 1946). We took several steps to ensure that the process of participatory action research would be congruent with its values: empowerment, supportive relationships, and learning (Ochocka, Janzen, & Nelson, 2002; Park, Brydon-Miller, Hall, & Jackson, 1993). First, we decided to use a Steering Committee, composed of key stakeholders, to guide the research, and to use qualitative methods that give voice to people's experiences (Lord & Hutchison, 1993). We fostered supportive relationships among various stakeholders (researchers, youth, family members, teachers, and service providers) by communicating widely findings and actions and by creating a sense of community for all involved. We also hired and trained youth as research assistants and used research findings for education and advocacy.

The Steering Committee—composed of the authors and representatives of immigrant youth, their parents, schoolteachers, service providers, and other groups with a stake in the issues of immigrant youth settlement—met every month. The committee actively collaborated in research process by reviewing, discussing, and approving all decisions regarding research process and research outcomes. It also developed recommendations for future actions.

The research design was flexible and consistent with the value of learning as an ongoing process (Lincoln & Guba, 1985). The interdependency between the research component and action component of the study included the opportunity to confirm experiences and understanding of existing supports, to clarify issues, and to mobilize the community for finding solutions and acting on findings.

Multi-phased Methodology

We used a multi-phased research methodology, in which new phases were built on the lessons from previous phases. In the first phase, we strove to understand the policy and immigration context for youth in Waterloo region. We reviewed policy documents, statistics, and demographics of immigrants and immigrant youth in the region. We also conducted an inventory of existing local services and supports for immigrant youth by reviewing documents and contacting service agencies.

In the second phase, we interviewed sixty-one people: youth (thirty), family members (seventeen), and schoolteachers and service providers (fourteen). During this stage a total of eleven focus group interviews took place. The size of the focus groups ranged from three to nine participants.

The third phase included a community forum and developing recommendations and action steps. The community forum was an opportunity for research participants, the Steering Committee, and other community members to discuss research findings and prioritize strategies for future actions. As a result of this open forum, the Steering Committee came up with practical steps to support immigrant youth in the Waterloo region.

Focus Group Interviews

Participants were selected from a list formulated through a network of local service providers, school boards, and steering committee members. We advertised the recruitment on a local radio station and made presentations to teachers at the public school board. A recruitment flyer was given to all teachers and service providers.

Participants were selected purposively considering such primary criteria as regional representation (i.e., some groups were held in Kitchener-Waterloo and others in Cambridge) and a mix of gender (i.e., one youth group was for males only, one youth group for females only, mixed groups for parents and teachers). Secondary criteria considered included a range of ages, ethnic background, immigrant class, arrival in Canada in the past ten years, employment status, and language proficiency.

A focus group interview format was used with separate interviews conducted with each stakeholder group. A structured interview guide, developed by the researchers and modified based on feedback from Steering Committee members, was used. The main questions dealt with issues that immigrant youth faced, the present supports, and suggestions for future supports.

Focus group interviews were held in local organizations and schools. All interviews were conducted in English, although informal simultaneous translation was used in some youth and parent groups. Interviews were facilitated by two researchers with notes recorded both on a flip chart and a notepad. The interviews were also tape-recorded. The youth researchers facilitated focus groups with youth. Fully informed consent was obtained from participants prior to the interview. Participants were asked to complete an evaluation form and offered a small honorarium ($15) for their participation.

An open coding process (Strauss & Corbin, 1990) was used to analyze the data. While the three main research questions mentioned earlier were developed *a priori*, the coding of responses was inductive. The trustworthiness of the codes was determined by having more than one person code the data, and by using feedback meetings with participants (Patton, 1990).

In addition to these focus groups, we received short essays from seventeen ESL high school students, detailing the challenges they faced while in Canada. These essays were written for an ESL class assignment, and were used in this research with the consent of the students.

Community Forum, Developing Recommendations, and Dissemination

A community forum was used for verification and feedback. It was also an opportunity for all focus group participants and other interested community members to meet and discuss immigrant youth issues and prioritize strategies for support.

The forum was widely advertised across the community and well attended. Despite a snowstorm earlier that day, forty-five people showed up, representing a good mix of various stakeholder groups and other community members. These included a local politician, a local television network, and a journalist from a regional newspaper.

Representatives of youth, family members, and service providers were instrumental in carrying out the forum. For example, the summary of focus group findings was presented by youth and parents teamed with a researcher. Several youth read the stories of anonymous ESL students about being an immigrant youth.

After presenting the findings, the floor was opened to suggestions and comments from those in attendance. These comments were used to shape the emerging list of suggestions for supports. Participants were then asked to indicate which strategies they felt most strongly about by placing two stickers beside the appropriate idea(s). The final list and the number of votes for each suggestion were compiled following the forum and presented to the Steering Committee to develop recommendations.

The Steering Committee met twice following the community forum and developed recommendations that were diverse and comprehensive. For example, these recommendations targeted different levels, including the government/policy level, the education system level, and the neighbourhood level. Recommendations also involved youth, parents, and service providers. Finally, the recommendations also included a combination of formal services and informal supports.

The final stage of this project was to disseminate the research findings. This happened in a variety of ways, including information packages available at the community forum, a written report and fact sheet distributed to many local service providers and interested community members, and a ten-minute live interview on a local radio station.

A series of workshops and conference presentations were also made to local service providers, provincial settlement workers, and at the fourth International Metropolis Conference (attended by academics, policy-makers and non-governmental organizations interested in immigrant issues from around the world). Finally, meetings were held with politicians, including a local city councillor who requested information about the project findings and the implications for the local community. A brief presentation was also made to Elinor Caplan, federal minister of Citizenship and Immigration, to highlight issues arising from our research.

ISSUES FACED BY IMMIGRANT YOUTH

The struggles that immigrant youth face while adapting to their new home country are many (Canadian Council on Social Development, 2000). Not only do they have to overcome the challenges shared by their parents (e.g., language proficiency and finding new networks of support), they also live in difficult times for all youth. For example, the employment prospects for youth across the country are challenging (Canadian Council on Social Development, 1998; Canadian Youth Foundation, 1995). Yet immigrant youth face the additional barriers to employment traditionally shared by many immigrants, such as lack of English language skills, no Canadian work experience, and discrimination (Henry & Ginzberg, 1985; Janzen, 1992; Janzen, Ochocka, & Wing Sang Wong, 1998; Commission of Inquiry on Equality in Employment, 1984).

In this section we highlight issues immigrant youth faced in their first years of living in Canada. While past literature has contended that the experiences of immigrant youth vary a great deal (Hicks, Lalonde, & Pepler, 1993), we wanted to better understand these diverse experiences by hearing the voices of immigrant youth, parents, and service providers. We have organized this section by using the ecological model (see Figure 1.1) to understand the specific issues facing immigrant youth as they relate to the various spheres of influence on their lives. We end this section with four stories written by the ESL students.

FIGURE 1.1: SPHERES OF INFLUENCE ON YOUTH

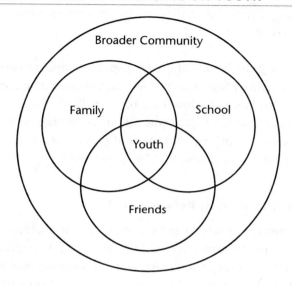

Issues Youth Faced Because of Who They Are

The first level in the ecological model was that of immigrant youth as individuals. English language acquisition has long been identified as an important factor in facilitating adaptation within English-speaking Canada (Barankin, Konstantareas, & deBosset, 1989; Ima & Hohm, 1991; Janzen, Ochocka, & Sundar, 2001; Rumbaut, 1991). While immigrant children and youth generally learn the English language more easily than their parents (Hiebert, 1998), during the time it takes to learn English, youth may experience difficulties such as alienation and poor academic performance (Johnson & Peters, 1994).

Our study participants confirmed that learning English was a major personal challenge that youth needed to overcome upon arrival in Canada. Learning English was seen as a key to entry and acceptance in their new world. Without it youth said that they felt "lost" or "nervous, shy, and terrible." In a few cases the inability to speak English led to isolation from their peers and to loneliness:

> They feel that they cannot express who they are. They may be
> quiet in class, but after you get to know them, you discover that

this is not their true self. People make judgments about who they are because of their inability to express themselves. (ESL teacher)

But learning the basics of the English language was not always enough. Speaking with an accent was also seen as a barrier to peer acceptance and an occasional source of ridicule from peers. The time it took to lose the accent was difficult for some, in light of the peer pressure to conform. "My accent was a big issue," said one youth. "It let everyone know that I was different."

Issues Youth Faced in Relation to Their Peers

It was not surprising to hear from youth that relationships with their peers figured prominently in their lives. In fact, speaking about peer relationships was a very popular topic of discussion among the youth we interviewed. (Interestingly, parents and service providers talked relatively little about how immigrant youth related to their peers.)

One topic of discussion was about the friends they had left behind in their home countries and whom they missed:

> At first I thought of being here like a holiday and I was eager to go back and tell my friends about it. But then it began to sink in that I wasn't going back. (Immigrant youth)

Attempts to connect with old friends only added to the frustration. Whereas they once shared things in common, old friends now led different lives, as both parties moved on. As one youth commented, "It is terrible to leave friends behind. I write, but it is not the same."

Making new friends in Canada was a challenging experience for most youth we spoke with. For some the challenge was considerable. They confided that they felt very isolated and lonely, particularly during their first few months in Canada. One youth admitted, "Friends are hard to come by. I can count the number of true friends I have on one hand."

When friendships were first made, they were typically with other immigrants, regardless of their cultural background. Culture seemed to matter less than the common bond in sharing the immigrant experience:

> When I first came I was friends with another immigrant. He was not from my culture. But he understood because he was an immigrant too, and he tried to help me. (Immigrant youth)

We did hear a few stories about immigrant youth feeling accepted by Canadian-born peers, but these seemed to be the exception rather than the norm, at least in the early years after their arrival in Canada. Breaking into the friendship circles of Canadian-born peers was challenging for a number of reasons. Visible distinctions, such as wearing different clothes or having a different colour of skin, were reported as barriers to acceptance. Other barriers were more subtle and related to differing cultural expectations and practices (such as relating to peers of the opposite sex). Youth also noted either a general apathy or an open hostility of Canadian-born peers toward immigrants:

> In my home country, you are who you are. Here they think you are a different creature or something. (Immigrant youth)

> Canadians have friends already, so they don't need to be friends with me. They don't show any interest in immigrants, they never ask about my home country. (Immigrant youth)

Taken together, these challenges in relating to Canadian-born peers led many youth to feel caught between two cultures. We noticed that on the one hand, immigrant youth wanted to feel accepted by others and conform to mainstream expectations and practices. On the other hand, youth also wanted to maintain and affirm their own personal identity—an identity stemming from their cultural background. This sentiment was well captured in the words of these two youth:

> You're stuck in the middle. You're not like people from your country and you're not like Canadians—you're right in the middle. (Immigrant youth)

> I don't feel comfortable with the way that Canadians talk, and they
> don't feel comfortable with they way that I talk. (Immigrant youth)

A few immigrant youth tried to make sense of these conflicting cultures by talking as if they rejected one culture in favour of the other. An example was the youth who commented that he was "almost embarrassed" by his culture and sometimes, he said, he wanted "to leave my culture behind and be like Canadians so that I would fit in." On the other extreme were those who attempted to segregate themselves from mainstream society. A good example was the person who "wanted to stick with people from my same culture because it reminds me of home and will help me to keep my language and cultural values."

Yet for the vast majority of immigrant youth, the balance was somewhere in between. They worked hard to forge a new identity and find new ways of relating to peers. They were innovators in building relationships across cultures. Youth realized that the tension of living in the middle of two cultures required a balancing act—they needed to discover for themselves what parts of their background culture they would maintain, and what parts of mainstream (and other) cultures they would adopt as their own. And in doing so, they also offered an opportunity for their Canadian-born peers to go through a similar process.

The success stories of immigrant youth who, in the end, were able to find ways to make deep and trusting friendships were inspiring. These stories demonstrated how youth could take charge of their situation and change it for the better:

> Students stay in their own groups and don't try to get to know
> other people. In my home country, everyone wanted to be friends
> with the new student. But that is not true here. It's hard to break
> into groups. This happened to me after a while, only because I
> took the initiative [and after] I saw that people weren't going to
> come to me. It took a lot of energy, but I did make friends.
> (Immigrant youth)

Issues Youth Faced in Relation to Their Family

Youth, parents, and service providers alike talked at length about the changing dynamics within immigrant families as a result of immigration. In fact, these discussions led us to conclude that the issues of immigrant families needed much further exploration, resulting in a new major provincial research study on immigrant parenting (Ochocka, Janzen, Anisef, & Kilbride, 2001).

In the present study we encountered four main themes related to immigrant youth and families: (1) a clash of cultures, (2) changing roles in the family, (3) pressures faced by parents, and (4) changes in family closeness. These themes were common across stakeholder perspectives (i.e., youth, parents, and service providers), although the interpretations of these themes were not always the same.

Clash of Cultures

The first dominant theme confirms the observations of other researchers (e.g., Anisef & Kilbride, 2001; Rosenthal, Demetriou, & Efklides, 1989), namely the clash between old and new cultures being played out in the home setting. If youth felt "caught in the middle" in relation to their peers, they felt it equally strongly at home. At home they continued to grapple with the dual sources of identity, conflicting values, and language differences between the old and new countries:

> Kids have two personalities for a while—one that lets them fit in at school and one that lets them fit in at home. As adults they become the integration of the two. (Service provider)

Some parents responded to this struggle between cultures by resisting the new culture. Youth attributed this resistance to a lack of understanding their parents had of both Canadian culture and the pressures that youth were facing to conform. "Parents don't understand that this is a different culture," said one youth. Another pointed out that her parents had not adapted to Canadian culture, and as a result had trouble understanding and accepting the fact that she had changed. Consider the similar opinions of these youth:

> My mom thinks family is number one, more important than friends, and didn't understand some things that people do here with friends. For example, she didn't understand the reason for sleepovers when I have a bed in my own house. She didn't like me acting like my new friends. (Immigrant youth)

> Mom wanted me to eat foods traditional to my home country [i.e., rice and beans] at school. But all the other kids would have sandwiches. It was such a clash and the other kids didn't understand. (Immigrant youth)

Not all parents rejected their children's struggling between cultures. In some cases parents and youth worked together toward compromise, combining old ways with new Canadian norms. For example, one youth mentioned that if there was something she did not like about her culture, she mentioned it to her parents and they talked about it. Her parents recognized that there were good aspects to Canadian culture and adopting these would not change their daughter's core personality. Other youth echoed that parents and children need to develop flexibility, trust, and mutual respect:

> My parents want us to keep our culture and I'm OK with that. My sister says that the Canadian way is better and my parents think that's OK too—as long as we don't do drugs. (Immigrant youth)

> It helps if parents trust their kids. If they do, the parents and kids will have a good relationship. If they don't trust, the kids will not care about their parents. (Immigrant youth)

Changing Roles in Family

The second theme dealt with the changing roles, and the resulting changing power dynamics, within the family. Children tended to learn the English language and to understand Canadian ways more quickly than their parents. As a result, youth acted as interpreters of language and culture for their parents—roles that parents usually play for their children.

The impacts of these role reversals were significant. For youth, they recognized that they needed to grow up faster and become more adult-like in their relationship with their parents. This was particularly true for older siblings. They often had to take care of younger siblings more than previously, because of the many pressures their parents were now facing. "In my home country," said one youth, "my parents took care of me. Now I have to take care of my siblings."

For their part, parents seemed to struggle with how to be parents in their new home country. "Parenting is tough regardless of being an immigrant or not," noted a service provider. "But being an immigrant parent adds another dimension of difficulty." Parents mentioned that they became insecure as their parental position was undermined, and when their power and control lessened (Ochocka, Janzen, et al., 2001). At other times there was a rift between parents and children because children knew much more about the Canadian system:

> It is more difficult for parents to learn the language and they get a distorted view of Canada. They are alienated from Canadian society, because they see it interpreted through the eyes of their children. (Service provider)

Dealing with Pressures Parents Faced

The third theme related to the way in which youth within the family dealt with the many pressures parents themselves were facing. The parents we spoke with welcomed the opportunity to express at length the many pressures that they were personally dealing with. Youth, too, were quick to point out their parents' worries about money and employment, and the limited time they are able to spend with their children. Observing their parents struggle in these new ways was hard for them, and they saw the pressures on them as negatively affecting their ability to be parents:

> My parents came here because of us [children]. And now they find themselves without jobs and they are ashamed. (Immigrant youth)

> I don't want to worry my mom. So I don't want to talk to her about my problems. (Immigrant youth)

53

Changing Family Closeness

The fourth theme focused on the changes in family closeness as a result of the immigration process. Immigration had caused some families to become less close and more fragmented. Family members (e.g., parents, siblings, or extended family) had been left behind in home countries. But not only did youth have to deal with the loss of leaving loved ones behind, they also could no longer rely on these important people for support. The resulting isolation and emotional turmoil caused one youth to state, "I left behind all my family. This made me kind of depressed in the beginning."

On the positive side, we heard stories about how immigration had in fact made families closer. Difficult times caused the family to look to each other for strength and resolve. Consider these words from one youth and parent:

> Here in Canada we are closer. I feel that I grew up in our relationship because of the hard work. We cried many times. Hard times made me grow up. (Immigrant youth)

> The first year I needed to help children in every way. My relationship with my sons improved because I was able to help them. I made them trust me. (Immigrant parent)

Issues Youth Faced in Relation to the School System

The majority of the immigrant youth we spoke to spent a large portion of their day in school. It was no wonder that they had many opinions about their school experiences. Through their comments we heard two main and interrelated themes: (1) how youth are adapting to their new school environment, and (2) how the school environment is adapting to immigrant youth.

Challenges in Youth Adaptation

Adapting to a new school in a new country was a stressful experience for many youth. "It was like starting all over again," said one youth. The first few days and weeks of school were particularly difficult. "It was scary," a youth commented. "I was so nervous . . . and just wanted to stay at home," admitted another.

The challenge of language was the greatest obstacle when they started school. Without understanding or speaking English, much of their early school experience was shrouded in confusion and frustration. Students felt like they were observers rather than participants in school ("I would just sit around and watch"). Homework took a long time to accomplish. Even knowing what question to ask was difficult because, as one student commented, "I didn't understand anything that happened the whole day."

Youth also needed to learn how to fit into a new educational system that in many cases challenged their assumptions of what school should be like. The closer, more open relationships between students and teachers were strange for some, as was the practice of some Canadian-born students to challenge the authority of teachers. Differences in curriculum and pedagogy were noticed (most often Canadian academic standards were seen to be lower, but the language barriers made it more difficult). Even the hours of instruction were unusual for some students. One student laughed when recalling how he left for home at noon on his first day, thinking that school was finished, as was the daily practice in his home country.

ESL classes helped students to overcome language barriers. More than this, the classes also gave them an opportunity to be with others who were going through the similar experience of being an immigrant. ("People are more similar, even if they are from different countries.") These new friends could help them interpret their new school system. And in many cases ESL teachers were described as being a very helpful source of support in adapting to a new school and a new country.

Yet students also saw the merit of integration within the broader school. They did not want to be treated by a different standard to other students. This was particularly true as their time in Canada lengthened. They wanted to be included in the mainstream of school. After all, the special help that they may have once received was not because they were any less bright, but because they needed to overcome (and consequently learn from) challenges that mainstream students did not experience.

Challenges in School Adaptation

There are many challenges for school systems to adapt to immigrant youth. Yet it is a school's willingness to accept, be open to, and respect diversity that can welcome immigrant students to the school culture. As suggested by Anisef and Bunch (1994), in the past immigrant youth encountered significant challenges in Canadian schools, which continue unless the school system learns to accommodate their differences and needs.

In our study we heard mixed reviews about school accommodations. On the positive side, some youth talked about feeling welcomed and stimulated by the school environment, particularly through their involvement with ESL classes and ESL teachers. "If the students didn't accept you," noted one youth, "at least the teachers did."

Other youth (and many parents and service providers) were critical of the school system. Much of the criticism was directed at schools for not looking beyond the cultural and language differences to recognize and advance the potential of immigrant youth. More to the point, youth and parents complained that academic expectations for immigrant youth seemed to be lower, and that access to after-class support was not easily available in mainstream classes:

> Teachers put limits on youth's capacities, saying that because they
> are immigrants and English is not their first language, they should
> be happy with lower marks. (Service provider)

For their part, parents were often frustrated with the school system. Much of their frustration dealt with differences between their past experiences with schools and their present perception of schools in Canada (e.g., lack of discipline, lack of respect shown toward teachers, the requirement of "non-essential" courses, etc.).

But perhaps the most striking observation was the lack of perceived control that parents felt about their child's education. Parents felt limited in the extent that they could advocate on behalf of their children. In part this was due to language barriers, but it was also due to a lack of information about the Canadian school system. Consequently, they did not have the tools, awareness, or platform needed to address their concerns:

There is a breakdown in communication between parents and educators. Parents are not aware of what is happening in schools, what children are being taught. Since parents often don't understand English, it's hard to communicate with teachers and understand the papers that children bring home. (Immigrant parent)

Issues Youth Faced in Relation to Society as a Whole

The broadest sphere of influence on immigrant youth's life was what we call the "broader community." This sphere included everything in society outside of the relationships that immigrant youth had with their peers, families, and school.

Youth recognized that a multicultural country such as Canada has both challenges and benefits. On the positive side, youth talked about appreciating the freedom, safety, economic security, health care, and general opportunities that Canada afforded. "We're very happy," exclaimed one teenage boy. "I'm here two years, but I feel like I am here all my life." Others acknowledged how moving to an ethnically diverse country had broadened their horizons. Being in Canada had enabled them to come into contact with and learn from so many people in ways that enriched their lives:

Being in Canada has opened my eyes to the world. I have met so many different people, with different values. Now I feel like I could go anywhere in the world. What could be worse [i.e., better] than this? (Immigrant youth)

But the dark side of Canadian society was also discussed. Despite its official rhetoric and long history of receiving immigrants, immigrant youth were aware of the difficulty Canadian society had in welcoming and adapting to the immigrant reality. They often perceived a general non-acceptance of immigrants by people within their community and the media (e.g., the negative characterization of Apu [the South Asian owner of the local convenience store] on "The Simpsons" as "the stupid guy"). They saw systemic social barriers that their parents faced in securing employment or gaining recognition of their professional qualifications.

And some participants described their personal experiences with racism and discrimination. For example, we heard stories about youth being ignored, taunted ("We hate you"), insulted (called "Black one"), or physically hurt ("My son gets beaten up") by others because they were immigrants. And youth also were beginning to experience barriers to employment that their parents also experienced, such as previous work experience "not counting" here in Canada.

LEARNING FROM YOUTH

In reflecting on the issues immigration youth faced, we came to see two dominant themes interwoven across all study participants. One was the immense pressures that immigrant youth experience, and the other was the resilience and capacity of immigrant youth to transform their own lives and society.

Through the participants' personal accounts, we noticed that immigrant youth were aware of their personally demanding predicament of integrating and adapting to a new home country. We noticed that they not only experienced the pressures common to most other youth in Canada, but also the challenges of being an immigrant.

While our research identified pressures and challenges, there was another storyline of capacity and strength. We heard about the resilience that immigrant youth and their families demonstrate through the their attempts to creatively transform their lives from what they once knew into something new and innovative.

But more than wanting to transform their own personal lives, we also noticed their desire to see Canadian society transformed. With the energizing idealism of youth, participants longed for a more welcoming Canadian society. An improved society would be one in which adjustment and adaptation would be mutual among immigrants and other Canadians. It would take full advantage of the mutual learning opportunities offered by diversity. It would encourage the immense potential of social capital to be released through the equitable and active participation of all members of society. There was an underlying recognition that the immigrant youth and their families were leading the way in shaping this new society.

To be accurate, not all participants explicitly articulated this vision of a transformed society. We observed, rather, three groups of youth that were progressively clearer in their realization of, expression of, and response to the need for social change. It was not uncommon to have participants within each focus group belonging to two or all of these groups.

In the first group were those who tended to be grateful and appreciative of Canada, and who either ignored or were unaware of the negative aspects of Canadian society. People in this group were not so much interested in transforming society as in focusing on its positives. Often, but not always, it was those who were most recent to Canada that belonged to this group. Theirs was a "honeymoon period" when everything seemed new and exciting, and where the strengths of Canadian society greatly overshadowed any weaknesses:

> Some youth are very excited about having a new life in Canada. Sometimes this is just a honeymoon period and reality hits them very hard. They suddenly feel that everything is going wrong and then they face depression. (Service provider)

As this quotation suggests, the pressures of being immigrant youth often led to frustration and disillusionment. For this second and largest group, the "dream" (as one immigrant youth called the time immediately after his arrival) had ended. Despite their frustration, there were frequent calls for constructive change. Youth articulated what they saw as being wrong about life in Canada, and offered their own vision of how to fix the problems:

> I am living in your world [i.e., in Canada]. You [peers] should be helping me, not making fun of me. (Immigrant youth)

It was the third group, fewer in number, who moved from critique and suggestions to concrete action. Immigrant youth in this group wanted to build a more just society. For them it was an issue of social justice. Having the fortitude to overcome their own personal pressures, they worked to make their schools and community more responsive to and supportive of immigrants' experiences. Examples

of these youth included the courageous youth who spoke passionately at the community forum about their struggles and their
suggestions for change. The small group of youth who took the
results of this research as a platform to mobilize other youth in their
schools was another example.

We end this section by hearing the written stories submitted by
four ESL students. When reading these stories, notice the different
spheres of influences on their lives that these youth mention. Also
notice the many pressures that they face, and their capacity to
respond to their situation.

Students' Stories

Student #1

As an immigrant I face many challenges like different community
and culture and like meeting new people to grow up with. As an
immigrant youth I faced problems, for example, I couldn't speak
the language, do the stuff Canadians or others do, not wear the
same clothes. But eventually you get over these things because
they will change toward you and understand the way you are, or
will change to the way they are living, whichever fits you better.
But after a long time you will feel like you are at home, nothing is
bothering you, and you will feel normal.

Some other problems may be teachers are treating you different than others because of your background. And sometimes you
don't get to hang around people that you want because you're not
accepted because they have an idea about your background. . . .
So there is a good side and a bad side to being an immigrant, so
it's not ugly because there is a pretty side to it. That's my point of
view. Other fellow students might not agree with my point, but
that's the problems I personally ran into when I got to Canada 3.5
years ago. So I know what it's like, but I got over these problems.

Student #2

As an immigrant youth I face many challenges. It wasn't easy for
an immigrant youth to come to another country for it was very

difficult. The most difficult thing was to understand the language. I had a lot of problems in school because I didn't understand. I was very depressed. I wanted to go back to my country. Another challenge was the weather because it was very cold. But my family and my teachers helped me a lot to understand and now I speak English and I love Canada.

Student #3

As an immigrant youth I face many challenges because it's hard to learn the language and when you don't know how to speak it, people will say things about you and when you go to find a job, sometimes they will give you a job and sometimes they won't, because you don't know anything or don't speak English or because you are from a different country. Your parents have a hard time finding a job because they won't give them a job because they come from a different country or because they don't speak very well English. Even your teacher says things about you too because you don't understand anything and the teacher gets tired of teaching you. Getting fired from a job that is something people experience because they are immigrants.

The best thing about Canada is that you are allowed to express your religion and celebrate your culture. You are free from everything. You could do things you would like to do. The worst thing about Canada is when you do something that is not very bad, they might send you back to your country because you've just did something by mistake.

Student #4

As an immigrant youth I experience a lot of challenges. First challenge is to learn how to live in a place where you're at. Second thing is language. That's OK when you have parents with you. But another problem begins when [you] start high school. Some Canadian kids are being mean to us immigrants. Same with the teachers. Some teachers are being mean. All of them say no racism, but they all actually do it. I am personally very disappointed in Canada. Canada is a nice and free country, but I'd rather want to be in Yugoslavia without food like I was for seven years. It's really hard when you're here, strange world, everything so different, and then you find out that you're not wanted here.

All of the people are saying no racism, we're all the same. But they don't mean it. Same with the teachers. Some of them treat you like you're nothing and nobody. Some of them think that we're stupid and we don't know how to talk back, and some of them think that we don't understand enough. Anyway, they think, some of them, that we're stupid. You know, it really bothers me. I hate when a person with a smile is telling horrible things to me and smiling like we're talking about heaven! All I'm telling you is, people are the one that make me cry. It's true I have everything here. I thank Canada for saving my life, that she welcomed me and my parents and sister. But there's something that bothers me. And all I'm saying, some people are bad racists.

Present Sources of Support

We asked immigrant youth about the people and places that have been particularly helpful in making them feel comfortable in Canada. Most supports mentioned were informal in nature and came from such sources as friends, family, people within their own ethnic community, neighbours, and those within faith communities. The message was simple and clear: immigrant youth typically look to those natural supports closest to them for help in dealing with their concerns.

As I got friends, it got easier for me. (Immigrant youth)

My family is closer here. We talk a lot about our struggles here. (Immigrant youth)

The youth we spoke with had trouble finding help beyond their natural supports. This was due in part to the fact that they were in a new country, and were dealing with new pressures that they had never experienced before. The general disorientation that came with being an immigrant also made it hard for newcomer youth to know how and where to reach out for help, let alone articulate their concerns to service providers.

Some youth said it was hard to ask for help because they felt ashamed of their circumstances. Or if they did ask for help, they were not understood. For some, the initial experience of being an immigrant was overwhelming and paralyzing, as described by this participant:

> You don't even know what you need help with; you just need help with everything. (Immigrant youth)

Participants also said that there were few formal services from settlement and mainstream organizations available to immigrant youth. Some formal services that did exist had recently lost their funding (e.g., ESL summer school programs). Those mainstream formal services for youth that did exist were sometimes inaccessible because of language, financial, or various cultural barriers.

ESL classes were the only formal services that seemed to be helping immigrant youth deal with their concerns. Parents and youth alike discussed the importance of ESL teachers in facilitating youth's transition to a new culture and school system:

> ESL teachers are helpful—they understand, they don't laugh, they spend time with you. They don't embarrass you because you don't know the language. (Immigrant youth)

Table 1.1 summarizes the different sources of support mentioned by focus group participants. They have been organized according to the spheres of influence highlighted earlier.

Suggestions for Future Supports

The various stakeholder groups made suggestions for future support during the focus group sessions. The collection of these suggestions was presented to participants at the open forum for feedback. Participants had the opportunity to add and prioritize the suggestions. The suggestions are listed below. Again the findings are organized according to their fit within the different spheres of influence highlighted earlier: youth and their peers, parents, schools, and the broader community.

TABLE 1.1: SUMMARY OF PRESENT SOURCES OF SUPPORT

Source of Support	Examples	Limitations
Friends	Friends	• Get involved with wrong 'crowd' (e.g., gangs) • Less incentive to make new friends when peers are only those of one's own culture
Family	Family	• Financial hardship (e.g., unemployment) • Parents have slower cultural integration
School	ESL teachers	• Teachers do not all share the same approach to supporting immigrant youth integration
	Informal supports in schools	• Few to begin with, but now diminishing because of reduced funding
	Own cultural/ethnic groups and faith communities	• Mixed messages: "Don't forget old culture's ways," yet "Important to become Canadian" • May be barriers to cultural change
	Formal community supports	• Scarce
	Other community supports	• Scarce

Youth and Peers

All three stakeholders talked about the importance of informal support for youth. This support will help to facilitate social opportunities and peer support among youth (immigrant and Canadian-born combined) to help them gain a better understanding of Canadian context and culture and build Canadian friendships. One immigrant youth stated strongly that "immigrant youth should get help from Canadian youth." Other stakeholders suggested practical implications.

> We have to provide structured opportunities for immigrant and mainstream youth to mix, to get to know each other. Sports is a very good vehicle for this—it breaks down barriers. (Service provider)

Other specific examples presented in the focus groups and the forum were as follows:
- summer language camps for youth
- tutoring from immigrant youth
- get youth together to define "services" and "supports" for youth
- support groups for youth
- recreational and social opportunities to make friends
- field trips to see Canada
- a community place to connect with other youth
- cross-cultural exchange evenings
- information for youth about Canadian culture/context

Support for Parents

It was evident in the focus groups that parents who have immigrated to Canada face many of their own difficulties. Understandably, their difficulty in finding work, earning a steady income, and learning about the Canadian culture themselves affect their children as well. As highlighted in earlier sections, new Canadian families are limited in how much they can help children because of factors such as financial hardship, slower cultural integration and knowledge, and their concern for their children in a strange environment.

The majority of participants talked about the importance of providing supports for parents so that they will be in a better position to help their children. They talked about how "teenagers needed to be teenagers, not to have adult responsibilities," and that "better stability for parents means better opportunities and quality of life for kids." Additional suggestions for supports for parents included:

- parents need opportunities to learn practical English
- parents need network opportunities to connect with other Canadians
- parents need to have information about Canadian society
- parents need summer language camps
- parents need to find meaningful work

School System

Mostly youth talked about the need to improve the school system. They stressed that school is an important place to learn, interact, and also help children with their problems. Consequently, it is important that the school environment promote these qualities in an effective and successful way. Some of the parents' suggestions were to "place youth in classes according to knowledge, not age" and "to meet youth where they are and talk to them more often."

Further comments on this topic and ideas for improving the school system are presented in the following list:

- develop ESL classes for concrete subjects
- integrate ESL classes with the rest of the school
- include immigrant parents on school councils
- teachers need to meet youth where they are and understand the situation from which they come
- include co-op opportunities for youth to gain Canadian experience
- provide recreational and social opportunities after school

> A kid who never talks in class can be so free and have so much fun when involved in social events. Sometimes tears come to my eyes watching them have genuine fun—it's totally different than what they experience in class. (Service provider)

Broader Community

Primarily youth and parents talked about the larger Canadian context. They explained that the attitudes and perceptions about immigrants are just as important (and potentially harmful) as the actual types of provisions and supports that are set up for immigrants.

Their suggestions were related to helping Canadians change their attitudes and increase their knowledge about immigration, multiculturalism, cultural meaning, and respect:

- create regional immigrant youth council and strategy/plan
- have agencies reflect on how to be more responsive to immigrant youth
- continue research on immigrant youth
- link schools with broader community
- disseminate research findings to youth group, regional council, and policy-makers
- create a "broker" group to coordinate immigrant youth strategies
- educate Canadians not to make assumptions about people based on language abilities
- canadian and immigrant parents to talk about raising kids (as partners)
- have a community place for immigrants and host Canadians to learn about each other
- develop a regional plan with commitment from the municipal government

Action Steps

Based on the above suggestions made by members of the forum and focus group participants, and taking into consideration their prioritization, the Steering Committee developed action steps to be taken by local community members. The steps were aimed at different levels within the community (i.e., local government/policy, local educational system, service organizations, and neighbourhood levels) and included:

- disseminate and present findings to local school boards
- form a regional immigrant youth council
- create peer support programs for youth
- facilitate meetings of service providers to explore future supports and research

CONCLUSION

This project was developed in response to a lack of research exploring the issues that immigrant youth face in Canada. There is a diverse immigrant population in Waterloo region, yet there are gaps in supports for immigrant youth. The purpose of this research project was twofold: (1) to understand the diverse settlement issues of immigrant youth (aged sixteen to twenty) within Waterloo region, and (2) to develop specific and concrete strategies for supporting youth to address their issues.

The findings from the project indicate that the issues that immigrant youth face are diverse and complex. They include difficulties in learning a new language, challenges in building relationships with peers, pressures their families experience, and barriers in adaptation in schools and in the broader community. Most existing supports for immigrant youth are informal in nature (e.g. friends, family). Few formal services for immigrant youth exist. Of those that do, ESL teachers were seen as key in helping youth's transition to a new culture and the school system.

Suggestions for future support emphasized: support for youth (e.g., peer mentoring, social/recreational opportunities); support for parents (e.g., opportunities to connect with other parents); improvement of schools (e.g., integration of ESL, parents on school councils); and improvement of society (e.g., multicultural events, public education).

The participatory action research approach used in this research project resulted in developing comprehensive action steps based on participants' suggestions. The resulting action steps touch on different levels within our society: local government/policy, educational system, service organizations, and neighbourhoods.

CHAPTER 2

Employment Needs of Newcomer Youth in West End Ottawa

RISHMA PEERA

Pinecrest-Queensway Health and Community Services, Ottawa

INTRODUCTION

Immigrants to Canada encounter numerous difficulties in settlement and integration, especially newcomers from "visible minority" ethnic groups. One of the recurring themes in the process of settlement and integration is that of employment. The ability to secure gainful employment is a critical element in the successful integration of newcomers to Canada. In community-based philosophy, employment is believed to be highly correlated with the global health of individuals as well as that of society.

Much of the research on employment issues to date has focused on the adult experience. The goal of the research presented in this chapter is to explore the issues that newcomer youth face in the context of employment as it relates to integration. This interest in newcomer youth and employment arose when results from consultations and planning initiatives conducted through Pinecrest-Queensway Health and Community Services (PQHCS) in Ottawa pointed to the importance of employment to newcomers, in particular to youth. Through these consultations, it was determined that newcomers between the ages of sixteen and twenty-four often have the most difficulty fitting into Canadian society.

OBJECTIVES

The limited information on the issue of newcomer youth and

employment seems to be a key reason why their needs have not been taken into consideration in employment program designs or in policy development. It is therefore essential for community-based service providers and funding bodies to acquire a contextual understanding of the issues facing newcomer youth with regard to employment.

The objectives of this research, conducted in the west end of Ottawa, were to:

- explore the key issues, causes, and effects of unemployment among newcomer youth
- identify the key barriers for newcomer youth in becoming participants in the labour force
- derive strategies to support the newcomer youth population's entry into the labour market, including immediate interventions as well as preventative measures

NEED FOR RESEARCH

Recent research has established the key barriers and needs of newcomers in terms of employment. As previously mentioned, the focus has been on the adult experience. Newcomer youth and employment issues have not had much attention, despite the fact that specific issues arise in their integration into the labour market. Many of the newcomers' needs are similar to Canadian youth, namely in terms of their transitions from school to work, but with many added challenges because of moving from a different country.

Employment Environment

There are numerous economic issues that constitute barriers to employment for youth (Canadian Youth Foundation, 1995, 1999). The recession of the 1990s, which led to organizational restructuring and downsizing, has affected the youth population the most. The most disturbing trend is that the economic recovery of these past few years has only increased the gap between adult and youth employment, with youth lagging behind.

Understanding Transitions

Human Resources Development Canada (HRDC) describes school-to-work transitions as the way young people move among and within the worlds of education, training, and work (Human Resources Development Canada, 1995). The boundaries between these environments are not as clear as they once were, so HRDC refers to "transitions" rather than a single straightforward "transition." In order to facilitate youth transitions, an institutional approach that organizes partnerships among businesses, schools, and governments has been deemed important. The Canadian system, however, remains very flexible in terms of entry into the labour market, so that one can go back and forth between school and work.

Distinguishing Risk Groups within the Youth Population

Marquardt (1998) notes that all youth bear some risk of being unemployed, but the risk is not spread evenly across the population. He defines youth at risk in terms of the social and economic factors that stand in the way of their becoming productive members of society, and highlights their potential marginalization as a result. He explains that the youth with the lowest levels of education are most at risk and adds that they are most likely to come from low-income families, have their own family responsibilities, or have disabilities. He points out that these are but a few of the predictors of being at risk and that more often than not it is a combination of many factors that creates a "cumulative disadvantage."

In order to categorize risk factors, the Canadian Youth Foundation (1996) has distinguished three segments within the youth population based on educational attainment. The "high-risk" youth are those who do not have a high school diploma and who therefore face higher unemployment rates, low wages, and low literacy. The second group is the "medium-risk" youth population, who have a high school diploma and some post-secondary education, but who cannot access jobs that would enable them to launch a career path. The third group of youth, who are "low risk," have a post-secondary degree or diploma and can make a successful transition into a career path.

Newcomer Youth Issues

Newcomers intrinsically face risks of not integrating into the labour market and hence into society. There are many issues that compound the difficulties in settling down in a new country—the country of origin, socio-economic status, education, and language—as well as numerous other variables that create a high level of complexity in addressing the issue of unemployment. It is generally agreed that education is key to providing opportunities for success. For newcomer students entering schools in Canada, there are many challenges that have far-reaching consequences for segments of youth who are deemed most "at risk," especially those with a cumulative disadvantage.

Language and School Integration

One of the key issues newcomers have to grapple with is language. It is a very serious preoccupation for newcomers who speak neither of the two official languages. As Westermeyer and Her (1996) argue, language fluency is a critical skill in psychosocial adaptation and mental health for newcomers.

For youth, especially those who arrive at high school age, integration into school poses challenges. The system welcomes these youth into programs, such as English as a second language, in order to facilitate their integration into the mainstream. Unfortunately, the structure and culture of school do not sufficiently support and address the complex needs of newcomer students.

Poverty

A key issue that newcomer youth face frequently upon arriving in Canada is poverty, which may be a transient condition to resettling in a new country (Human Resources Development Canada, 1996). Some of the issues linked to poverty and social housing, however, are lack of aspirations for the youth and lower performance in school, as well as violence, criminal activity, and substance abuse.

For the Ottawa region, and the west end of the city in particular, two of the largest newcomer refugee populations are the Somali and the Lebanese communities. These two groups are highly represented in the west end social housing areas and live in situations of poverty, often with a single parent—factors that increase the challenges they face in integrating into society.

Parental Education

Since the new immigration policy based on education, skills, and occupational qualifications was adopted, many newcomer groups have entered Canada with educational levels that are often higher than the Canadian average. However, as pointed out in recent literature (Anisef, 1994), despite the higher levels of education, there are income differences associated with ethnic membership, such as for people from the Black, Chinese, and Greek communities. For these groups of newcomers, the downward occupational mobility that occurs with moving to Canada directly affects the youth, who tend to doubt the value of the educational opportunities school can offer.

Fitting in: Issues of Integration

Newcomers to Canada are a diverse group and, depending on their life experience, adapt differently to the new society. In general, however, newcomers who arrive as refugees need to deal with issues in addition to language. Dealing with emotional trauma is an essential step for the future integration and well-being of entire families. However, this is compounded by cultural differences, literacy problems, problems of identity, perceived lack of support, and racism, to name but a few, that affect the integration of newcomer youth.

The majority of issues youth face in attempting to adapt to their new society are the same both at school and later in the labour market. Ali (1995) has identified several factors that impede youth integration into Canadian society, namely low language proficiency, extent of cultural shock, stereotyping, identity problems, and racial hostility from the community. Also, youth are less likely to adapt to the new culture if they lack a sense of belonging or support, and experience pressures from the family to earn an income.

Situational Analysis

Immigration to Canada has shifted considerably in the last two decades. The statistics show that patterns of immigration, notably in countries of origin, have shifted from European to Asian and African countries, with a higher percentage of refugee claimants. Issues regarding their integration into society have come to the forefront, notably because of the increased number of newcomers arriving in the Ottawa region and especially because they are visible minorities.

In Ottawa, this has meant a need for rapid adaptation of institutional structures and systems, particularly as 32 per cent of the total newcomer population settling in Ottawa in 1994 were refugees, many of whom were fleeing war-torn countries such as Somalia and Lebanon.

In 1994, PQHCS conducted the "West End Youth Needs Assessment," which revealed that one of the main concerns of youth, especially newcomers, was unemployment. In 1995, the needs assessments of both the Somali-speaking community and the Arabic-speaking community in the PQHCS catchment area underlined the fact that unemployment was a key issue facing newcomers.

METHODS

The project began in early December 1999 with the hiring of a researcher and two research assistants. One of the project's first steps was to establish an Advisory Committee to provide input into the process and act as a resource for the team. The committee held one meeting a month, which resulted in a total of four meetings during the life of the project. The committee was comprised of members from the following organizations: the Children's Aid Society, the Nepean Community Resource Centre, the Somali Centre for Youth, Women and Community Development, Woodroffe High School, the John Howard Society Youth Employment Services (West End), the Ottawa-Carleton Regional Police, Ottawa-Carleton Housing, and the Regional Municipality of Ottawa-Carleton.

The methodology selected for the study was mainly qualitative and comprised interviews and focus groups with three target groups: new immigrant youth, community members as key informants, and service providers who work with the new immigrant population. The research attempts to bring to life the realities of newcomers by exploring their experiences. The intention was not to tell the stories of any individual or group of people per se, but to highlight the key challenges some participants face in integrating into the labour market; the particular geographical focus was on the west end of Ottawa-Carleton.

The methodology involved conducting a review of the literature related to newcomer youth and employment in order to situate the issue. It was also determined that focus groups and interviews with newcomer youth, service providers, and community members would be conducted. Therefore, instruments were designed in the first three weeks of the project and presented at the first Advisory Committee meeting. Table 2.1 provides relevant information on the composition of each focus group.

DATA COLLECTION
Outreach Process

Outreach efforts to find newcomer youth participants were made to employment services, community and recreation centres, adult high schools and high schools in the west end of Ottawa, multicultural liaison officers, social service organizations, youth drop-ins, job fairs, and religious institutions. Various media were also used to find participants, including articles in local community newspapers/newsletters and public service announcements on radio stations. The use of the media was limited in order to avoid receiving an overwhelming number of responses and in order to remain within the PQHCS catchment area. Most of the youth participants indicated that they had heard about the study through word of mouth or through flyers that they saw at employment and community centres.

Interviews and Focus Groups

The interviews and focus groups took place between late January and early March 2000, and were conducted in several locations to promote access. A total of eleven focus groups and twenty-five interviews were conducted with youth participants, service providers, and community members (see Table 2.2).

TABLE 2.1: FOCUS GROUP PARTICIPANTS

	Group Composition	Language/Cultural Groups	Number of Participants
YOUTH	Female and male youth ages 17–22	Somali, Jamaican, Cambodian	7
	Female and male youth, ages 18–21 in ESL adult school	Russian, Spanish, Croatian and Ukrainian	6
	Male youth 17–20	Somali, Russian	4
	Female and male youth from Canadian African Women's Organisation Youth Employment program	Somali, French	6
	Canadian African Women's Organization	Somali, French, English	8
	Woodroffe High School	Somali, Arabic, Vietnamese, English	13
TOTAL YOUTH IN FOCUS GROUPS			**44**
COMMUNITY MEMBERS	Cultural interpreters	Arabic, Somali, Spanish, Ukrainian	5
	Somali Community members	Somali	10
	Multicultural Liaison Officers	Somali, Arabic, Spanish, Cambodian	16
TOTAL COMMUNITY MEMBERS IN FOCUS GROUPS			**31**
SERVICE PROVIDERS	Members from the West end Youth Service Providers Network		17
	Representation from 1 employer, OCISO/World Skills Project, Algonquin College, John Howard Society Youth Employment Centre, HRDC Youth Initiatives		5
TOTAL SERVICE PROVIDERS IN FOCUS GROUPS			**22**

TABLE 2.2: SUMMARY TABLE OF FOCUS GROUPS AND INTERVIEWS

	Total Number of participants	Total Number of focus groups	Total Number of interviews
Youth	57	6	13
Community members	31	3	8
Service providers	26	2	4
TOTAL	**114**	**11**	**25**

LIMITATIONS

Due to time constraints, some of the individual youth interviews—which required identifying, scheduling, and conducting the interviews—were replaced by focus groups. The researchers opted to tap into youth who were affiliated with an institution, whether in an employment program, in a recreational centre, in an adult education facility, or a high school. The early attempts to bring independent interested youth together for focus groups were time consuming and relatively unsuccessful. One of the challenges that we faced in the course of this research—a challenge that has been highlighted by other researchers—was the poor attendance of youth at some of the focus groups. Although the research offered a $25 honorarium, youth did not always attend.

The limitation of having selected pre-existing groups and youth who attend the same school or recreational centre is that not enough representation was given to youth who are not affiliated and who therefore might face even greater challenges such as isolation (teenage mothers, youth with addiction, youth in trouble with the law).

The identification of newcomer youth who are unemployed, especially those who have dropped out of school, was a continuing challenge. As they are disengaged, they were very hard to identify and involve in the project.

Another limitation lies in the outcomes of the research. As the data collection process extended past the deadline, the volume of qualitative data could not be entirely analyzed. In fact, the data needed to be coded, analyzed, interpreted, and the report written in a very short time. Consequently, some critical issues emerging from the data are undocumented in the present chapter. For instance, issues discussed by participants regarding role models, definitions, and their concepts of success and what would constitute good jobs, are not presented in this report. An analysis of the gender differences, specific cultural components, and discussions of soft skills are not documented either. These issues are, however, present in the data and could eventually be explored further in follow-up research.

Finally, there are some implicit limitations in how this research was conducted. Although focus groups allow for an in-depth examination of issues, the information they yield is not representative of the entire population. The qualitative nature of this research, therefore, does not allow for information to be generalized.

DESCRIPTION OF FINDINGS

The findings from the disparate groups of participants revealed some common perspectives on certain issues, but also some divergent views based on the concerns identified by each group. However, as an overall outline of the findings, youth were primarily concerned with their immediate needs to find work; community members highlighted the role of employment in an overall integration perspective; and service providers offered information about the institutional gaps that exist in addressing the needs of newcomer youth.

Participant Profile

The following profile was compiled of all the youth participants. A total of fifty-seven youth participated in the study in either interviews or focus groups, 57 per cent of whom were male and 43 per cent female. They ranged in age from sixteen to twenty-nine with 41 per cent between fifteen and eighteen, 36 per cent between nineteen and twenty-one, and the majority being eighteen or nineteen.

In terms of their employment status, 49 per cent reported being unemployed and 24 per cent stated they had part-time jobs. Other youth, representing 22 per cent of participants, were enrolled in a full-time employment program. With regard to enrolment in school, 66 per cent were out of school or attending school part-time, while the others were enrolled in adult education or attended school full-time.

While 34 per cent of the participants had not completed high school, 21 per cent had some college or university experience in Canada or in their country of origin. The remaining stated that their highest educational level attained was Grade 12.

Regarding their immigration status, 63 per cent reported having arrived as refugees, while 33 per cent reported arriving as landed immigrants. Of these youth, 42 per cent had arrived in Canada less than three years ago and 39 per cent had arrived more than six years ago.

A high number of Somali participants reflected the large population that has settled in Ottawa in recent years, with 53 per cent of the youth participants indicating that their mother tongue was Somali. The second highest group represented in our sample was the Russian-speaking community, which constituted 14 per cent of participants. Other participants' languages included Arabic, Spanish, Cambodian, Croatian, Ukrainian, Gujerati, and Farsi, which altogether represented 33 per cent of the sample.

Regarding their living arrangements, 40 per cent lived in social housing, 35 per cent lived with a single mother, and 37 per cent with both parents. Of the remaining participants, many lived alone, with other relatives, or with a spouse. Seventy-one per cent of the youth lived in the west end of Ottawa.

There were thirty-eight community members who participated in interviews and focus groups. They included parents, community leaders, multicultural liaison officers, and cultural interpreters. Twenty-five were female and thirteen were male. There were a few language groups represented, but the sample was clearly dominated by the Somali-speaking group, which constituted 66 per cent. The other language groups represented included Arabic, Spanish, Ukrainian, Cambodian, Bulgarian, Vietnamese, Chinese, Haitian, and Persian.

Cumulative Disadvantage

In the case of our sample, it was apparent that the majority of the youth had a cumulative disadvantage that places them at risk of not successfully integrating into the labour market: 63 per cent arrived as refugees, 40 per cent lived in social housing, 35 per cent lived with single mothers, 46 per cent were not in school, and 34 per cent had an educational attainment lower than Grade 12.

In addition to having been uprooted from their country of origin, and having experienced the trauma of war, separation, and persecution, youth who arrived as refugees have been faced with numerous settlement issues, such as the lack of identity papers. Refugee claimants to Canada who have no proper identification must first have their case heard in order to be admitted as convention refugees. Those who have been admitted as convention refugees, however, do not automatically gain work permits. Although they can request a work permit, employers recognize their immigration status by their social insurance number and avoid hiring individuals who might be in Canada for a short while.

Another factor related to newcomers, especially refugees, is their low socio-economic status, which leads them to rely on public housing. This was an important issue that the disparate groups in the research discussed. The service providers and community members were adamant that neighbourhoods make a difference in terms of the self-confidence and self-esteem of youth. They also alluded to the fact that employers were influenced by where job applicants live. The youth themselves were cognizant of the fact that employers discriminate against them because of their neighbourhood.

Service providers and community members echoed many local studies, which highlighted the fact that single mothers with large families do not have options other than to live in social housing. Some families with two to four children have been able to move out of public housing and into apartments, which allows them to avoid the stigma associated with living in public housing.

Newcomer Youth's Desire to Belong

A large proportion of the youth participants had a cumulative disadvantage that combined their low socio-economic status with being part of a single parent family, living in social housing, and having arrived in Canada as refugees. Although all these factors create tremendous integration challenges for youth, the findings clearly indicate their strong desire and need to belong, whether it be with friends and their own community members, or by adopting elements of their new cultural environment.

Peers and Community Groups

Friends are extremely important for newcomer youth. Peers of the same origin and culture tend to spend time together because of their common bond. Friends therefore become the prime source of information regarding services, jobs, and activities, as well as role models. Most youth who had found jobs in the past mentioned having found them through a friend.

The newcomer youth participants in the study also tended to rely on relatives and community members to create a sense of belonging. The youth alluded to the fact that they could relate much better to people who could understand their culture. This perspective was echoed by others who work with newcomer youth. Knowing that a person has the same culture or religion automatically creates a bond of trust for the youth.

Educational Opportunities

In order to integrate successfully into the new society, newcomer youth indicated a strong interest in taking advantage of educational opportunities. For the majority of newcomers—those who had arrived less than a year ago or who were in the settlement phase (three to five years in Canada)—learning a new culture was dominated by learning the language. For youth in the integration phase, their cultural adjustment was more complex, but included going to school or being in transition between unemployment and/or leaving school.

The strong desire to belong to their new society was evidenced by the fact that the majority of youth wanted to take advantage of the educational opportunities offered in Canada. Indeed, education was believed to be the single most important element that would determine a person's success in Canada. The youth participants believed strongly that those who do not have an education would have very limited employment prospects. Community members also believed that employers look for employees with a good education, and that without a good education, youth would end up in menial jobs below their potential.

Motivation for Working

In their desire to integrate into their new society, newcomer youth want to feel that they have the same opportunities as others. In expressing their reasons for wanting to work, the youth participants said that they needed to save money for college or university and wanted to be independent. The notion of independence was seen as very important, especially for male youth, who also felt that they needed to provide for their families, particularly their mothers. Community members and service providers mentioned that newcomer youth from certain cultures are responsible for supporting their families here and abroad.

Another key motivation for these youth to work is to accumulate experience. Youth mentioned that working would enable them to acquire experience, which would enable them to access other kinds of jobs. Many of the youth who have been in Canada for a few years have learned that they can gain experience from volunteer work or part-time jobs.

Struggling to Fit in: Barriers

Lack of Experience

According to the research, the most cited barrier that newcomer youth have faced is their lack of experience. Employers want them to have Canadian experience. Youth who have gone to school in Canada are still told by employers that they need to have experience. First-time job seekers face the dilemma of not being hired because they do not have experience, and yet they will not acquire experience if no one hires them.

Youth's lack of experience was combined with the fact that they have limited established networks. Those who have an established network need to complete their higher education before their support system can help. The majority of the youth we spoke with, however, had a sense that Canadians are advantaged in many respects because of their networks. Newcomer youth felt as if they were sitting on the sidelines and could not access the world of their Canadian-born counterparts.

Limited Networks and Information

As mentioned earlier, friends are the major source of information about jobs. However, because these youth tend to remain within their own communities, their access to information and networks is limited.

Youth consistently mentioned that having a friend at the company where they are applying provides them with support from within. Youth have said that an employer is more willing to give someone a chance when the reference is already working there.

Most of the youth mentioned that, apart from relying on their friends (most often close friends), the method they use to look for work included submitting applications or resumés to stores, restaurants, fast food outlets, and other places that advertise job openings. Most of them also stated that they had applied to the same places, which in turn may have created a high supply of labour for a limited demand.

Newcomer communities are not always linked with mainstream service providers such as employment centres, which means the youth are unaware of these sources of support. Some learn about these services through friends at school and in the community. However, the negative experiences of a few spread much faster than the information about the benefits of using these services. Youth tend to believe what their friends tell them because they trust them.

Discrimination

The majority of newcomer youth who are also visible minorities clearly sense that they are not treated fairly, let alone equally. Many of the youth who applied for jobs and were called for interviews felt discriminated against because employers would not call them back. One of the most unsettling aspects of going through the job search process was the uncertainty as to the real reason why they were not selected; they did not know if employers rejected them because of their lack of experience or used it as an excuse to discriminate against them.

Youth who have had work experience had other challenges. They consistently perceive being treated differently from other staff members and felt that their cultural differences were not respected. In a work situation, a few of the youth pointed out that they are perceived as untrustworthy and the opportunities afforded them are therefore limited. They are not given the same responsibilities as others (such as handling cash), and they feel excluded because important information is not shared with them, or they are singled out when something negative occurs.

Discrimination has a debilitating effect on newcomer visible minority youth. The fact that they feel discriminated against in many aspects of their integration process has a tremendous impact on their self-perception and their self-esteem. These youth have had to face the transition from one country to another, which requires cultural adaptation; they also face, like all other youth, adolescent transitions in terms of their personality and identity. These transitions, however, are deeply affected by the new society's perception of them as individuals, which in turn affects their views of themselves.

Language

The data indicate that for the youth who participated in our research, the most recent arrivals were the most likely to encounter language barriers. Language was not as big an issue for some youth because they knew English before settling in Canada. Youth who spoke only French faced the same issues as those who spoke other languages. This eliminated their access to most services and job opportunities because they did not speak English.

Although learning English was an issue for the recent arrivals, not being bilingual was another barrier that youth who had been in Ottawa longer were facing. In a region considered bilingual, many service jobs require both languages. This constitutes a key barrier for newcomer youth who need to learn two new languages in order to be successful in entering the labour market.

As service providers and community members have noted, some

youth have difficulty with the written language, which might be a barrier in applying for and functioning in certain jobs that require fluent literacy skills.

Long-Term Employment Opportunities

As discussed in the previous section, education was highlighted by all participants as being crucial in newcomer youth integration and full participation in the labour market and in society. However, as community members and service providers outlined, there are major difficulties for many newcomer youth in Ottawa, especially visible minority youth who are dealing with issues of poverty, which hinder them from taking full advantage of the benefits of education.

The biggest barrier many refugees in Ottawa, notably in the Somali community, faced is that their legal status as refugees was not changed to landed immigrant status within a reasonable time. This has hindered many youth from accessing higher education, and created a group of newcomer youth who have been denied proper settlement and integration into their new society.

Furthermore, community members from the Somali community—especially parents who have high expectations for their youth—are becoming increasingly aware that the school system does not respond to the needs of their young people. Other community members also echoed the fact that youth were dropping out as a result of the system's failure to integrate them. They were cognizant that a number of combined factors, including socio-economic status, economic needs, and the downscaling of expectations, play a role in explaining why many newcomer youth do not take advantage of educational opportunities.

What it means in the long term is that the prospect for "good jobs" is considerably reduced, if not eliminated. It takes time for newcomers to become full participants in the labour force and society. Some say that the next generation might integrate better; however, if parents have downscaled expectations, their children might simply repeat the cycle.

Effects of the Barriers

The youth in the study mentioned being frustrated and wanting to give up searching for work. Their discouragement is compounded by how they think people perceive them.

The perception of being purposely overlooked by employers creates a sense that they are not meant to belong here. A few youth mentioned wanting to move to the United States, where they felt the opportunities would be much better for them, or to move back to their countries of origin. Some expressed a desire to become entrepreneurs, in order to have control over their own environment and to be treated as they wish to be treated.

Community members mentioned that, in the past year and a half, because the economic situation has improved so dramatically, unemployment for many of the newcomer youth has changed. In fact, high-tech companies that have hired many people in the last year have also hired young newcomers to work as assemblers. This included youth who were in school, others who were out of school and unemployed, youth who were having difficulty in school, and those who could not find work in their field. Community members see the clear advantage in an economic sense, but also consider the negative long-term effect on the opportunities of these youth who have opted for this short-term solution.

Lack of Meaningful Support and Opportunities

Parents and Community Members

Parents of the youth, who are also new to the country, have high expectations for their children's future. They are, however, also unable to provide the support required to help them make a successful transition into school or in the labour market. The sample of youth indicates that many of them come from single-mother-headed families and families who have arrived as refugees, for whom it is extremely challenging to integrate. Because mothers are overwhelmed with their large families and often have a low level of education, the youth are often expected to fend for themselves and perform despite the lack of parental support.

As many community members have stated, parents are an essential source of support for their children. It was clear in our research that the youth who have parents who push their children to complete their education and to perform in school are the ones who were most able to perform, to remain engaged, and to have access to more information. They were also the youth who mentioned their parents as being good role models.

Schools

Community members suggested that schools, which are there to provide opportunities to their youth, are actually not responding to their needs. It has been mentioned that support was not provided to address the high emotional needs of children and youth who have arrived as refugees. The feeling that schools try to hold back newcomer youth was also put forward by community members, who feel unable to communicate with the institutions.

With regard to employment-related programs, the co-op model was mentioned by a number of youth. Some found them useful, if only they resulted in an actual job at the end of their placement; others thought they were used to perform tasks no one else wanted to accomplish. The most frequent comment about co-op placements was that they were not related to the long-term interests of the youth.

Employment-Related Programs and Services

As a source of information about jobs and job search techniques, employment services and programs are theoretically very beneficial. However, the majority of the most sustainable programs and services are designed for mainstream youth, whose needs have been identified or at least explored. Little attention has been given to the specific needs of newcomer youth, which explains why these have not been taken into consideration in program or service designs.

The services and programs that are offered seem to address some needs directly related to employment and employability skills. However, what the youth, community members, and service providers themselves indicated is that the newcomer youth most at risk of not successfully integrating the labour market do not take advantage of these services. According to the youth, the reasons are multiple: some mentioned not being aware of these services or programs; others were aware of one or two employment centres or services, but were not using them; and still others who had used some services and participated in programs before felt they were limited in their usefulness. A minority found that the services were very useful and supportive.

The fact that these services are available but are not accessed or do not seem to respond to the needs of the newcomer youth who use them means they are not very relevant to newcomer youth. Service providers and community members mentioned that there are many programs that focus on particular skills, such as resumé writing and other job search techniques. However, newcomer youth need a more integrated and sustained approach, especially those who are most disadvantaged and dealing with added issues of trauma, poverty, and family separation, all of which affect their self-esteem and ability to make positive changes in their lives.

Employers

Service providers and community members indicated that employers tend to have little or no understanding of the value and background of newcomers. Data available indicates that newcomers in general are highly educated. However, their educational and professional qualifications are systematically rejected because they are not Canadian. This, in turn, affects the youth's perception of educational and professional opportunities for them in this country.

Service providers have mentioned that some programs are available, such as apprenticeships, but employers have not shown an interest in participating. This limits youth opportunities tremendously. However, with financial incentives from the government, the participants were convinced that more employers would participate.

DISCUSSION OF FINDINGS

The first broad theme that emerged from the data indicates that newcomer youth from the study, not unlike other youth, have a strong desire to belong. They seek the company of those to whom they can relate, such as friends and community members, and they seek role models with whom they can identify. They also adopt, at least in theory, elements of the new culture such as the desire to take full advantage of educational opportunities because they believe that higher education leads to better jobs in this culture. In fact, most of them stated that they wanted to pursue their education at college or university.

Another characteristic that the newcomer youth have adopted from their new society is their desire to work in order to achieve the same opportunities as Canadians. In fact, some of the main reasons for wanting to work were linked to being independent, supporting their families, and saving for their education. As the majority of the youth had a limited educational attainment and wanted to pursue their education, most of them were looking for temporary, low-skill, or part-time jobs to earn an income.

The second theme that emerged from the data relates to the challenges youth confront in trying to fit into the labour market. The barriers they face include:

- lack of experience
- limited networks and information
- discrimination
- limited language skills
- limited overall skills
- limited prospects due to limited education

Another barrier for newcomers is the fact that they do not always speak the language when they arrive in the country. This factor alone impedes them from quickly integrating as full participants in their new society. As has been clearly documented in the educational literature (Perkins, Pohlman, & Brutten, 1988), it takes up to seven years for newcomer children to catch up to the level of their English-speaking peers.

Although education was identified as the key to success by the three disparate groups of participants, parents and newcomer youth themselves have a limited understanding of the process of securing a job. Community members and youth need to understand that one needs to start early to accumulate experience to secure a job. Indeed, the data from the youth and community members indicate that they do not always understand that extracurricular activities, volunteer work, and part-time or summer jobs help to build skills for future employment.

Also, society needs to understand and accept the diverse interests and capabilities among newcomers. Depending on individual abilities and interests as well as factors relating to support systems within the school, some newcomer youth would benefit from other educational alternatives, such as vocational education, entrepreneurial training, or employment programs. Youth and their parents need to understand that these alternatives are extremely valuable choices for youth who have dropped out (or might), or for those who have opted to settle for menial jobs.

Service providers and community members emphasized that when youth's self-esteem is high and they believe in their potential, they can look to the future with confidence and expand their prospects considerably. Youth from poor socio-economic backgrounds, who live in social housing, and who are visible minorities have serious issues related to self-esteem, largely because of the stigma associated with those factors.

Issues of discrimination surfaced quite prominently in the data because most of the youth in our study were visible minorities. Discriminatory practices—signs of societal rejection—indicate to newcomer youth that they are not wanted, thus making them feel they do not belong. This issue has been discussed and studied from many perspectives, but needs to be emphasized again due to the tremendous impact it has on the lives of young people.

The last theme that emerged from the data is the lack of meaningful support for these newcomer youth. Parents and community members, for the most part, are taking care of their own integration process and are therefore unable to fully support their youth. The most disadvantaged families—those living in poverty and those with parents with low education levels—are less resourceful. Consequently, their youth are often expected to fend for themselves.

In terms of employment support, there are many programs and services available. These services, however, are not accessed by newcomer youth for several reasons: youth are not informed of their existence, they feel they will not help in finding a job, or they feel intimidated. Those who access services feel that their needs are not always addressed. It was also noted that for youth who are most at risk, including those who are out of school and out of work, there are too many other issues in their lives that affect their ability to access established programs.

The key findings of this research, therefore, indicate that although some risk factors originate from the individual background and experiences of newcomers—such as socio-economic status, education, parental education, status on arrival, country of origin, and lack of fluency in the language—others are due to personal factors such as fragile self-esteem, learning abilities, motivation, the drive to succeed, and the ability to set goals. Still others are due to the lack of institutional support mechanisms to address their needs through government, municipal, or community-based programs directly related to employment or integrated interventions.

What seems to have guided policies related to employment is an interpretation based on individual characteristics that inherently attributes flaws to the individuals rather than to the system (low education, not enough experience). As it is the responsibility of newcomers to make adjustments and efforts in integrating into their new environment, so it is society's responsibility to provide meaningful support and opportunities for them to integrate successfully.

The institutional factors are those that can be tailored to meet the needs of this constituency, as varied as it might be, and to provide the support that newcomer youth need to get an equal opportunity to integrate into the labour market. The institutional support to meet the needs of newcomer youth is therefore key to their successful settlement and integration, especially the youth who are most disadvantaged.

RECOMMENDATIONS

This research has outlined the issues that the newcomer youth from our study have faced in seeking to join the labour market. Some of the needs of newcomer youth are similar to those of other youth. However, there are also many differences from the issues Canadian youth face, as well as differences among the group we have opted to call newcomer youth. Indeed, the case of refugees is quite unique in that the issues to be dealt with are more complex, so the integration process takes longer. Based on the findings of this research, a multi-pronged approach is recommended involving multiple partners from different sectors.

Creating a Newcomer Youth Information Network

Creating this network would address the present gaps in access as well as information. This network would have the mandate of working in partnership with community services, settlement agencies, and employment services to identify newcomer youth and their families and to support them in accessing present services as well as creating new initiatives to cater to their multiple needs.

Network Objectives

- Coordinate information on existing youth employment programs and services, and refer newcomer youth and their parents to existing services. This requires contact with mainstream youth services and programs, HRDC, provincial and municipal health and community services, and community organizations.
- create links between organizations and educational institutions in order to make newcomer youth aware of opportunities, and create linkages between newcomer youth and those institutions.
- identify employers or potential mentors (with newcomer experience) to be used as resources for programs in employment centres, so that newcomer youth may have mentors to whom they can relate.
- provide ongoing cultural liaison between newcomer youth, employment resources, and employers by establishing key contacts via networking sessions and job clubs hosted by employment services; provide support to accompany youth to employment agencies and design a monitoring system to follow up.
- develop an advocacy component to educate employment services and employers about key issues facing newcomer

youth; create partnerships with the Canadian Youth Foundation to disseminate information.

Outreach Responsibilities

- Advertise existing employment services in ESL programs. An educational component of the ESL curriculum should include an introduction to the different employment services in Ottawa-Carleton and their roles.
- liaise with outreach workers, multicultural liaison officers (within the school setting), and other key informants in order to identify youth who might need support.

Integrated Program Following the Youth Development Model

Based on the model developed and perfected by Somerset West Health and Community Services in Ottawa, adopt or adapt the program for youth-at-risk. This model operates in a holistic manner, taking into account that employment needs are related to global health and thus addressing all the needs of youth by providing life skills, counselling, soft skills, computer training, and a twelve-week job placement. This program also has a monitoring and evaluation system to follow up on the success of their youth after completion of the program.

Meeting Other Global Health Concerns

Investigate and develop active liaison with research projects in other Canadian cities dealing with the mental health of immigrant and refugee communities. Due to the comparable circumstances of the Somali refugees established in Ottawa, similar research would enable community-based organizations to get more in-depth knowledge of some of the issues facing Somali youth.

Preventative Measures

There should be services available that assist youth who have dropped out to return to school by providing such support as adequate subsidies for meeting basic needs and a program of social, cultural, and linguistic support within schools to facilitate their learning. Remaining in school or in an environment where learning occurs would ideally provide a better long-term solution for these youth. Vocational training programs should be a serious alternative. The most important facet of prevention, however, should come from society in general, with leadership from the government in addressing the real issues related to discrimination. The fact that these youth are discriminated against creates a sense of rejection, which leads them to create environments of their own to obtain the sense of belonging they need so desperately.

Employment Services and Organizations

Existing employment services should self-reflect and attempt to create critical linkages with newcomer communities as well as increase the latter's representation among their services.

CONCLUSION

The objectives of this research were to document the issues that newcomer youth encounter in accessing employment opportunities; to explore the barriers to employment for these youth; and to identify strategies that could support them in making easier school-to-work transitions. Newcomer youth have been identified as being at risk of not successfully integrating into the labour market because of cultural differences and language issues. Other factors, such as the trauma of war and the stigma of being a refugee, compound the difficulties for youth who have arrived as refugees. Frequently youth are also coping with social housing and poverty.

The discussion of risk factors for youth has indicated that some background factors constitute a cumulative disadvantage, which often impedes newcomer youth from integrating fully into their new society. In this research, it was found that living in social housing neighbourhoods, in large families, in households led by single mothers with low levels of education, and being a visible minority presented a cumulative disadvantage. The risk in coming from such a background is that youth will not be able to take full advantage of educational opportunities, which in turn limits their employment prospects in the long run.

Employment is therefore instrumental for newcomers in their integration into society. In a society driven by consumerism and where experience is gained by working, the sense of belonging to the new society includes integration in the workforce. For newcomer youth dealing with poverty, employment becomes even more important for their livelihood as well as their self-worth.

CHAPTER 3

English Language and Communication:
Issues for African and Caribbean Immigrant Youth in Toronto

JACQUELINE L. SCOTT
Coalition of Visible Minority Women, Ontario

INTRODUCTION

This research explores the language and communication issues faced by English-speaking Black youths from Africa and the Caribbean as they settle into their new lives in Toronto. The study was commissioned by the Coalition of Visible Minority Women, Ontario.

The Coalition of Visible Minority Women, Ontario, is a small non-profit agency in Toronto. The agency serves African, Black, Central American, Chinese, Filipino, Indonesian, Iranian, Korean, Japanese, South Asian, and Vietnamese women living in Toronto, Hamilton, Ottawa, Brampton, and Sudbury. The mission of the Coalition is to acknowledge and affirm visible minority women as full participants and contributors to the economic, social, and political life of our society through advocacy, education, research, and support services.

The Coalition has offered a variety of programs and services to its clients over the years. These include: preventing family violence workshops, counselling and referral services, AIDS education project, seminars on menopause and aging, building a 133-unit housing co-op, Multilingual Access to Social Services Initiative (MASSI), and Language Instruction for Newcomers to Canada (LINC).

The Coalition's interest in this project stemmed from two observations. First, a large number of its English-speaking African and Caribbean clients were experiencing language and communication problems that hindered their settlement. Second, the English as a second language (ESL) program that the agency was delivering at the time did not successfully address these issues.

The Coalition's clients faced a paradox. Those from the Caribbean defined themselves as unilingual, with English as their mother tongue, yet many found mutual incomprehension when talking to other speakers of English. The clients from anglophone African countries had a variety of language needs. Some were native English speakers, yet found that their accents and vocabulary were viewed negatively. Others had a minimum grasp of English, as it was their second or third language.

This project aimed to identify gaps in programs for youth who are suffering chronic unemployment because of insufficient communication and language skills and other integration barriers. The research focused on youth between the ages of sixteen and twenty-four from the Caribbean and English-speaking African countries.

There were some key limitations to this project. First, for this small-scale qualitative research, participants were selected from those attending programs at four social service agencies. Obviously, this represents a small sample of the immigrant population. It is also possible that the recruitment through social service agencies resulted in an oversampling of those who are working class and poor.

Second, in this study "Caribbean" specifically refers to Black youth from anglophone islands. "African" denotes Black people from English-speaking African countries.

Third, this study is not a true comparative analysis of African and Caribbean immigrants' language issues. While both groups share a common identity based on being Black, there are enormous cultural differences between them that were outside the parameters of the project. The more limited aim of the research is to point out similarities and differences between the groups on language and communication issues.

THE NEED FOR RESEARCH

Adolescence can be a challenging time for youth and their families. Both have to deal with the physical, social, and psychological changes as youth leave childhood behind and begin the process of becoming adults. Migration complicates an already challenging phase of a young person's life. It may force youth to renegotiate not only their individual identities, but also their cultural identities. In the case of African and Caribbean youth, they are moving from countries where they are the majority to one where they are the minority. Their adolescent and settlement issues are compounded by discrimination based on race and cultural differences.

African Youth

There is a paucity of studies on the migration and settlement needs of Black people from continental Africa. In the literature, the terms "Black" and "African" most often refer to those from the Caribbean. While they share some commonalities with the diaspora, the specific needs of Africans are submerged in the larger picture and hence unrecognized. The first group of African immigrants to Toronto arrived in the 1970s. They tended to be highly educated. Many came to Canada to attend university to study medicine, engineering, and business (Mwarigha, 1991). Despite their higher level of education as compared to the population, Africans had a high rate of unemployment when compared to the norm for Toronto (Kasozi, 1986).

Significant African immigration to Canada began only during the 1980s and 1990s. The major sources of immigrants were from South Africa, Tanzania, Ethiopia, Kenya, Ghana, Uganda, and Nigeria. Some came as part of the African brain drain to the West in search of better opportunities. Others were refugees fleeing war, political instability, and the economic malaise in their home countries.

The African newcomers quickly organized community associations to help deal with their settlement needs. The majority of these associations run on a shoestring budget, lack core government funding, and rely heavily on volunteers. They have limited capacity to meet the needs of their clients. As they are institutionally weak, the agencies find it difficult to meet the criteria for more stable long-term funding (Ainsah-Mensah, 1996).

English is the medium of instruction from school to university in the anglophone African countries. However, one's facility with the English language depends on the number of years in school, class, gender, and rural/urban location. English language skills were identified as a key service that was needed in the community (Mwarigha, 1991). Specific language difficulties—such as accents, the use of idioms, and speaking styles—were identified. Some community groups tried to meet these language needs by holding ESL classes for their members (Opoku-Dapaah, 1993).

In Kasozi's (1986) study, some 60 per cent of the research subjects stated that their accents hindered their integration into society and in finding employment. Some 28 per cent lost or left their former employment due to language problems.

Caribbean Youth

People from the Caribbean have lived in Canada since 1796 with the migration of the Maroons from Jamaica to Nova Scotia as part of the settlement of the British-Maroon War (Winks, 1997). In recent years, large-scale Caribbean youth migration started in the 1960s. Typically the mother came and settled, and later the children and their father joined her (Anderson & Grant, 1987).

This pattern of Caribbean migration is unique among immigrants, and it has had enormous consequences for Caribbean youth. Issues include dealing with a reconstituted family that may have been separated for up to ten years. The difficulties can be compounded if the youth has other siblings who were born in Canada, or has to deal with step-siblings who are now part of the new blended family. The youth may still be emotionally attached to an extended family back in the Caribbean, especially a grandmother. Now, however, they find themselves living in Canada in a family in which their place is insecure. Caribbean youth come from a culture where education is a scarce resource that in most cases has to be paid for. Teachers are highly respected members of the community, classrooms are formal, discipline is strict, and expectations are high. By contrast, in Canada education is seen as "free." The youth and their families recognize education as the most important vehicle for advancing in Canadian society, yet numerous studies show the underachievement of Caribbean students in the Canadian system (Lewis, 1992).

Caribbean youth face pressure in school from their parents, teachers, and peers. Teachers' expectations significantly affect the progress of students in school. Caribbean students are often stereotyped as having poor language and communication skills, and low levels of participation; males are perceived as aggressive (Anderson & Grant, 1987; Foster, 1996). Furthermore, Caribbean youth are confused by the Canadian education system when they are assessed as not speaking English. A disproportionate number are put back several grades, assigned to special education classes, or placed in English as a second language programs. The teachers' low expectations of students and misunderstanding of their culture all compound communication problems for Caribbean youth (Edwards, 1986).

Parents assume that schools operate in the same way in Canada as they do in the Caribbean. They do not always understand the dilemmas that their children face in school. Caribbean parents are more likely to be concerned with the discipline problems in school and the limited amount of homework. They have high confidence that the school as an institution is meeting the needs of their children (Brathwaite & James, 1996).

Caribbean youth may find themselves failing in school, isolated, and frustrated. Their parents do not understand their dilemma and are more likely to blame the children for their failure. Teachers have low expectations of them, and there is little in the curriculum with which they can identify. In addition, the Caribbean way of socializing is seen as negative. All of these factors contribute to the underachievement and high dropout rate for Caribbean students (Dei, 1995, 1997).

Language and Communication

Depending on how a person speaks English on the telephone, one can infer a range of information, including the speaker's age, gender, level of education, whether English is the person's mother tongue, and even his or her ethnic identity. In short, one can ascribe to the person a social identity based on his or her use of language.

English, like all other languages, is not monolithic. There are dialects within the language, reflecting particular social, educational, economic, and historical conditions. For linguists, the notion of "dialect" refers to a way of speaking a language, and not to an incorrect way of speaking it (Taylor, 1990). All dialects of a language are linguistically legitimate. However, some dialects are more socially prestigious than others. The dialect spoken by the educational, socio-economic, and political elites becomes the standard dialect of a country. It is the language of culture, social mobility, and education (Trudgill, 1974).

Standard English is the acceptable dialect in Canada. It is the medium through which people from different linguistic backgrounds communicate with one another. While there are regional and social differences within the dialect, it is spoken by some members of all ethnic and cultural groups.

Non-standard dialects exist in all languages. Occupying the other end of the social spectrum, non-standard dialects are most often spoken by the powerless, the less educated, and the poor. While legitimate linguistically, non-standard dialects tend to be unacceptable to the elites of society.

Standard English is the language of the Caribbean middle class, and it can be understood by anyone in Canada. Working-class youth and those from rural areas may speak English on a continuum from standard to patois (Coelho, 1998). The more grounded they are in patois, the more likely it is that they will have limited comprehension of standard English, and standard English speakers will not understand them. In Canada, Caribbean students encounter problems in terms of intonation, grammar, and vocabulary (Beserve, 1976).

African and Caribbean youth need to master standard English for academic success, and for career and social mobility. Any difficulty with standard English severely limits their opportunities.

METHODOLOGY APPLIED

The data for this research project were collected using six focus groups. The participants were located though four social service agencies. The four youth focus groups consisted of youth aged sixteen to twenty-four years. Separate sessions were held for African females, African males, Caribbean females, and Caribbean males. The last two focus groups were for African and Caribbean parents of immigrant youth. The groups consisted of both females and males.

Each focus group session was taped. The first part of the guided discussion covered general issues on adjusting to life in Canada. Topics included differences in values, beliefs, and behaviour between Canada and "back home," and organizations and individuals that helped the participants with the settlement process. The second part of the discussion specifically addressed the issues of language and communication.

Additional information on each participant was gathered from a short questionnaire. This included demographic data such as place and date of birth, level of education completed, occupation, and languages spoken at home.

The tape from each focus group was transcribed. Data from the transcript was then integrated with data from the questionnaire. The data were analyzed using the following matrix of similarities and differences between: females and males, African and Caribbean, parents and youth.

WHAT WE LEARNED

The focus groups yielded a wealth of data covering the social, psychological, economic, and cultural aspects of youth migration and settlement. Due to limits of space and time, only the findings that relate to language and communication are presented here.

Overview of the Participants

African Females

The members of this youth focus group were originally from Ghana and Zambia. All were high school students, except for one woman who was attending university. Their parents' occupations ranged from taxi driver, to secretary, to environmental chemist. Their fathers were most likely to have completed university and their mothers high school. The languages spoken at home were English, Twi, and Fanti.

African Males

This youth focus group consisted of immigrants from Ghana and Nigeria. Most were in high school, typically in grades 10–12. One male was attending college. Their parents' employment included store clerk, restaurant manager, and social worker. Their fathers were most likely to have attended university and their mothers high school. These African males were relatively recent immigrants, most arriving in Canada in the last five years. The languages spoken at home were English, Twi, Akan, and Beni.

African Parents

This group was made up of women from Ghana and Nigeria. Their employment ranged from factory worker to community worker. The parents were most likely to be in their mid-forties and most had a high school education. Edo, Twi, and English were the languages spoken at home.

Caribbean Females

The members of this youth focus group were originally from Jamaica, and Trinidad and Tobago. Most were high school students in grades 9–12. One had just completed her first year at community college. Their parents' occupations ranged from labourer, to dressmaker, to nurse. Fathers were most likely to have a high school education, while mothers tended to have completed college. These Caribbean females had immigrated to Canada when they were very young, and most had lived here for about ten years. All indicated that they spoke only English at home.

Caribbean Males

This youth focus group consisted of immigrants from Grenada and Jamaica. Most were high school students, and one was attending university. Their parents' jobs ranged from social worker, to nurse, to phone technician. Both parents were likely to have a college education. The Caribbean males had also immigrated to Canada when relatively young, and most had lived here for about ten years. English was the only language spoken at home.

Caribbean Parents

This focus group comprised both females and males who were originally from Barbados, Jamaica, and Grenada. Their employment ranged from assistant chef to health care aide. Most parents were in their mid-forties and had a high school education. English was the only language spoken at home.

There are both similarities and differences between the African and Caribbean groups based on the demographic data. The African youth are relatively recent immigrants, most arriving within the last five years. In contrast, the Caribbean youth have been living here for ten years. There were distinct cultural and gender differences in the education of the youth parents. The Africans mothers were most likely to have a high school education while the fathers had attended university. In the case of the Caribbean youth, the pattern was reversed. Their mothers were most likely to have higher or the same level of education as the father. In terms of language, the Africans spoke English and other languages at home, while those from the Caribbean spoke only English.

Cross-cultural Communication Themes

This section analyzes the general cross-cultural communication themes that emerged from the focus group discussions. Specifically, the section examines the similarities and differences between the groups in terms of manners and respect, discipline, and interactions between parents and children.

Manners and Respect

There were remarkable similarities between the groups in terms of their experiences of manners and respect in Canada as compared with "back home." The groups expressed astonishment and disappointment with the lack of respect for elderly people in Canada. They saw this lack of respect most keenly in the school system. Instead of teachers being respected by youth, the teachers were more likely to be disparaged. The following are typical sentiments from the discussions:

Where I come from you are suppose to give teachers the most respect. They take their time to teach you things that you don't know. When you come here, you see that too, but it's mostly about disrespecting teachers. And then you have the teachers who disrespect the students too. (Caribbean male)

I found it odd that here students are being disrespectful to the teacher. In Ghana we have a set of values such as: it is the teacher's responsibility to be like your third parent, so you respect the teacher. Here it is different. (African male)

I've gone back to Jamaica a few times since I left. What my mom notices and what I notice is the manners. She sees how some of my friends conduct themselves, and I have some White friends, when they are in the street, they swear on the bus. My mom says that if you were back home and you did that, anyone would talk to you. The woman sitting across from you, she would probably know your mother or your father or your grandparents and would say something. It would be an embarrassment to your family; you would be dealt with when you got home. You are called on for bad behaviour. Usually when you are back home, you know how to conduct yourself. Here it's kind of accepted as this is the way teenagers act. They can talk loud on the bus and disturb others. (Caribbean female)

Discipline

Discipline was one of the topics most passionately discussed in the focus groups. For both Africans and Caribbeans, corporal punishment was the culturally acceptable way of disciplining a child. As one youth explained:

My older sister came home with a really bad report card and my mom beat her. My sister called the police on my mother! She got beat worst. The officer that came was this old White man. He goes, "When I came home with a bad report card, my father beat me too." He pretty much accepted what my mom did. He said, "She probably did that out of anger, knowing that you could have done better." But I think if it were a younger officer, he would have got more upset with my mother. But the whole fact that my sister called the police on my mother upset my entire family. Grandma, grandpa, aunts, and uncles came to the house and beat my sister. They were so upset with her. It's like you cannot call the police on your mother, especially for something that she could have prevented too. That report card was really bad. (Caribbean female)

In my country, if you disrespect the teacher, and the teacher calls your mother, your mother will tell the teacher to beat you! And after, when you go home, you'll get beaten again. (African male)

One person doesn't born a child. If a child is doing something wrong, you smack them for it. Here you can't do that. Everything is law, law. Here you can't control your children. That's a big problem. (African female parent)

In the Canadian context, physical punishment is unacceptable. Neither the youth nor their parents favoured the Canadian way of disciplining. As one youth noted:

Kids up here get punished by time out, or you are grounded! What kind of punishment is that? (Caribbean female)

The Caribbean parents saw the lack of discipline as resulting in their youth having problems with the police. As one parent stated at length:

One of the biggest issues as I see it is that they don't allow you to deal with your kids in the respectful way that you were brought up. The way in which I grew up it was "Yes, ma'am, no ma'am. Yes, sir, no sir. Please can I have this?" Here your kids come and it's "Yes" and "No." You call him, and it's "What?" You try to discipline your child. The first thing they do is they try and remove your child from home. They will take your child from you. They are suppose to allow the people who come here to grow their kids in the way in which they grow up. Do not take that away from them. As soon as they do that, do you know who start kicking their butts around? The cops because they don't allow you to discipline your kids. When they get out of hand, they are the same ones who come in, put a bullet in his butt, or their foot. Why? Because you didn't get the chance to bring the child up the way you wanted to bring the child up. You bring the child up to their system and that's what their system gives. No discipline. That's one of the things that the government here should look into. Allow the people from their culture to deal with the kids the way in which they want to grow them with respect and manners. If this is taken away from you, your child is not yours anymore. (Caribbean female parent)

Parent-Child Interaction

The differences in discipline standards affected interactions between parents and children. This was seen as negative by both the youth and the parent; both knew the parents had lost control. As one youth noted:

> You come here as a child and you feel that you have power over your parents and over your teachers because they can't raise a hand to hit you. Up here as children and young people, we know that we have the power. And at times we abuse it, because we know that they are powerless against us in this society and in the law. We have the power, and they don't. (Caribbean female)

The parents echoed these sentiments:

> Say you left them there for three years and now they are here. Up until that point, every time the kid misbehaves, you disciplined that kid by tanning his behind. Kid comes here, after five or six months, understands the system as in "If my mom hits me, I pick up the phone and I call 911. My mother is wrong." There you go in terms of being able to discipline your kids; it is taken away from you. That is a serious issue. What happens is that you lose the rein on your kids. There goes your kids doing things that you do not want them to do, but you cannot correct it the way that you want to. So your kid is either moving into a life of crime, of jail, etc., and

you feel helpless towards them. This is [a] serious issue that has to be dealt with. (Caribbean male parent)

While the youth enjoyed more freedom here, they were also aware of the consequences of this:

When you do something bad back home, your parents can beat you. But when you come to Canada, when the parents shout at you, you can call the police. That's the Canadian way. Or sometime children think that their parents don't like them. But it's not like that. You are not from here; you weren't born here, so if they put you into a foster home or something, you can't adapt to that. You are not going to be happy. That's what's wrong with a lot of the kids here from back home. They end up as juveniles because of the Canadian way. (African male)

There were many communication and language themes that emerged from the focus groups. These were categorized as *comprehension, language in the school system*, and *language and employment*. On this topic there were major differences between the people from Africa and those from the Caribbean. Another important theme arising from the focus groups was the issue of *gaps in services*.

Comprehension

Words are symbols that represent things—ideas, events, objects, desires, and so on. In English, as in all other languages, there are rules that dictate the way in which symbols can be used. The most basic of these deal with syntax (the structure or ways in which words can be arranged) and semantics (the meaning of words). Dialect speakers of a language may use different syntactical structures and ascribe meanings to the words other than those used by non-dialect speakers. Add to this situation difference in accents, intonation, and the rhythm of the speech, and the possibility for mutual incomprehension between the dialect and non-dialect speakers increases substantially.

Constantly being misunderstood eventually affects a person's self-esteem. Those with low self-esteem tend to perform poorly when being watched, as they are sensitive to possible negative reactions.

They may become quiet and passive so as not to draw attention to themselves. This in turn may lead to feeling rejected by others. In the words of the research subjects:

> I'm from Grenada. I had to adjust to speaking, because I spoke Creole, which is totally different, and it was hard for anyone to understand me. So I had to get used to that, which was pretty difficult. (Caribbean male)

> It was strange. People could not understand what I said. But my grandmother forbade patois to be spoken in the house. She has this mentality that it was the Queen's language, and nothing but. When I came I was able to understand as well as able to speak to people. It's strange because I speak more patois now with my mom than I do with my grandmother. And I speak it more here than I do in Jamaica. (Caribbean female)

The frustration for the Caribbean speakers was doubly so as they defined themselves as native English speakers:

> In the West Indies we have some words in our dialect which are different from plain English. And I think that is what made the problem in school for most of these kids. That's why they said they are not speaking English. The Jamaican dialect that we have, the Canadians don't understand. It's not that we don't speak English. (Caribbean female parent)

> I don't see patois necessarily being inferior to "standard English." Standard English is the language that is spoken in Canada, Britain, and other areas of the British Commonwealth. I think that patois is a language within a language. It's basically something within English. It's a kind of fusion. (Caribbean male)

The situation for the African subjects was somewhat different. Depending on their level of education "back home," they may have a range of fluency in English ranging from basic to native. As these youth noted:

In school your peers look at you differently, maybe because it's the way you express yourself. You might not have the full knowledge about speaking English, because at home you speak your own language. That was one thing that made it hard for me. (African male)

In Ghana our colonial masters were British, so most of us don't have a problem speaking English. But what makes it hard for us when we come here are the phrases and the jargon and all those terms that these people use. In the cafeteria in school, or even at work, the moment that you start talking, people can tell that you've not been here that long. This makes it hard for most of us. I finished high school back home, so I was o.k. with the English language. But for those of us who didn't, it's harder for us to control our English. In school when a topic is being talked about, you might want to express your opinion, but because it's in the English language, you don't want them to laugh or something like that, so you keep silent. (African male)

The differences in comprehension also affected the dynamics in the family. The youth may begin to use Canadian English expressions and idioms, which the parents are unfamiliar with. If the parents take the words literally, it may lead to confusion and tension, as the following illustrates:

Sometimes if you are talking to your parents and you say something like, "Mummy, what are you talking about?" they get offended. They demand, "What do you mean what am I talking about?" Or you say to them, "What are you saying?" That's taken as an insult. Or you might say "That's a dumb idea." They think you are telling them that they are dumb. It's little things like that they take straight as offence. It's like automatically you are insulting them, but you are not. It's just that you are really asking them the question "What are you talking about?" (African female)

Language in the School System

The perceptions and expectations of teachers powerfully affect students' self-esteem and performance. African and Caribbean youth's initial encounter with the school system was negative. Those from the Caribbean were most likely to be put back, regardless of their age and ability. As they were unfamiliar with the school system, their parents did not challenge this initial placement:

> I am from Jamaica. When I left I was between basic school and primary school. The difference is that basic school you start when you are about three or four. When I came up here they did not want to integrate me in Grade 1, so they put me in kindergarten! In basic school in Jamaica you learn how to read and write. You go to school to learn. But when I came, they put me in kindergarten where you play with water, blocks, and sand! You have a nap in the afternoon. I remember my mom coming to school and saying "This can't work. She knows how to read; she knows how to write. You need to put her in a program that will help her develop that." They refused to do that. (Caribbean female)

> That's the mistake. I did not know at the time that they couldn't put you back a grade if your parents didn't want them to. My mom didn't really know what was going on. They gave her some sob story like "He's too young to be in this grade." That was their excuse for putting me back. Now that I look at it, if you can do the work, what is the problem? I think that a lot of parents get tricked into having their kids put back a grade. If you do not agree to it, it won't happened. (Caribbean male)

Teachers expect less from Black students, whether they are African or Caribbean. The students are encouraged to take non-academic courses and/or are encouraged to focus on sports. The youth were particularly incensed by the advice they received from guidance counsellors. Most often the message was that the student did not have the ability to go very far:

> Teachers take it out on the Black kids. If they do well, they are wrong. If they do it right, they are wrong. When the kids do good, nobody believes them. My son did a great assignment. The teacher did not believe that he did it himself. His self-esteem dropped. (African female parent)

When my brothers moved from Ottawa to Toronto, they went to see the counsellors. The counsellors didn't care that their marks were in the 80s. They just picked any course for them. My Daddy was so angry that he went to school, and forced them to drop the drama and all that stuff and take science and other hard subjects. When you are talking to the counsellors, they say "What college are you going to?" They don't say what university are you going to because they don't care. Because you are Black, they think that you are going to college. Last time we were doing something in school and they gave out books on college, and one of my friends picked up a university book. The counsellor told him to put it down, and to take a college one instead. (African male)

In a sense if the child is not what the teacher expects the child to be, the child will be neglected and will be targeted. These are things that are not good for the child. They make the child feel as if he's not worthwhile. Now my son is just getting the confidence that he's a somebody, that he is worthwhile. All those years of going to school, whatever the problem was, he said it didn't interest him. Now is the time that he is trying. He's thinking of going to college now. (Caribbean female parent)

The counsellors tell the person that from what they're seeing, the person is going nowhere. They destroy the person's dream, so the person will feel like "What the heck?" and then drop out of school. I have a friend. All he thinks about is basketball. The counsellors tell him about basketball. He thinks he's going to join the NBA, yet he can't even read. It's all basketball. Stay in school, don't let those bullshit counsellors spoil your dreams. If you think you want to join the NBA, join the NBA. If you think you want to go to university, go to university. Don't let people tell you what to do. (African male)

While teachers recognized the language needs of Caribbean students, the usual solution was to place them in ESL classes:

I already knew English. But when I came here I could understand them, but they could not understand me. They wanted to put me into an ESL program, probably because I had an accent and I spoke fast. (Caribbean female)

In the case of the African youth, ESL classes were seen as either appropriate or inappropriate depending on their fluency in the language, class, and age:

We don't want to be in the classes with the Russians who don't speak English. We need a class where we can pay attention to things like our accent. (African male)

Older people in Ghana were taught proper English in school, and should not need much help with their English here. If you are younger, like elementary age, then you do need help with your English. (African female)

However, the consensus was that Africans needed ESL classes as they were more likely to speak other languages at home:

But we do need the same kind of ESL classes like the Russians. In Ghana English is only taught in class; we don't speak it at home. If you put that person in the same class, they should be a step ahead of the Russians. Because the official language of Ghana is English, it does not mean that everyone speaks it. Most of us actually don't. (African male)

I don't think you should be there in elementary school if you just came here, especially if the teacher is speaking full 100 per cent English and you are speaking 100 per cent Twi. You won't be able to communicate. You won't be able to translate anything. It will help you later on if you have a basic understanding [of English]. (African female)

Language and Employment

The research participants recognized the link between employment and language. Standard English was the language of the workplace and school. Dialects, patois, and Creole were used only with friends, family, and in situations where the subjects were comfortable. As one parent noted:

> When I had my first job interview here, I was asked "How long have you been here?" I told him that I had been here for a year. So I asked him "Why did you ask that?" He says it was because I spoke very good English. I trained myself. I watched my friends. When they are around certain people, they talk differently. When you go out, you have to conduct yourself in a certain manner. If you present yourself to certain people in a certain way, they will look at you and they will respect you. But if they don't understand, they will feel that something is up. If you are working and you see two people who are talking differently, and you don't understand it, you feel a way! (Caribbean male parent)

> I won't make a presentation at work because I know they will giggle at my accent. (African female parent)

Gaps in Services

For the African subjects, there were issues regarding access to services. In the first place, they may not know what services exist. And even if they are able to find the right services, they might not be accessible because of cultural differences and language barriers. The Africans were more likely to rely on friends and family for help, as the following quotes illustrate:

> There are different types of resources, but I don't think that they are accessible to all people. For example, even though there are different clinics and centres that can help you to adjust to life here, you don't know how to start and how to go about finding them. There are guidance counsellors in schools, but oftentimes they don't give you the correct information. So you mostly turn to your parents. That might be a problem too as they might not be familiar with all the things that are available to you as well. As newcomer parents and newcomer children, I don't know where, plus my mom doesn't know where to turn. And I don't understand my guidance counsellor. (African female)

> As a newcomer, if you are not familiar with the language, and even if you do find out what is here, when you get there you have to fill out an application, but you can't read English. Who are you going to talk to if nobody there speaks Twi? After that experience you're not going to want to go out because you feel that you are isolated, no matter where you go. (African female)

While the Caribbeans identified access to services as a key issue, they did not cite language as a barrier. The Caribbean youth were also more likely to go to friends and family for help, which had more to do with culture:

> If you are from the islands, if you have a problem, it's private. I wasn't really comfortable telling my problems to anybody, except maybe my friends who I grew up with. To this day, I don't tell my problems to strangers. I'd rather talk to my friends and family. (Caribbean male)

Several of the African and Caribbean youth mentioned that they got help from the counsellors at sports and recreation programs:

> My friends helped me out. Or I went to the rec programs, where you play sports, to get rid of some of the stress. I know some people in the rec programs so I could talk to them. (Caribbean male)

A number of the youth also mentioned that they went to the youth groups in their church for help. However, they cautioned that only a minority of youth attend church. Many youth still went to their school's guidance counsellor for help.

The best way of closing the gaps in services was for more established newcomer youth to help the new arrivals—in other words, a buddy system:

> Newcomers need support from other youth who might have been here a little bit longer, just so that they could teach them some of the ways that we have here. If they are not speaking good English, then an ESL type of class may help them with their language. You

might need an organization just for newcomers so that they understand each other. Because sometimes if you are a newcomer and you are trying to tell me your problems, I might not understand if I were born here. Maybe an organization for newcomers so that they can share their experiences with each other and get different feedback from each other. (African female)

I believe that when a child has just arrived, they should find somebody from the child's culture, for the first year or two, in school who understands that child, or understands their culture. (Caribbean female parent)

RECOMMENDATIONS

The following recommendations resulted from this research project:

1. *Language Training for Africans:* African youth need to either learn English as a second language or to significantly upgrade their language skills.

2. *Standard English as a Second Dialect for Caribbeans:* Caribbean youth need help with their English. This must be grounded in the recognition that they speak a dialect of English and therefore need assistance in mastering standard English.

3. *Mental Health:* Both African and Caribbean youth and their parents need help with bridging the difference between parenting roles and responsibilities "back home" and here in Canada. For the African community, it is crucial that mental health services be delivered in their native languages.

4. *Schools:* Schools play a vital role in the integration of newcomer youth. Teachers, especially guidance counsellors, need to know more about the cultures of these young people. Teachers also need to confront their racial stereotypes and increase their expectations of the capabilities of both African and Caribbean youth.

5. *Buddy System:* Youth are more likely to go to their friends for advice. Therefore, Citizenship and Immigration Canada should explore the possibility of creating a buddy system that links more established immigrant youth with newcomers.

6. *Recreation Centres:* Youth also use their local sports and recreation

centres as sources of advice. Citizenship and Immigration Canada should therefore investigate the feasibility of providing settlement services in these centres.

7. *Future Research:* Further research is needed on the settlement needs of the Black African community. While their settlement experiences are similar in some ways to the African diaspora, there are unique needs in the community that have not been fully explored. The few studies that exist are anecdotal in nature.

CONCLUSION

This research focused on the language and communication issues faced by newcomer African and Caribbean youth as they settle into their new lives in Toronto. The research findings indicated that there were similarities and differences between these two Black communities. Language was the most significant of these differences. Africans spoke many other languages in addition to English, even if it is the national language of their home countries. Their familiarity with English depended on their level of education "back home," age, class, and rural/urban location. The Africans interviewed cited the need for English as a second language training as the most pressing in settlement services for their community.

The people from the Caribbean also had difficulties with language. While they were unilingual, native English speakers, they spoke a dialect of English. This dialect is sufficiently different from standard English that it can lead to mutual incomprehension. As the Caribbean dialect is seen as negative, it hindered the youth in school and contributed to their underachievement. Most often schools dealt with the language difficulties of Caribbean students by placing them in ESL classes. However, this lowered their self-esteem and further contributed to their underachievement.

Implementation of the policy recommendations developed through this research would significantly improve the process of settlement for Black newcomer youth from the Caribbean and Africa.

CHAPTER 4

Colour, Culture, and Dual Consciousness:
Issues Identified by South Asian Immigrant Youth in the Greater Toronto Area

SABRA DESAI AND SANGEETA SUBRAMANIAN
Council of Agencies Serving South Asians and South Asian Women's Centre

INTRODUCTION
Purpose and Rationale

South Asian youth have immigrated with their parents to Canada for any number of reasons—better overall life, better economic and educational opportunities, safer and healthier lives, and, in some cases, to escape civil war. The youth, regardless of their families' reasons for immigrating, are faced with high unemployment rates, peer pressure to fit in, and significant pressure from their families to succeed academically and pursue professional careers, as well as strict codes of behaviour regarding relationships with the opposite sex and dating (Council of Agencies Serving South Asians/South Asian Legal Clinic [CASSA/SALC], 1999); Kurian, 1983, 1991; Wadhwani, 1999).

The Council of Agencies Serving South Asians and the South Asian Women's Centre undertook this research to explore and document settlement issues faced by immigrant youth of South Asian background who came to Toronto at or over the age of eight and who are now between sixteen and twenty-four. The research is part of a larger study on the gaps in settlement services for newcomer youth in Ontario, conducted under the aegis of the Joint Centre of Excellence in Immigration and Settlement, Toronto (CERIS) and the Centre for Refugee Studies, York University, with financial assistance from Citizenship and Immigration Canada, Settlement Directorate Ontario Region.

This study is about exploring, deciphering, and decoding the lived realities of South Asian immigrant youth living in Toronto. It should be noted that although the collective term "South Asian" is used, the collectivity is very diverse and nuanced in a myriad of complex ways. The term is also used in a political way to define individuals and groups whose roots can be traced to the Indian subcontinent. More importantly, the term reflects a consciousness and a self-definition arising out of dialectical relations between the dominant culture and cultures within it that are considered outside the ruling relations and no more than marginal because of racism (Hill Collins, 1990; Smith, 1987, p. 1; Tatum, 1992).

South Asian youth, for the purposes of this research, includes those who are sixteen to twenty-four and whose origins or ancestors would be from the Indian subcontinent, which includes the countries of Bangladesh, Bhutan, India, Pakistan, and Sri Lanka. Thus, youth coming to Canada after the age of eight or later as newcomers from countries like Bangladesh, India, Pakistan, Sri Lanka, as well as South Asian youth born in England and countries of Africa and the Middle East, are included as participants in the study. The study focused on youth from the various ethnocultural and linguistic groups to reflect the diversity within the South Asian community in Canada. This included youth from Gujerati-, Hindi-, Punjabi-, Tamil-, and Urdu-speaking communities. Moreover, by reaching out to different groups we included South Asian youth from the major religions—Christianity, Hinduism, Islam, and Sikhism.

The purpose of the research was to explore the settlement challenges and concerns faced by immigrant youth of South Asian background; to help meet their needs; and assist them to integrate in a new culture while maintaining their cultural identities and strengthening their family structure and support.

Objectives of the Study

The objectives of the study were:
- to explore and document issues faced by immigrant youth
- to identify challenges in the settlement process of immigrant youth

- to identify and lay the groundwork to bridge the gaps between the views of youth and those of their parents
- to outline the first steps toward building alliances between parents and youth

The research findings will be helpful for policy-makers and practitioners in educational and social and community agencies, and will assist staff within the health system to make effective interventions when working with South Asian youth and their families. It is hoped that the findings will not only enhance the services delivered by South Asian agencies through the ongoing participation of youth and their families in identifying barriers to accessing appropriate services and support, but also inform organizations and agencies within the broader Canadian society of the need to remove the prevailing systemic barriers.

LITERATURE REVIEW

For the purposes of this study, a literature search of Canadian sources was done to locate existing studies on South Asian youth in Canada. The search was done not so much to start the current work with a set of formal propositions but to see what was available to help locate this project within a context of existing material on South Asian youth.

Although there are studies on South Asian immigrant needs and the adjustment and adaptation of South Asian families in Canada, they do not deal directly with the experiences of youth. The experiences, concerns, and difficulties are dealt with indirectly through discussion of issues faced by South Asian families in general. There are reports on youth living in the Greater Toronto area within the broader societal context. These reports are about youth issues and needs in general; the only study we found dedicated specifically to South Asian youth was by Wadhwani (1999).

The reports on youth issues and needs have been usually undertaken by mainstream organizations, such as the City of Toronto's *Toronto Youth Profile* (City of Toronto, 1999) and the Central Toronto Community Health Centres' *Making Money* (Gaetz, O'Grady, &

Vaillencourt, 1999), to name just a few examples. These reports provide a good overview of youth profiles, issues, and needs, as well as new policy and programming initiatives to stimulate discussions about difficulties that youth face. The stated purpose of all these studies is to help improve educational, recreational, health, and social services for youth in general. The latest report, *Toronto Youth Profile*, states clearly that "it is hoped the profile will contribute strategy for youth that engages youth as partners in shaping the city's future, builds on best practices, and forges partnerships to create economic and cultural opportunities for youth" (City of Toronto, 1999, p. 1).

While these reports are necessary to help set policy and programming to meet the needs of youth, they are superficial in dealing with the specific challenges and concerns of ethno-racial youth, such as South Asian youth. Merely citing statistical information on current demographics is not sufficient for exposing or revealing the lived realities of South Asian youth. The presence of South Asian youth and youth from other so-called visible minority ethno-racial groups is quite evident and has, in fact, been evident for many years. Simply knowing about the presence of visible minority communities and their youth has not made any significant changes in structural or systemic barriers with regard to services (James, 1995b). Moreover, while statistical information is necessary, qualitative data is equally important for providing insights into the psychosocial processes that youth experience. Therefore, it could be argued that mainstream organizations and their commissioned studies typically continue to consciously or unconsciously either obfuscate or render invisible the lived realities of racial minority youth. This conscious or unconscious expression of racism would undoubtedly be reflected in policies and programs because one cannot develop a policy or program for that which one does not see. Hence the maintenance and development of policies and practices predicated on domination, segregation, and marginalization of racial minorities continue. This does not surprise many marginalized groups because members of these groups have come to learn first-hand that often truth lies outside the establishment. Many members of marginalized groups also know that their indigenous knowledge and wisdom is negated by the establishment whose decisions affect the quality of their lives by continuing to make decisions based on partial truths.

It is interesting to note that the role of racism and its impact on employment opportunities for youth is evaded by merely stating that "differences in employment patterns and income levels do exist but that it is too complex to determine what caused these differences" (City of Toronto, 1999, p. 10). Moreover, these differences are dismissed not only by stating that these are too complex, but also by indicating that long-established ethnic communities, such as the Chinese community, have their own infrastructure and that these communities provide a wide range of opportunities for their own youth (City of Toronto, 1999, p. 10). The reasons for this are not examined. Could it be that youth from the so-called ethnic communities face barriers in accessing jobs in mainstream organizations and have little choice but to look for opportunities within their communities of origin? This report alludes to the possibility that by accessing opportunities within their own communities, youth might be restricting their mobility (City of Toronto, 1999, p. 10). The way this restriction is constructed is problematic because it blames visible minority communities and youth instead of examining the structural and systemic racism within the larger dominant Canadian society. Discrimination experienced in accessing jobs is a serious difficulty, sometimes posing impenetrable walls for first-generation racial minority immigrant youth.

Another important report dealing with concerns and challenges that youth in Ontario face is the study commissioned by the Ontario government, *Report on Race Relations to Premier Bob Rae* (Lewis, 1992). This report deals with racism as the central systemic issue and its implications for racial minority youth with regard to educational, recreational, social services, and employment opportunities. It is about anti-Black racism, as Lewis himself concluded: "it is true that while every visible minority community experiences the indignities and wounds of systemic discrimination throughout Ontario, it is the Black community which is the focus. It is the Black employees, professional and non-professional, on whom the doors of upward Equity slam shut" (Lewis, 1992, p. 2).

However, while a focus on Black youth is not an issue per se, the report does not examine and explore or problematize Black/African-Canadian identity. In other words, the study does not examine complex questions such as how, why, by whom, and for what purpose or utility is this identity constructed in Canada. In fact, some would say that this report is about Caribbean African-Canadians and not continental Africans, and that the diversity within Black/African-Canadians is not addressed. Moreover, the social construction of Black/African-Caribbean Canadians also poses difficulties because it often seems to refer to Jamaicans of African descent. The question then is whether anti-racism has become defined as Black anti-racism, and specifically anti-racism for Blacks from the Caribbean and not inclusive of the racism experienced by continental Africans and other racial minority groups.

Again we see the experiences of South Asian youth made invisible even in broad or general studies on racism and anti-racism. Perhaps a partial answer for this lies in Henry's explanation of how racism against South Asians is constructed. Henry explains that contradictory stereotypes of South Asians as both visible and invisible are created by racism (Henry, 1983, p. 46). Hence, there is a racist phenomenon of "Now I see you, now I don't" when it comes to perceptions of the South Asian presence and realities in Canada.

While it could be argued that studies dealing with general issues of adaptation and settlement of South Asian adults and families do in fact deal with youth issues, there is a gap because the focus is from the adult perspective. As mentioned earlier, the only study specifically on South Asian youth issues—albeit suicidal ideation—revealed through our literature search is the one by Wadhwani (1999). Since it is the only one focusing solely on South Asian youth, it will be dealt with specifically.

Wadhwani's study was prompted by the recent notable increase in suicides among South Asian youth (Wadhwani, 1999, p. 4). The study reveals a disturbing and distressing trend. She reports that 30 per cent of the 104 participants in her study indicated that they had considered suicide; of those who considered suicide, 50 per cent said that "family pressures" were the number one cause or reason for thinking about suicide as an option. As well, 60 per cent of her participants cited school as the main source of stress; 80 per cent of those who had admitted to having engaged in suicidal thoughts were female; and 60 per cent of the participants who indicated that they were "always depressed" had considered suicide (Wadhwani, 1999, p. 77).

Wadhwani's study is significant because it is the first one (known to us) that deals specifically with South Asian youth. Her information on the sites of conflict and contestation are useful, especially her section "To Be Young and Brown in North America—Issues of Identity" (Wadhwani, 1999, p. 21). The information on intergenerational differences, dating, and marriage are helpful in thinking about factors affecting South Asian youth settlement and integration.

Most of the existing literature on South Asians in Canada reviewed for this study can be broadly or arbitrarily categorized under the following headings:

1. *Literature on Immigration, Settlement, and Adaptation:* Basran & Zong (1998); Buchignani (1987); Henry (1983); Israel & Wagle (1993); Kurian (1991); Kurian & Ghosh (1983); Siddique (1983).

2. *Literature on Needs and Settlement Services:* Arora & Mutta (1997); Coalition of Agencies Serving South Asians (1994); Council of Agencies Serving South Asians (1998), Council of Agencies Serving South Asians (1999); Saidulla (1993); Zamana Foundation (1997).

3. *Literature on Family and Women's Issues:* Agnew (1993); Kurian & Ghosh (1983); Riverdale Immigrant Women's Centre (1993); Shakir (1995); Srivastava & Ames (1993).

These categories are not mutually exclusive; however, for the purposes of this study, the literature explored, as mentioned earlier, is arbitrarily categorized only to facilitate discussion.

Literature on Immigration, Settlement, and Adaptation

The literature—especially earlier works on immigration, settlement, and adaptation—do not consider historical and structural factors that affect adaptation patterns (Basran, 1993). The researchers do not examine the reasons for South Asian immigration within the context of colonialism, imperialism and/or capitalism, and globalization

(Shakir, 1995). Moreover, the researchers do not provide a critical analysis of the implications of immigration, or of state policies such as multiculturalism. The earlier writings do not examine the ideology or principles on which the policies are predicated. Some authors seem to assume an inherent neutrality and objectivity in Canadian policies. For example, the immigration policy and practices that favour educated and skilled immigrants are not questioned. The adverse effects of devaluation, demoralization, unemployment, and underemployment are not examined, so the undeniable reality of racism is left unexamined.

Within this literature on immigration, settlement, and adaptation some authors do attempt to negate racist notions that immigrants are a drain on Canada and its social institutions, especially the social services sector, by statistically arguing that immigration is, in fact, economically beneficial to Canada (Kurian, 1991, p. 425). Many of the authors do not problematize the Canadian institutional policies, programs, and structures and their differential impact on South Asians and other immigrant communities. Kurian, for example, states: "While the general successes of Indian immigrants is quite evident, there are some aspects of their life which could be remedied making their lifestyle in tune to life in urban North America" (Kurian, 1991, p. 421). Thus, it can be said that many writers and their earlier works placed the burden of adaptation entirely on new immigrants and do not regard it as a burden to be shared by Canadian society. Adaptation is not seen as a mutually reciprocal or interactive dynamic between Canadian society and new immigrants; as a result, most of the earlier works pathologize immigrants who face difficulties. Their focus is on individuals, and immigrants' difficulties are analyzed in relation to the specificities of individual situations rather than the failure of Canadian society to meet the needs of all its members. Lastly, the earlier works could be described as apolitical in that issues of power, privilege, control, and their distribution are largely overlooked.

Literature on Needs and Settlement Services

Literature on needs and settlement services clearly articulate the extent and nature of services needed because of cultural and linguistic specificities, as well as immigration trends. For example, Tamils, as the largest ethnocultural group in the broader South Asian community, have unique linguistic needs as well as issues related to the need to immigrate because of the civil unrest and open warfare in Sri Lanka (CASSA, 1994, 1998; CASSA/SALC, 1999).

These studies also explore the reasons why mainstream agencies are failing South Asians. They report that mainstream agencies are unable to provide culturally appropriate and sensitive services because of systemic racism and language barriers.

The needs outlined by these studies focus on employment, language, and family issues (CASSA, 1994, 1998; CASSA/SALC, 1999). It was found that South Asians do not access mainstream services because clients are very aware that the mainstream agencies do not understand South Asian culture, and that they have racist stereotypes (CASSA/SALC, 1999).

It is interesting to note that the identified needs seem to remain the same no matter when the study was done. However, the extent of the need seems to increase. While the studies on service needs are very useful for policy and programming, the continued shortage and inadequacies within existing services persist because of a lack of funding. In fact, it could be argued that the rate of cuts or availability of funding dollars is diametrically opposite to the rate of growth in the demand for settlement services (CASSA/SALC, 1998).

Within this political reality of funding restraints, existing settlement services are faced with funding organizations' unrealistic expectations to increase efficiency and financial accountability despite double or triple the need for services. While financial accountability and efficiency are not bad principles to uphold, the implied message is problematic because it suggests that the settlement sector is not good at managing money. This perspective sidesteps the more important issues of access, availability, and effectiveness of services, which are all tied to funding. Instead, as Richmond (1996) states, settlement service agencies are strongly encouraged to forge partnerships and collaborate. This approach to surviving funding cuts is not very healthy because it does not take into account the inequities in resources among settlement agencies. In a sense this proposed strategy is fostering partnerships among unequals. As Richmond states, this is ironic because funding structures are encouraging partnerships while also encouraging competition among agencies for the limited supply of dollars. In fact, this is quite evident in an example he cites in which larger and more powerful agencies collaborate with smaller agencies to build up their own organizations at the expense of the smaller agencies (Richmond, 1996, p. 10). He goes on to say that the funding climate is, in effect, generating fear and a sense of crisis among agencies.

These studies also argue that mainstream agencies are known to make only superficial attempts at addressing the needs of South Asians and other racial minority communities. For example, some mainstream organizations have employed some racial minority staff, but have not made fundamental changes in their policies and structures. In short, these attempts amount to mere tokenism. According to Agnew, even White feminists or organizations run by White feminists end up exercising tokenism because, while they have included some of the interests of South Asian women in their work, they remain structurally unchanged (Agnew, 1993). Thus, as Shakir (1995) states, "the cultural/linguistic/racial 'inappropriateness' of mainstream services to South Asian immigrant women's needs is not a case of neglect or oversight, but a manifestation of 'cultural imperialism'" (p. 1). As a strategy to transform this, Shakir suggests "that a true model can only be achieved if the very articulation of South Asian women's needs and experiential reality decentres the mainstream discourse and leads it to develop a new epistemological map which, along with the concrete struggles of the marginalized classes, changes the structural relations of power that exist in Canadian society" (Shakir, 1995, p. 2). Therefore, Shakir's analysis and critique are very helpful in understanding how South Asians in Canada find themselves facing and negotiating problematic institutional policies and programmatic services located in the context of cultural imperialism.

Literature on Family and Women's Issues

Literature on women and the family, especially the earlier works, focused on husband-wife relations, decision-making, structure, and changes in the face of a new environment. Most of the studies, except

Shakir's analysis, are predicated on the notion that South Asian culture is pre-modern and hence preoccupied with the persistence and perpetuation of patriarchy. Many believe that cultural tradition-alism or pre-modernity is at the centre of greater gender inequities among South Asian families. Thus, many authors hold the view that assimilation and/or acculturation of South Asian women into the modern Canadian culture or "westernization" will lead to gender equality. Implicit in this is the assumption that gender equality is a creation of advanced industrial or modern societies (Kurian, 1991; Siddique, 1978, 1983; Srivastava, 1983).

Naidoo and Davis (1988) deal with what they call the transition and duality of the experiential realities of South Asian women in Canada. According to these authors, South Asian women in Canada have an unflinching commitment to their family and home, deeply held values entrenched in their cultural heritage, and also future-oriented aspirations that are very contemporary.

The problem with many of these writings is that they see gender oppression of South Asian women in Canada as simply being located in South Asian culture. This is not only a simplistic view of gender inequality within South Asian families in Canada, but also very reduc-tionist. Most of these works not only reduce South Asian culture, but also ignore gender differences as well as differences among South Asian cultures. The traditional/modernization or westernization dichotomy framework is simplistic because it is binary and ignores the complexities by treating South Asian women as an unproblem-atic universal category. These authors also fail to identify the specific ways in which gender inequities and oppression among South Asian families in Canada are uniquely created and maintained by histori-cal factors such as racism, classism, and cultural imperialism.

South Asian feminists like Shakir, Srivastava, and Ames challenge this reductionist view and White socialist feminists by pointing out that their analyses are based on racist stereotypical assumptions of South Asian women as passive victims of oppressive cultural struc-tures like the family (Shakir, 1995; Srivastava & Ames, 1993). These authors highlight the need for a critical analysis of Canada's multicul-turalism policy and racism, and how these homogenize differences (Shakir, 1995; Srivastava & Ames, 1993). Srivastava, Ames, and Shakir help us understand the prevalence and persistence of gender inequities experienced by South Asian women in Canada, identifying not only the historical specificity of South Asian women's gender oppression, but also the impact of cultural imperialism, racism, and classism in the construction of gender relations in an advanced capitalist society like Canada.

Unlike many studies on issues facing South Asian families, Shakir locates her analysis within a larger reality of disempowerment, marginalization, and racism. She contextualizes these in a way that is specific to the historical experience of South Asians rather than a simple manifestation of male violence or patriarchy. By integrating culture, cultural imperialism, and racism, Shakir demonstrates that culture is important not only in creating oppression, but also in the social construction of resistance (Shakir, 1995, pp. 9, 16).

Shakir's work is also important in reminding us that the racist understanding and criticisms of South Asian cultural practices, and especially those related to the family and gender oppression, should be evaluated according to different criteria from those that apply to White culture. She also reminds us of the importance of challenging the racist view and portrayal of South Asian women as passive by identifying their sites of resistance as well as the social construction of resistance. In short, Shakir proposes a more complex conceptualization of South Asian women living in Canada—their cultural, economic, political, and social locations—than what is conveyed in current literature. She helps us to challenge the stereotype of passive, impotent South Asian women constantly struggling and battling their cultural heritage or systems, and to *broaden* our perspective of South Asian women as constantly negotiating and renegotiating their identity and cultural location.

As mentioned earlier, there is little material on South Asians in Canada and even less on South Asian youth. This disturbing lack of information raises critical questions such as why there is a gap and what this gap means, particularly when one considers the history of the South Asian presence and their contributions in Canada. This project was undertaken within the context of identifying a significant lack of Canadian literature on South Asian youth. It is hoped that this study will help us understand the experiential realities of

South Asian youth living in the greater metropolitan area and its surrounding municipalities.

LOCATING THE RESEARCH AND SOME WORKING ASSUMPTIONS

The immigrant settlement and adaptation process can be particularly trying if the person is young and facing two environments that are dramatically different. Therefore, one must explore the process, recognizing that youth are confronted not only with the developmental challenges of adolescence, but also with adjustment problems because of intercultural conflicts between the values of the host culture and their culture of origin (Naidoo, 1985; Wakil, Siddique, & Wakil, 1981). Moreover, the already difficult process of adaptation is exacerbated when the contingencies mentioned above are at work in a racialized society like Canada. Therefore, the pivotal question "Who am I?" during adolescence takes on a myriad of nuances for ethnocultural and racial minority adolescents. In addition to the question, "Who am I?" South Asian youth also need to ask themselves "Who am I ethnically?" "Who am I racially?" and "What does it mean to be South Asian in Canada?"

Framework for Analysis and Some Underlying Assumptions

Identity is embedded in both psychological and social processes, so understanding how South Asian youth deal with questions related to identity development, construction, reconstruction, and maintenance become very important in a racialized country like Canada. Moreover, since identity is socially constructed with a complex of psychological processes, identity development must be understood in relation to its social and historical context. Identity formation is "a process of simultaneous reflections and observations, a process taking place on all levels of mental functioning, by which the individual judges himself [herself] in the light of what he [she] perceives to be the way in which others judge him [her] in comparison to themselves and to a typology significant to them; while he [she] judges their way of judging him [her] in the light of how he perceives himself [herself] in comparison to them and to types that have become relevant to him [her]. This process is, luckily, and neces- sarily, for the most part unconscious except where inner conditions and outer circumstances combine to aggravate a painful, or elated, 'identity-consciousness'" (Tatum, 1997, p. 19).

An underlying assumption for the researchers starting this project is the belief that skin-colour racism is a given in Canadian society. Therefore, in Canada, people's skin colour becomes extremely rele- vant in how they are treated, what they can access, what opportuni- ties are available, and determines the quality of their lives. The next contention is that oppression based on skin colour and other's domi- nation of certain individuals and/or groups is a reality. Therefore, an integrated anti-racism framework will be employed to understand and report on the issues of adaptation and settlement of South Asian youth in the context of Canadian society. It is an integrated frame- work because it offers a tool for analyzing and addressing racism and the other interlocking oppressions of "ableism," "ageism," "classism," "heterosexism," and "sexism." The framework is very useful in under- standing how the interlocking social constructs and categories of gender, class, ethnicity, and race affect people's lives in an overlap- ping and cumulative manner. It is particularly useful in understand- ing the complexities of the lives of youth living in a racialized society because "it moves beyond a narrow preoccupation with individual prejudices and discriminatory actions to examine the ways that racist ideas and individual action are entrenched and (un)consciously supported in institutional structures" (Dei, 1996, p. 27). Another reason for using an integrated anti-racism framework is because it helps to understand how differences affect and mediate people's lives, while also facilitating a discussion on how we can, within our differ- ences, create solidarity regardless of colour, culture, sexual orienta- tion, or abilities and capacities. This framework, according to Dei, also helps to "explore how difference is named, lived, experienced, imag- ined and acknowledged" and to ". . . define, conceptualize, and perceive 'difference' from the standpoint of those who occupy the margins of society and continually have to resist their marginality through collective action" (Dei, 1996, p. 37).

This framework also facilitates the exploration of South Asian intragroup similarities and differences, as in the case of Tamil youth who have a different pre-immigration experience of civil war unlike the rest of the South Asian community. In other words, the integrated anti-racism framework helps one to examine the heterogeneity within the larger collective group known as South Asian without overlooking its diversity, as is often the case within a racist paradigm. The framework also allows for examining the impact and implications of religion, as in the case of Muslim and Sikh youth. The data will be analyzed in terms of the principal factors in the marginalization of South Asian youth and their identity development, construction, and reconstruction in Canada as they cope with the challenges of settlement and integration.

Having outlined why an integrated anti-racism framework is used, it would be remiss not to comment—even if only briefly—on the problems of language. The terms "colour" and "race" are inappropriate and misleading. "Race" is misleading because it is based on erroneous biological assumptions that physical differences such as skin colour and facial features, including hair colour and texture, are somehow related to intellectual, moral, or cultural superiority or inferiority. "Race," from an integrated anti-racism framework, is a socially constructed concept that has no basis in biological reality. Rather, it derives its meaning and significance from its social definition, which affects the world's majority people and racial minorities (Henry, Tator, Mattis, & Rees, 2000).

Moreover, to refer to groups who have little or no institutional power as visible minority or people of colour is objectionable not because they are loaded terms but because every person has colour—White is a colour just as much as Black or Brown. To limit the term to so-called "non-White" members of society is perhaps another manifestation of unconscious racism because it suggests that such people are reducible to their colour and that colour is their only significant feature. We do not suggest taking a colour-blind approach because it is also problematic in a racialized society.

Members of racial minority groups are also sometimes referred to by the seemingly less offensive term "immigrant." This may be less offensive, but is misleading because Canadian history is one of successive waves of immigration. The term "immigrant" is appropriate in this report when referring to someone who is a recent arrival (according to government policies, "recent" refers to up to three years). It can be argued that it is also quite acceptable if the term were strictly used, regardless of colour, to refer to members of Canadian society who are not naturalized or who have not gone through the legal process of becoming Canadian citizens. Language of colour becomes a problem when the term "immigrant" is indiscriminately applied to members of racial minority groups regardless of their length of stay or settlement in Canada.

Outlining some concerns with language shows that even supposedly innocent and even well-intentioned terms contain an ideological bias, and that they may be highly offensive to those they are meant to describe. Therefore, for the purposes of this study the term "skin colour" will be used instead of "race" since skin colour carries with it more than the significance of "colour" alone. Whenever it is necessary to make a particular point, the term "race" will be used with caution. The term "immigrant" applies to recent arrivals who qualify for services under the Immigrant Settlement and Adaptation Program (ISAP) or, as stated earlier, when referring to non-Canadian citizens regardless of racial or cultural identity.

Methodology

Methodologically we employed a qualitative research approach because it would be most appropriate in exploring the dialectical relationship between the culture of South Asian youth and the dominant mainstream culture. Capturing the stories and coping and survival strategies of South Asian youth in their own words could be done best through this methodological approach. The specific qualitative method of inquiry employed was focus group discussions.

A Project Advisory Committee was set up to provide guidance and direction to the researcher, outreach in the community, and help in recruiting participants. Once consent forms and publicity materials were ready, thirty organizations (settlement agencies, schools, community colleges, and universities) were contacted to help in recruiting participants.

A total of thirteen focus groups were held: six with girls, five with boys, one with parents, and one with both parents and youth. Of the thirteen groups, four were pilot groups, which helped us finalize the discussion guide. For the purposes of analysis, data from nine focus groups have been used.

The Project Advisory Committee was very helpful in developing the discussion questions. The questions were open-ended and used easily understandable language. It allowed the participants to really engage in a dialogue with each other and the facilitator. It also allowed room for probing and facilitated a fuller understanding of the issues and concerns. The participants also completed a brief questionnaire that helped us develop a socio-cultural profile.

The data analysis involved several steps. The first step was to transcribe the focus group discussions. The second was to summarize the quantitative data and attach numerical values to develop the participant profile. The third was structuring and coding the narrative data. We employed a flexible framework directed by the words of the youth and parents. The data was then arranged and cross-referenced according to the themes that emerged from the narratives.

Some Reflections on the Process

The project generated excitement, anxiety, and frustration. The excitement was largely evoked by the youth, who shared their experiences openly and candidly. It is quite a privilege to be trusted by the youth.

Tension and frustration resulted because often researchers are required to work with a methodology and tools for their study based on criteria and principles established by people outside the experience of the principal participants of the study. However, the biggest challenges we experienced were in recruiting participants because:

- youth had to meet the age criteria (sixteen to twenty-four), as well as other requirements pertaining to their immigrant history
- we could not plug into existing programs since there are very few services for youth; in some existing youth programs, there seemed to be a lack of trust or a level of disengagement experienced by both the youth and staff of various agencies and organizations

- many youth had to work and could not attend if they were called in for work
- some parents did not allow their youth to stay after school
- entry into some of the communities was not easy

We share these reflections in the hope that some of these challenges will be addressed in the future by policies, programs, and change in how we design and do research with some communities and population groups.

FINDINGS: DEMOGRAPHICS, PROFILE, AND DISCUSSION
Demographic Highlights of South Asians in the Greater Toronto Area

- South Asians constitute the second largest visible minority community (24.7 per cent) or 329,840 in the GTA (CASSA/SALC, 1999, p. 4).
- South Asians represent 8 per cent of Ontario's population (CASSA/SALC, 1999, p. 4).
- There are 49,305 South Asian youth between the ages of fifteen and twenty-four, with a majority (58.1 per cent) of the youth arriving between 1991 and 1996 (CMA Toronto, Census, 1996 in CASSA, 1998, p. 8).
- The employment to population rate for South Asian youth ages fifteen to twenty-four is 37 per cent, with 35 per cent for females and 40 per cent for males (CMA Toronto, Census, 1996 in CASSA, 1998, p. 8).
- The unemployment rate for South Asian youth ages fifteen to twenty-four is 24 per cent, with 27 per cent for females and 22 per cent for males (CMA Toronto, Census, 1996 in CASSA/SALC, 1999, p. 8).
- The unemployment rate for South Asian youth is about 22 per cent, while the rate for youth in general is about 15 per cent (Ornstein, 1996).
- South Asians speak many languages—Bengali, Gujerati, Farsi, Hindi, Punjabi, Tamil, and Urdu—to name but a few (CASSA/SALC, 1999, p. 4).

- A study done by the *Toronto Star* found that 38 per cent of South Asians surveyed earn less than $30,000 per year. Of these, 15 per cent earn under $20,000. Only 10 per cent earn more than $75,000 per year (CASSA/SALC, 1999, p. 5).

Participant Profiles

Ninety-four youth participated in the project, of whom thirty-one were part of the pilot focus groups and the remaining sixty-three were in the focus groups. The data gathered from the sixty-three youth were analyzed and used to produce this report. A brief profile is given below.

Of the total number of sixty-three participants, thirty-two were female (50.8 per cent) and thirty-one were male (49.2 per cent).

The majority of the youth were between the ages of sixteen to eighteen, with eighteen (28.6 per cent) female and twenty (31.7 per cent) male. With this overall age breakdown, most of the participants (both males and females) were in grades 11–13.

Eighteen females and fourteen males, totalling thirty-two (50.8 per cent) of the participants, were from Sri Lanka. The next largest representation—eleven (17.5 per cent), or five females and six males—were from India, followed by five females and five males totalling ten (15.9 per cent) from Pakistan; two (3.2 per cent) males from Kenya; and one (1.6 per cent) female each from Bangladesh and Saudi Arabia.

In line with the above, thirty-two (50.8 per cent) of youth indicated that their mother tongue was Tamil. Thirteen (20.6 per cent) of the youth spoke Urdu; seven (11.1 per cent) spoke Punjabi; two (3.2 per cent) spoke Gujerati, and only one (1.6 per cent) each belonged to the Bengali, Hindi, Katchi, and Sindhi language groups.

With respect to religious representation among the participants, thirty-one (49.2 per cent) were Hindu, sixteen (25.4 per cent) were Muslim, nine (14.3 per cent) were Sikh, and two (3.2 per cent) were Christian.

With regard to their parents' level of education, the youth indicated that fifty-five (or 44 per cent) of their parents had post-secondary education. Of the fifty-five, thirty (24 per cent) were fathers and twenty-five (20 per cent) were mothers. The percentage with the lowest level of education (only some high school education) was greater for the mothers—nineteen (15 per cent) compared to seventeen (13.5 per cent) for the fathers.

Of the 115 parents who are in Canada with their children, thirty-eight (33 per cent) of the fathers and twenty-two (19 per cent) of the mothers were working.

Of those who responded on family status, twenty-four (38.1 per cent) were from a nuclear family; seven (11.1 per cent) were from extended families; one (1.6 per cent) was from a single, sole-parent family; and the remaining four (6.3 per cent) indicated "other" without explaining what it meant.

Highlights from Focus Groups: Findings and Discussion

As human beings we are social and need a sense of belonging. This need is most pressing in our adolescence when we are trying to find our place in the world as potential adults and defining who we are. South Asian youth involved in this study shared their stories about how they deal with the questions of identity and belonging as they adapt to a new culture.

Negotiating Identities: What the Participants Had to Say about Identity

> I speak Punjabi all the time. . . . I am proud of my culture. If I'm going to speak English and act like a White person, that ain't going to make me White, right? . . . So I just say . . . if you're going to be classified by culture or your colour, represent your culture all the way. (Male)

> Ultimately it is about a person making a choice. Sometimes one decides to wear it in spite of your parents not wearing it because of your own consciousness of your religious identity. (Female)

The participants brought all the dimensions of racialization (language, colour of skin, and culture) into focus and used them almost as interchangeable constructs. This reflects the fact that racial minorities face prejudice and discrimination because they speak differently, dress differently, have a different skin colour, and follow different religious and social customs. All these factors, which are an integral part of their cultural identity, make them targets for racist behaviour and consequently these factors are seen as key to developing pride in one's cultural identity. As a response to racism and the indignities that they face in everyday encounters with the dominant culture, for example, Muslim girls choose to wear the *hijab*,[1] or Punjabi youth take pride in speaking their mother tongue as a form of resistance. The youth do, in fact, begin to focus on their cultural identity of origin in the face of racism. Tatum (1992) explains that this is in keeping with Parham's Immersion/Emersion stage of identity, which is "characterized by the simultaneous desire to surround oneself with visible symbols of one's racial identity and an active avoidance of symbols of Whiteness" (p. 15).

The educational institution is often the first place where youth encounter skin-colour racism. The schoolrooms and playgrounds become arenas where visible minority youth learn more than science and basketball—they learn that regardless of their skills and capabilities, they will always be seen as inferior because of the colour of their skin. These narratives clearly illustrate that children from the South Asian community are targets of racial harassment, which includes racial slurs, ethnic and racial jokes, threats, and physical assaults. They also illustrate that youth have had to come up with their own responses to this form of harassment. There were no quoted instances of how institutions or authority figures such as teachers dealt with such incidents:

> We support each other. [It] doesn't matter what kind of South Asian you are. We get in there to help our guys out even when they are not part of our small group. I can remember even in school . . . there were . . . twenty White guys [who] . . . were making fun of us. They were . . . calling us Pakis and stuff. And we just jumped them. (Male)

The youth informed us that they had to come up with their own strategies to deal with harassment in schools because principals, teachers, and other educational officers hesitate to deal with racism. This is supported by McCaskell (1993), who reported that teachers were reluctant to report racist incidents because they did not want to be seen as lacking control over their classes; department heads did not report them because it "looked bad"; principals were reluctant to report them because they reflected negatively on their school; and superintendents did not report them because they were supposed to provide leadership:

> If you are Indian, Pakistani, Sri Lankan, you may have frictions between each other . . . but if an outside group, say like, West Indian or Black people come or White people come, or Chinese people come and try to mess with any one of us, they are all going to combine and they are all going to go after that group. (Male)

Even though under normal circumstances the diverse South Asian ethnocultural groups see themselves as culturally distinct and not part of a homogeneous South Asian community, when threatened by another racial group they see their solidarity as the best defence against White supremacy and everyday racist harassment. Therefore, this solidarity is also how individual youth come to adopt a consciousness of the collective South Asian identity. Thus, the collective known as "South Asian" is constructed through a dynamic created by both internal and external factors, namely interracial relations of dominance/subordination or the dialectical nature of oppression and activism (Hill Collins, 1990, p. 95). According to Tatum (1992), this happens in response to "a society where racial-group membership is emphasized, the development of a racial identity will occur in some form in everyone. Given the dominant/subordinate relationship of Whites and people of color in this society, however, it is not surprising that this developmental process will unfold in different ways. . . . Faced with the reality that he or she cannot truly be White, the individual is forced to focus on his or her identity as a member of a group targeted by racism" (pp. 14–15).

All We Want Is to Fit in

> . . . when people from outside come here and they don't have a job . . . they go out and do drugs, gangs and violence, and everything. I think the reason they try to do that is . . . to fit in. . . . it seems people

here do drugs, they are in gangs, they go clubbing, whatever. So, you think, in order to fit in, you must do all of these things. (Male)

But they should know themselves that if I have to do that to fit in, then that's not worth it. But they want to fit in so badly. . . . (Male)

The participants in the study clearly reveal the limited options that South Asian youth have in terms of making life choices and the tremendous pressure they face to "be cool" or "one of the gang." Faced with racist attitudes and racial harassment, the youth are drawn toward other racial minority youth, namely Black youth, who are respected or even feared by the dominant group. Belonging to or becoming a part of this "select" club often brings "power" and "privileges" that are otherwise denied because of the colour of their skin. It is not surprising then that the youth find the pressure to belong to this group difficult to resist since male youth know that they are "respected" for the real or perceived physical strength that these groups supposedly have because of prevalent racial stereotypes. Therefore, several youth spoke of adopting elements of pop culture associated with the Black youth culture because it is the "hip thing to do." Hence many South Asian youth were described as "Black Wannabes." The disturbing reality is that many racial minority youth resort to violence to solve problems that should be addressed systemically. This also reveals that they are responding to a broader culture that sanctions physical and psychological violence until it fosters fear and implicitly supports violence as a solution.

The girls, however, had a different perspective. While the boys clearly stated that they come together regardless of their inherent diversity, the girls seem to face the challenge of being accepted by their own cultural group as well as the dominant White group. The girls did not face overt physical violence. Some of the females who had spent a longer time in Canada said that as they had strived so hard to "fit in" and be "accepted," they feared that if they attempted to support newcomers, they might be excluded from the group they have strived so hard to fit into and be accepted by. This perspective arises also because young South Asian girls are told in many ways that it is not desirable to "stand out" in a crowd or to draw attention to themselves. In a society dominated by Whites, this might get translated into acquiring some kind of pseudo-White status. This dual consciousness in many South Asian youth results when they "become familiar with the language and manners of the oppressor, even sometimes adopting them for some illusion of protection while hiding a self-defined standpoint from the prying eyes of dominant groups," as explained by Hill Collins (1990, p. 91).

It is also evident from the study that youth attending schools with a significant number of South Asian students are able to adapt and fit in better than youth attending White-dominated schools. Moreover, the youth in schools where South Asians are the majority expressed a sense of confidence and a stronger self-concept as opposed to internalized inferiority. Also, youth who have been in Canada longer play a mentor role for newcomers:

> . . . the school that I go to is very multicultural and it's kind of really interesting to be in a school of this sort because you feel confident. (Male)

> You're new in the country and you have no one. If you have someone who talks your language and then could translate stuff for you, it's much easier for you to communicate with other people. And you have some kind of support rather than being alone. (Female)

Some schools seem to have recognized the very important role that peers from similar backgrounds and cultures can play. Pairing a new student with another student who acts as a cultural broker, a "buddy," makes the process of settling in and making sense of the new environment much easier.

The youth negotiated their identities during the process of controlled enculturation/acculturation to maintain a duality or bicultural identity through their dual consciousness. They also exhibited a critical understanding of media as an apparatus of the ruling class. Many of the participants saw television in particular and the media in general as perpetuating many existing stereotypes about minority ethno-racial or ethnocultural and religious groups. With this knowledge and understanding of media as part and parcel of the "ideological apparatuses of the society" (Smith, 1987, p. 17), the youth were critical consumers of media messages. The youth explained clearly how this exclusion meant that their ethnocultural or indigenous knowledge, values, and beliefs were not recognized as having a part in developing a contemporary Canadian identity. Many youth who demonstrated this awareness did, however, acknowledge how media in general, and television in particular, were powerful socializing agents. Some participants, as revealed by the following quotes, felt that watching television had helped them learn how to speak, how to act, and behave like a "typical teenager":

> It was basically see what the culture and the ways are—the behaviour—on the TV and I saw all these things. . . . I was . . . able to adjust quite easily. (Male)

Parents Just Don't Understand . . .

> I think a lot of Indian families—South Asian families, for that matter—don't understand the youth or today's culture. They just go back into their days when they were young and say, "We couldn't do this when we were your age, so why should you be able to do it?" (Female)

> I think that parents need to understand what you're going through in school. You are going through different stuff . . . they need to change their ways too, a little. (Male)

The issues regarding conflicts between parents and children because of cultural differences between the country of origin and Canada came up more in the female groups. In the South Asian tradition, women and girls are seen as the "custodians" of family values and culture. Consequently, parents are more anxious about their daughters retaining traditional values and customs. As an extension of the double standards that prevail in patriarchal societies, many male siblings within the South Asian culture also seem to appropriate the role of parents when it comes to deciding what is "acceptable" for their sisters and female cousins. However, patriarchal dynamics within immigrant families must be understood in relation to racism and cultural hegemony. Often excessive insistence and adherence to "culture" and "tradition" is a reflection of relations of power in Canada as opposed to something intrinsic in the culture of origin or its traditions. Altered notions of "Western" culture and values are pitted against "our culture and traditions," not because of naïveté but in response to power relations and delegitimization and the threat of losing one's identity. Therefore, many South Asian parents here are reacting to this perceived threat of cultural eradication when imposing "excessive" demands on their children:

> . . . she [his sister] can't go to school wearing . . . a mini skirt and . . . a little top that shows her stomach, because I know how guys think, too. . . . And I refuse to let her wear that. (Male)

Parents, as evidenced by the quotes below, also seem to seek affirmation from their peers that they have been "good" parents and have done a good job of raising their children with their culture and traditional values intact:

> You're the middle-class, working folks, you know. You don't want your children to go astray because you have a reputation to keep. (Female)

This is partly because of a desire to recapture some of the lost social and economic status through children who are doing well academically or professionally and retaining traditional values. The manifestation of this could range from dressing appropriately, to speaking the mother tongue, to knowledge of religion and scriptures, to marrying the girl or boy that the parents choose. The greater the difference between the economic circumstances in the country of origin and Canada, the greater the level of discomfort and conflict because of the perceived loss of power and control over the children who are seen as becoming something else by adapting more rapidly to the new culture.

This is also a reflection of parental anxiety that if the children become too well integrated into the Canadian culture, parents will be "abandoned" to institutionalized care facilities, such as homes for the aged—a very "Western" concept. Therefore, the parents also want to control the friendships and peer group contacts that the children make. They want to control and limit external/Western influence by encouraging their children to maintain friendships within their own ethnocultural linguistic group or the larger South Asian community:

> It's diverse out here. They somehow don't want us to blend, unless we are blending with people they like. . . . (Male)

> I can have Indian friends over, [but] not others. (Female)

Parents who participated in the study felt that they should impose some restrictions on where their children went, with whom, and for how long. While some parents were of the opinion that the children should go straight to school and come back home, others felt that some exposure to society was good as long as they (the parents) had control over the process of acculturation. This need to maintain parental control should be understood in the context of the broader "immigrant" experience. In other words, it is important to understand this intergenerational gap in the South Asian community from the perspective that there is a gap between main-stream cultural-social values in relation to power as experienced by "immigrant" parents in their everyday realities in Canada. In real-ity, parents in the face of external forces of dominance have to legit-imize their values and the children/youth must simultaneously negotiate and "construct" a new reality that is inclusive of them in Canada. In essence, both the parents and their children/youth are reacting to structures of dominance. Parents are reacting to domi-nant social value structures that are culturally specific to "Western" society, and the youth are reacting to parental as well as societal structures of domination. Ironically, within this process, larger soci-etal structures such as the media and education tend to "delegit-imize" and weaken parental structures.

There was greater parental concern about the daughters. Many parents were reluctant to let their daughters go out alone, even to the library. In addition to the gender dimension, there is also clearly a religious dimension to the conflicts within the home arising out of cultural differences. Girls from Muslim families seem to face maximum parental pressure, though there are significant differences from one family to the next. The girls felt tremendous pressure since they have to fit into a certain mould to be accepted among their peers and, at the same time, adopt a completely opposite set of behaviours for their parents. One of the coping mechanisms that girls seem to develop to survive this schizophrenic existence is to lead dual lives:

> I know some people who come to school and change the way they dress 'cause they don't dress up like that when they come out of [their] house because of their parents. They come to school and they change the way they look and everything. They put on their makeup. . . . they have makeup stored . . . in their lockers and they just come to school plain and they would never do all that stuff at home. (Female)

There has been no documentation of what effects this has on the girls' mental health, but several female youth in the study indicated that "feeling stressed out" or depressed was not unusual:

> It's really hard for the girls. Do you know how many of the girls are depressed . . . ? [general agreement in the group] (Female)

As parents come from a culture where the concept of dating did not exist when they were growing up (and even today dating in this culture is not really common practice), they have a hard time dealing with their children's relationships with the opposite sex in their newly adopted country. First, for the parents it means having to acknowledge their children's growing sexuality and sexual awareness. Second, this seems to symbolize an erosion of cultural values and all that is "bad and wild" about Western culture as far as the parents are concerned. Third, this is a culture in which arranged marriages are still practised to some degree. Some parents here are concerned that their children might not only select their own partners but might choose someone from a different ethnocultural, racial, or religious background. Again, as mentioned earlier, it is very important to understand that parents' concerns and fears are related to their sense of not always understanding the workings of this new society where they feel pressured to succeed, and hence of experiencing a loss of power in the dominant culture. They are also afraid that their children might lose their ethnocultural identity.

However, participants also cited instances in which the parents, while not being completely supportive or understanding of their children's actions, still did not disown them. Instead, they worked together to find a more positive outcome. Some of the participants also suggested that the children might be underestimating and prejudging the parents:

> [The] parents [of a friend of mine] didn't kick her out of the house; they were supportive. Okay, you were stupid, you made a mistake, you were young, it's over with. Let's just start fresh. And they know she's still with the guy. There's no point in breaking the relationship now that you've gone so far, so might as well talk, and in a couple of years get married. (Female)

There is also evidence that parents are trying to change and adapt to the new culture's different norms, including parenting and the relationship between parents and children. Sometimes when there is more than one child in the family, the older children rebel, which may lead the parents to adjust their expectations:

> My parents have changed because they realize that . . . things aren't the way they are back home. (Female)

The parents who participated in this study were very aware of the pressures that their children were experiencing. Yet they were torn between what they had been brought up to believe was right and had accepted unquestioningly, and the need to justify any restrictions they may place on their children in terms of clothing, food, friendships, etc. Some of the parents felt they were engaged in a losing battle in urging their children to delay gratification, persevere, work hard, and persist. However, their children did not share the perspective that these behaviours would be enough to over-come and address racism. Parents who are still struggling to find economic security also expressed difficulty in meeting some of their children's lifestyle expectations. The children understood the diffi-culties their parents were facing and why they will stay in Canada in spite of the problems and challenges. In fact, the children were often told that their parents were willing to endure these hardships and indignities so that they (the children) can have a better life here, thus instilling in them a sense of responsibility and obligation. Perhaps it is this strong sense of indebtedness to the parents that helps to keep the family together and retain cultural identity.

Some parents said their children needed advice, but were reluc-tant to take it from parents who were seen as too old or out of touch with the way things are in Canada. In the process of resettling and trying to fit into the new culture, parents—in the face of external realities imposed by the dominant culture—lose some of their tradi-tional authority and their children start looking elsewhere for posi-tive role models. But there is still much reluctance in seeking counselling or joining programs that would facilitate adaptation and settlement largely because parents and youth do not think that the programs (designed and developed within the structures of the dominant society) will understand the cultural values and beliefs of those considered "outsiders." Moreover, both parents and youth believed that society would automatically deem their culture as problematic rather than locating the difficulties within the complex "immigrant" experience as mentioned earlier. Several youth said that often the suggested solution to their problems was to leave home, which was regarded as an entrenched authoritarian envi-ronment beyond change. This, according to many youth and their parents, was untenable and totally unacceptable.

The parents are sensitive to the fact that their children often had very little say in the decision to immigrate and in most cases were very reluctant to leave the home country and all that was friendly and familiar for a new country that was unfamiliar and at times overtly hostile.

After coming here they face such a different environment and so many stress and strains here that they can't cope with that. It is a shock and if we pressurize him more, he will break. . . . (Male)

My Mom Is More Understanding

Even within the parental relationship, there are differences in how mothers and fathers deal with parenting issues. Mothers are usually referred to as the emotional support, the mediator, the buffer between the children and the father, and are often the people with whom the youth feel closer and more able to discuss their problems. The mothers traditionally play this role in many South Asian families. Even if they are working outside the home, they are still seen as responsible for the children's upbringing and will often be blamed if they rebel:

Yeah, I think my father is more strict than my mother. My mom's more into "They're young now, so if they're not going to go to the movies now, when are they going to go the movies? If they are not going to wear the clothes now, when are they?" Not that she promotes it, [but] she's more liberal. (Female)

My mom knows . . . all of my friends. And she knows who I hang out with and who I had a fight with, or whatever. . . . my mom's sort of close to me so she knows certain aspects of life pretty well. (Male)

All participants reported that they are more comfortable talking with their mother. They said that at times their mothers know about their friends, especially those of the opposite sex, but would not tell their fathers, so it appears that the mothers are not averse to practising some deception on behalf of their children!

I Don't Want to Become a Doctor

Many parents are willing to sacrifice upward mobility in their careers and social status to ensure a better future for their children. Even when parents had come here because of civil war or conflict in the home country, they felt that their children had benefited because Canada had better educational facilities than their home country:

So [the] purpose of coming to this country is all for the betterment of the career opportunities for children. (Father)

In Canada the choice is more varied and, moreover, technology—the application of technology in learning—no way we can compare to Canada. (Mother)

This translates into much pressure on the children to perform well academically. They are also expected to go into careers that are valued in their community. Children who want to pursue careers other than the professions or computer technology find that their parents are not very supportive:

Our parents want us to have . . . office jobs because . . . they . . . now . . . have the low jobs. (Male)

How you are doing at school is always a big impact because remember, that's the main reason all of our families came here. (Male)

[Parents] want their children to go into an educated career instead of [an] athletic career. . . . if the kids want to go into an athletic career, they don't support them enough. (Male)

Many of the girls wanted non-traditional careers. It raises the question of whether the girls would have been able to have such non-traditional career aspirations if they had remained in their home country:

I want to be computer teacher. (Female)

I want to be an air force pilot. (Female)

Oh My God! You Can Speak English!
Language and whether and how one speaks English is one of the major issues that children from racial minority groups have to face in school. It is also a way in which the system distinguishes and

discriminates. Aptitude and skills tests that are not appropriate for someone who comes from a different country and a different educational system are used, and often students of South Asian origin are denied access to advanced level courses based on these tests:

> They see a brown person who doesn't speak English well and think that all brown people can't speak. They'll stick them in ESL. (Male)

> They just look at your English knowledge and they'll put you in ESL for other subjects too. (Male)

There is also a tendency for counsellors and teachers to have lower expectations of these students. Often the counsellors seem to encourage these students to think about alternatives to university education, such as community colleges or trade schools, even when the children have good test scores and overall good grades. Such reactions reflect the racism that is so ingrained in White Canadian consciousness. It is also very ironic because most participants in the study said that "better educational opportunities" was why their families immigrated to Canada:

> They took my tests in math and English. My scores were well above average. The counsellor told me, "You should go into community college and maybe handy-work is good for you."

In recent years, the largest category of immigrants from South Asia has been the "independent" or "skilled worker" category. Thus, increasingly these children have parents who are often very highly educated, and who place a great deal of emphasis on education as a way to improve one's position in life and society. Unless counsellors and teachers recognize the importance of education as a vehicle for upward mobility and increased life chances, South Asian youth will not get a fair deal out of this education system.

The participants also offered some wonderful insights about how the curriculum content and design could help in dealing with racism and prejudice because there is very little knowledge or understanding about racial minorities and their contributions to

Canada. This brings up the very critical question: What role does the education system have in building a nation that is inclusive, equitable, and accepting of all minorities?

> We should learn about different cultures, their countries, their histories, their importance in the world. I'm not going to stop a person on the street, you know, I'm Pakistani and this is my culture. You seem to learn it at school, that's the general thing. (Female)

Even schools that have a number of students from a specific ethnic community do not have courses for their mother tongue. Even if they are offered, they are offered on Saturdays and not as part of regular a curriculum—almost like an extracurricular option. Also, many of the students work weekends, which makes it difficult for them to attend these classes:

> [At] West Humber, at least 65–70 per cent of the school was Punjabi. . . . [At] TCI, there's a lot of Punjabis there too. I think they should . . . have Spanish courses. (Male)

> . . . Spanish is not an official language of Canada, so why not Punjabi? (Male)

Even in other activities like sports, schools often do not offer options that the South Asian youth excel in such as cricket or soccer as opposed to hockey, football, or basketball. The youth also pointed out that sporting activities were largely limited to competitive sports. Students who could compete for their schools had access to space and sports equipment, leaving youth who were simply interested in "having a good time" with no access to these resources.

Cultural stereotypes are reinforced by teachers' racist behaviour. No amount of anti-racist policy statements can counter the powerful impact of seeing role models behaving in a discriminatory manner.

According to some students, sometimes the teachers are not "consciously racially discriminatory," but they may place demands on the students without being aware of their special needs and challenges.

Female: Sometimes they don't know how to explain to class, right. So, he just embarrass everyone in front of the class.

Male: I don't think any teacher who sits in a class and hands out assignments and expects them back the day or the day after who doesn't know what your real life is . . . after 3:00 you are working 12:00 in the morning or whatever. He doesn't know what you are going through. But he expects his work done just because that what he gets paid for. He doesn't care what you going through, right.

Students also demonstrated an understanding of how racial minority teachers, who could be positive role models to the youth, are often themselves victims of discrimination and powerless to counter racist behaviour from students. The following words reveal this:

. . . he's an Indian teacher. And all the students are really very bad with him, even [saying] things like "Shut up, stupid." They just don't listen to him. (Male)

At the same time, many of the participants also felt that the school system was very good despite all its limitations. They felt that the schools offered more choices in terms of courses, and there was not so much emphasis on performance in standardized exams and ranking on the basis of their academic performance:

I love the access that we have here, the electoral options and things like that. I love the opportunities that are here. (Male)

The youth also shared experiences of having teachers who were supportive and the difference this made in the process of adaptation:

I had a nice teacher. . . . He doesn't look like he was going to come after you. He tells you everything word by word so we could understand. (Male)

It helps when you talk to teachers, ask them if you will be able to handle the course and they help you after school. (Female)

These stories focus on the critical role that educational institutions and teachers play in this phase of young people's lives, and how making schools safer for visible minority children needs to become a priority.

All the participants in the study have learned to cope and find "happiness" through their "dual consciousness" prompted by their experiences in their new environment. For some, Canada has provided opportunities that were not available in the home country. Many of them who have been here for three years sadly said that they still do not feel they belong. Canada is not yet home.

CONCLUSIONS

Freedom to speak one's language, and practise one's culture and religion are enshrined in various human rights legislation and policies at both the provincial and federal levels. As Canadians, we are bringing up our children with the belief that—no matter who you are, regardless of class, race, or gender—you have equal access to Canadian political processes and services within the economic, education, health, and social sectors. Yet the experiences of the South Asian youth who participated in this study bear the hallmarks of a fundamentally non-egalitarian society. Their experiences reveal that injustices are at work, despite the professed ideology of egalitarianism and meritocracy. This persists because of an entrenched and rooted ideology of language superiority and cultural supremacy buttressed by the established "ideological apparatuses of society" (Smith, 1987, p. 17), such as education and media in a racialized society.

Skin-colour racism is the most powerful social reality that compels them to become conscious of their status as "other." To survive the accompanying devaluation, many youth develop a knowledge of and pride in their cultural, racial, and religious identity to ground themselves. This experience of discrimination was also a very powerful unifier, as experienced and expressed by South Asian youth. The experiences of being marginalized took precedence over other difficulties specific to particular ethno-linguistic or ethno-religious or national origin and pre-immigration history. Regardless of pre-immigration history, or ethno-linguistic or cultural differences, youth revealed that the issues related to skin-colour racism and discrimination were most important to them, not the "uniqueness" of the diversity within the broader South Asian community.

The youth articulated and analyzed the tensions within their dual or bifurcated consciousness, generated by the conflict between how they see their culture and themselves and how they are perceived and treated by the dominant culture. Their comments reveal what strikes them as unjust and how they have devised strategies to survive. They demonstrate an understanding of the material barriers and existential experiences of everyday indignities in their everyday encounters. Some Muslim female youth and Sikh males involved in this study said that they sometimes have to comply with two competing values systems: on the one hand, their religious requirements and, on the other, their own need to fit in the larger youth culture within the Canadian context. South Asian youth have come up with creative ways to manage these competing demands. They combine two systems of values and expectations to create a bi-culturality.

No significant differences were found in educational expectations for males and females. Females expressed interest in "non–gendered" careers. This reveals the diversity of lived realities among South Asian women and challenges the commonly held stereotype of South Asian women as oppressed and restricted, an outdated stereotype that could have serious negative implications for youth seeking direction from teachers and guidance counsellors who might perceive South Asian culture as homogeneously traditionalist and sexist. Muslim females also expressed a strong sense of agency that came across through their comments about wearing the *hijab*. Some of the Muslim young women insisted that wearing a *hijab* was based on choice and freedom to decide, as well as religious pride and faith and not just because their religion expects women to be modest. Their decision was based on rejecting external definitions and the media's images of Muslim women. Hence the youth are engaged in constructing independent self-definitions as a form of resistance and self-valuation reflecting the dialectical nature of oppression and activism (Hill Collins, 1990, p. 95).

In the face of these experiences, South Asian youth have devised realistic and pragmatic strategies in order to cope, and to help them live up to their parents' expectations, which they feel they must honour because of the sacrifices their parents made by immigrating, and the difficulties and hardships their parents endure to ensure success for their children in a society where there is very little hope for themselves. The youth revealed an acute awareness of their parents' struggle to maintain their positional power as parents despite the odds stacked against them. Both youth and their parents find themselves experiencing shifts in their respective roles within the family and especially in the outside world. In the face of barriers such as language and an unfamiliarity with mainstream institutions, youth often find themselves in the position of intermediary, translator, interpreter, and negotiator for or on behalf of their parents. Some parents can access mainstream institutions only with their children as cultural brokers. Without the assistance of their children, they risk being isolated. This creates awkwardness for the youth and places an unwarranted burden on them. Parents, on the other hand, find their power, authority, and ability to control their youth somewhat compromised. Needless to say, these shifting roles places both parents and youth at risk, with profound implications for family dynamics. These differences in the existential realities between South Asian parents and children exacerbate the already challenging process of adaptation and settlement for youth and their families, hence the intergenerational challenges. However, a sense of unmitigated duty and obligation seems to keep the family in check to survive the complex challenges in a new country, as all members try to establish a sense of home.

Parental expectations are something all youth have to deal with. In the case of South Asian youth, this takes on special significance. They are under tremendous pressure to succeed because their parents endure many unwarranted burdens, especially when seeking access to employment in a society that does not recognize their credentials and experience. Within this reality, many South Asian parents tend to assert "excessive control." In the face of everyday struggles imposed by external constraints, parents try to create and maintain spheres of influence and control by exercising parental authority and control within the family.

Parents realize that in such an environment, South Asian youth have to swim upstream while non-racial minority youth can drift with the tide. The youth have to understand how teachers, counsellors, and others in this society operate against them and their culture, in order to overcome systemic barriers and achieve full participation and success. Regardless of gender, the youth consistently seem to suggest that maintaining an intact sense of cultural identity and keeping their parents' expectations in focus helps them to maintain a balance and to continue working hard. Implied in this is also a sense of cautious optimism that they will be respected and accepted if they work hard. South Asian youth, strongly influenced by their parents' attitudes toward work and education, reveal high aspirations of social class. Despite their awareness of systemic barriers, their aspirations remain unaffected.

Within the context of school, it seems as if much of the youth's time is spent in coming up with strategies to deal with teasing, harassment, name-calling, and systemic discrimination within the educational system that fosters Euro/Anglocentric cultural supremacy. Youth have to devise ways to avoid the effects of stereotypes and violence perpetrated by their non-South Asian peers and their teachers' low or negative expectations of them. Many of the youth did not believe the system will do anything about these problems. The coping strategies seem to indicate that they rely on their own abilities and achieve a sense of security by seeking out other South Asian youth to create a sense of belonging and cultural identity. The youth are very aware of the differences within the collectivity known as South Asian. They did not see these differences as operating antagonistically in the context of their lives here in Canada. The youth—regardless of their specific ethnocultural, linguistic, or religious identity—demonstrated the need to coalesce despite the intragroup differences when faced with an external threat. They revealed that this strategy was critical in fighting off attacks on their pride and dignity from non-South Asian youth.

While they recognized the invaluable assistance and direction given them by some teachers, they indicated that they have to struggle with teachers and guidance counsellors who ask them to lower their expectations. Many felt impeded by teachers' assessments of their abilities, and did not have good reliable information and advice about educational opportunities. Through this study, the youth tell us how the education system continues to apply culturally biased intelligence, aptitude, and general knowledge and skills tests to immigrant children. They also had serious concerns about being classified as inadequately prepared to deal with the demands of the curriculum, and as having insufficient ability or capacity or intelligence, which results in them being placed in an inappropriate grade level when they arrive as newcomers.

In addition, from what the youth told us, educators still do not recognize that much of what is taught is biased and offensive to immigrant children. Muslim youth expressed frustration with the representations of Muslims as terrorists, and as violent and evil. The youth said the education system must play a critical role in confronting and changing these stereotypes by having curricula materials that reflect the presence and contributions of South Asians not only in Canada but also in the global context. Having curricula activities and reading materials that reflected their diversity and their contributions would help them maintain their pride in their cultural identity as well as address their marginalization in Canadian society. They also said that the South Asian community should become actively involved in challenging the education system. They thought that South Asians should learn from the African-Canadian community about lobbying for change. The youth recognized that having Black History/Black Liberation Month is an important, meaningful, and necessary first step in the process. They said that the education system needed to go beyond this and to have curricula materials and activities that included all ethnocultural and racial groups.

Youth's school experiences have made them disillusioned and very suspicious of the system that is supposed to facilitate equal opportunity and access to better life chances. They consistently expressed the view that schools should be a caring place where all students feel they belong and have something to offer and contribute. Their comments reveal that they are acutely aware of systemic discrimination and how this places them at the centre of the struggle between the school's expectations of them and their parents' expectations, not to mention their own expectations, which might not be consistent with those of either the school or their parents. Conscious of these dynamics, many students did not have any recourse to challenge the discriminatory practices since in many cases they felt that they could not turn to their parents or the South Asian community for help. Often this left many of the youth feeling as if they had no control over their lives. Many of them felt angry and others said they were left with a vulnerable ego and weakened self-esteem because they had little or no control. Some of the females had experienced depression and some said that they turned the anger toward themselves. Some of the males coped by engaging in fights or turning to alcohol or drugs.

Along with comments about what the education system should do, the youth mentioned that the Canadian media should become more responsible in their treatment and representation of South Asians. They also indicated that the South Asian community had a role to play in ensuring positive and balanced representations in the media by using political processes to reduce the racial harassment targeted at South Asians.

Recommendations

There are very few services available for youth in general. Services for South Asian youth seem to be even fewer. In the absence of formal support services, many South Asian youth rely on informal supports, which are usually provided by friends and family. As services were scarce and discrimination evident, youth came up with these recommendations.

The participants proposed many suggestions on how parents, teachers, and the larger community can help make this process of transition an easier one. Their "needs for support" and suggested recommendations are organized under education, social services, parents, and the larger community. However, for many of the recommendations to be fully realized, we must, as Canadians, confront and deal with skin-colour racism before we can remove systemic barriers.

Education

1. Make the curriculum more inclusive by specifically including content that gives the students an understanding of other cultures

and traditions. Ensure that youth recognize the many ways in which ethno-racial minority groups have contributed to the development of Canada as a nation. Schools should actively promote anti-racism and anti-discrimination.

2. This inclusive framework needs to go beyond the classroom. After-school programs should be geared toward including students of all cultures. Sports that are more popular in South Asian countries, like cricket and soccer, should be introduced. This way the newcomers would find at least some activities that are familiar and it would also give them a sense of belonging.

3. Schools also need to give serious thought to how newcomers are systematically restricted from taking advanced level courses, even though they may perform well in aptitude tests, either because of discriminatory practices or because of how the ESL program works.

4. School guidance counsellors need to approach their counselling from an integrated anti-racism framework, which would help them make their interventions more insightful and address the needs of *all* students regardless of skin colour, culture, class, ability, sexual orientation, etc.

5. There is a need to develop more accurate ways of determining where a student should be placed in terms of grade and levels of study. School boards need to develop aptitude tests that are not discriminatory or Euro/Anglocentric.

6. ESL classes need to be flexible, graduated in level, and of a high quality to integrate students into their subject areas at the level of sophistication they need for their academic work, rather than the "same size fits all" structure that currently exists.

7. The mentoring or "buddy" system needs to be institutionalized, so that integrated youth can help newcomers gain an understanding about the school, its education system, and "Canadian" culture.

8. The Settlement Education Partnership in Toronto (SEPT) program should seen as an integral part of educational services, with full recognition of SEPT workers as part of the educational team and not as outsiders or interlopers "spying" on teachers. When students outside the City of Toronto heard about this program, other focus group participants expressed a keen interest in having SEPT extended to their areas.

9. Schools with a large number of students from a similar ethno-linguistic South Asian background should find ways to provide classes for the mother tongue during school hours rather than in the evenings or on weekends.

10. Schools should have more cultural programs to help foster a greater understanding of different cultures among the students.

Social Services

1. Counsellors are needed to act as mediators among youth, parents, and teachers, as intergenerational issues come up in the process of settlement and integration. Community centres should offer programs for youth and parents that would help resolve some of these issues.

2. The youth need drop-in centres where they can socialize, participate in games, and learn while having fun.

3. There is a need to provide youth with information about the services and opportunities available in Toronto and the Greater Toronto area. For example, youth who need to work to support or supplement the family income need to know how they can continue their education.

4. Agencies such as the Coalition of Agencies Serving South Asians (CASSA) and the South Asian Women's Centre (SAWC) could establish a South Asian Youth Council for the Greater Toronto area. The Council should play an advocacy, liaison, and facilitation role with local school boards and principals, settlement services, municipal departments, and other social/health institutions to implement some of the other recommendations.

Parents

1. Youth want a shift in their parents' attitudes and their desire to steadfastly hold on to traditional customs that are not necessarily appropriate in the new environment, otherwise the adaptation process is more problematic.

2. Parents need to recognize that their children go to schools that are multicultural and that they are likely to have friends who may not necessarily be from the same ethnocultural or ethno-racial background. They need to be supportive of this kind of

diversity, as it would help their children adapt in a multicultural, multiracial setting.

3. Parents need to become aware of how the educational system really works and the long-term implication of putting their children in ESL and not allowing them to take more advanced courses. Parents need to first educate themselves, so that they can combat discrimination in the schools.

The Larger Community

1. The larger South Asian community has the responsibility to take a more active interest in the way the schools are run. The community needs to get involved in making the educational system more inclusive and equitable.

2. The community needs to support youth initiatives that celebrate their culture and traditions. The youth today feel alienated, not just from the dominant White society but also from leaders and people of influence in their own communities.

3. The media should go beyond paying lip service to multiculturalism and human rights, and carry stories and articles that reflect the positive aspects of the South Asian community, especially its youth.

NOTE

[1] *Hijab* literally means a barrier or a curtain. It is a headdress, covering, or scarf that women use to cover their hair in public. This is in keeping with the Islamic regulations concerning modesty.

CHAPTER 5

Factors Affecting the Settlement and Adaptation Process of Canadian Adolescent Newcomers Sixteen to Nineteen Years of Age

RAJKO SEAT
Family Service Association of Toronto

BACKGROUND TO THE RESEARCH PROJECT

The Family Service Association of Toronto (FSA) has been serving families, individuals, and communities in Toronto for more than eighty years. Today FSA is one of the leading non-profit social service agencies in Canada, providing assistance to more than 20,000 individuals and families each year. FSA's services include a variety of counselling, education, intervention, and community support programs for those coping with depression and physical abuse, marital and family problems, developmental disabilities, and life challenges that the elderly face. FSA also works in partnership with various groups to help diverse communities provide care and support for their members.

Each year, approximately 200,000 immigrant and refugee newcomers arrive in Canada. Between 70,000 and 80,000 of them (over half of the total number of those newcomers who settle in Ontario each year) come to live in Toronto (Advisory Committee on Immigrant and Refugee Issues, 1997). It has recently been estimated that Canada receives between 25,000 and 35,000 new migrant children nineteen years of age and younger every year (Hicks, Lalonde, & Pepler, 1993). FSA sees the process of settlement, adaptation, and integration for these immigrant and refugee youth as a complex and multifaceted experience with an important psychological dimension.[1] It is also a process that in many cases can be extraordinarily intense and stressful.

A number of recent studies of newcomer youth challenge the notion that their settlement process is relatively easy (Chiu & Ring, 1998; Goodenow & Espin, 1993; Huang, 1989; Rivera-Sinclair, 1997; Rousseau, Drapeau & Corin, 1997; Pawiluk et al., 1996; Seat, 1997). Our own work with these youth (by the Community Action Team of FSA) confirms these observations and contradicts the oft-prevailing views among mainstream service providers in sectors such as health, mental health, and education that immigrant and refugee youth adapt quite quickly and easily in their new environment. It has become increasingly clear to FSA that these young people frequently encounter a variety of psychological challenges and problems related to the settlement process that can seriously interfere with their personal and social lives, their academic achievement, and their future well-being. Manifestations of these problems include disappointment with life, low self-esteem, dysfunction, tension, and a sense that they are not accepted by and are isolated from mainstream Canadian society.

With funding support from Citizenship and Immigration Canada, Ontario Region (OASIS) and in collaboration with other research teams investigating the problems of newcomer youth, this study had two basic and related goals. The first was to investigate and explore the role of some of the psychological factors involved in the settlement, adaptation, and integration process of newcomer youth. The second was to develop and promote knowledge and skills to improve services for these youth and to make mainstream institutions in an increasingly multicultural society more responsive to their particular needs.

OUR APPROACH TO THE RESEARCH
Theoretical Perspective

For immigrant and refugee children and youth, migration presents significant life changes in their environment, community, and interpersonal affiliations. Reviews of the literature on this topic highlighted many variables such as language fluency, age, sex, degree of identification with the host culture, and the amount of social interaction within the new environment (Berry, Kim, Minde, & Mok, 1987; Church, 1982; Furnham & Bochner, 1986). In Canada, in addition to facing the usual highly intensive developmental issues related to growth and independence, newcomer youth also must start a new socialization process (Seat, 1997).[2] Emphasizing that throughout adolescence youth participate in a variety of personal transitions, Seat pointed out that for newcomer youth, migration breaks down the socialization process, including the specific thoughts, norms, and rules for behaviour that were accepted and valued within their original cultures. Furthermore, according to Seat, relationships between newcomer youth and their parents change in the new living environment, affecting not only the socialization process but also the children's psychological and behavioural well-being. Seat also pointed out that during their process of settlement, adaptation, and integration, newcomer youth must cope with many new demands: they must meet new academic challenges, deal with new expectations from teachers and parents, gain acceptance into new peer groups, and develop new kinds of social competence. Throughout this process, they are also obliged to negotiate the differences between the cultures of their countries of origin and their new home.

As these youth go through settlement, adaptation, and integration, we can expect to see a shift in their cultural orientation or "ethnic identity." Cultural orientation is the degree to which a person is oriented or connected to the members and the values of her or his original ethnic or cultural group and to the members of other groups with which they have contact (Phinley, Lochner, & Murphy, 1990).

Erikson (1968) pointed out that developing a consistent self-conception and identity is a necessary task for every adolescent. According to Erikson, ego identity formation occurs through personal exploration and the formation of a coherent set of attitudes, values, and beliefs. Burke (1991) proposes that one derives the meaning of her or his identity from traits shared with one class of people in a given society; thus, the identity that one constructs represents a set of internalized meanings that one attributes to the self in a certain social position or role. According to Burke, the identity process is a continuously operating and self-adjusting feedback loop that adjusts behaviours to reduce discrepancies and achieve congruence between the identity portrayed or given by the environment and the identity with its own set of meanings constructed by the person.

Immigrant and refugee youth experience major differences in their social environments inside and outside their families. This has been documented in recent multicultural literature (Atkinson, Morten, & Sue, 1993; Rowe, Benett, & Atkinson, 1994; Wong, 1999) and verified in FSA's everyday work with newcomer youth. As these youth live through the stages of settlement, including various degrees of involvement with both the culture of origin and the mainstream culture, the process of identity formation is complex and multidimensional. As well, the obligation to adapt to both their parents' traditional cultural values and Canadian society's norms makes the process confusing and ambiguous. This is even more acute if the parents of these youth are preoccupied with their own issues and problems during settlement and their children in turn have more limited communication with them and do not view them as positive role models. All these factors can make identity formation stressful and indeed painful for newcomer youth, who try to see themselves as part of the mainstream culture, but struggle with the conflict between how they identify themselves and how others identify them.

Throughout its work with newcomer immigrant and refugee youth, FSA has sought both to understand the problem-solving processes and other strategies they use in their new environment and to identify the various psychological factors affecting, limiting, or impeding their settlement process. More specifically, it was a concern with the issues of socialization and identity formation specific to newcomer youth that led us to this research project. Our approach highlights the importance of the psychological changes and challenges that newcomer youth experience as key to their settlement, adaptation, and integration.

Much research has been done on the services for newcomer youth in Canada. However, very little research has been conducted on the influence of different psychological factors that either increase or decrease the probability of these youth experiencing problems in different aspects of their settlement. Nevertheless, the experience of FSA and of other community-based service providers working with immigrant and refugee youth and their families reveals the significant influence of newcomer youth's psychological factors and changes in their new Canadian life and the psychological dimension of the settlement process. Our project, therefore, addresses an area of research that is relatively new and undeveloped, yet also of great importance.

FSA's experience in working with newcomer youth suggests that interpersonal and intrapersonal demands and the corresponding outcomes of adaptation to cultural transition and change—such as relating successfully to a new school, peers, teachers, and other relevant parts of a new culture and gaining their acceptance—are not only highly salient to newcomer youth but also important in forecasting later settlement outcomes. Our experience with newcomer youth suggests that the cultural transition associated with the migration process is a significant life change that is discontinuous, sharp, and sudden. For newcomer youth, this change heralds the end of one lifestyle and the beginning of another. They are obliged to move from the old and intimate contexts of their previous life into a strange new environment. There is a sharp increase in feelings of anonymity—of knowing no one and not being known by anyone. Also, demands for further adaptation are always on the horizon.

Our work with these youth shows that their adaptation patterns are complex and highly differentiated. Outcomes such as peer rejection, depression, anxiety, and feelings of isolation may persist over many years and maintain or contribute to future problems of adaptation and integration such as prolonged psychological disturbances and mental health problems, or difficulties in academic achievement or personality and social and emotional development. It is clear, therefore, that for these youth the adaptation phase of their new life has significant psychological impacts and also presents significant challenges for the school system and providers of settlement, and social and health services. While this much seems obvious on the basis of our work with these youth, we still lack an understanding of the processes underlying the adaptation of newcomer youth. By researching the process of adaptation as a series of reactions to various life situations that these youth encounter, FSA hopes to shed light on one specific element that we believe to be key. In our view, the adaptation process for these youth can be better understood in terms of a coping framework that includes specific types of adaptation reactions to various situations encountered in their everyday life in the new Canadian environment.

Another potentially important outcome or expression of newcomer youth's settlement is the degree to which they become satisfied with different parts of their new life, including personal contentment and satisfaction with mainstream society. Our work with newcomer youth suggests that this is key in their identity development and settlement. Within the domain of developmental psychology, there are many authors (Adams & Looft, 1977; Erikson, 1968; Lipsitz, 1979; Rogers, 1985) who emphasize the importance of satisfaction, or degree of subjective well-being, as the focal point in adolescent identity development and its necessity in the acquisition of sex-appropriate roles and a commitment to social values and norms.

Within social psychological theory, attitudes are defined as one of the most important products of socialization. They consist of cognitive, affective, and behavioural components; they involve personal experiences and a permanent system of positive or negative valuing, and a disposition to take positive or negative action in various situations. Attitudes are consistent, stable, and complex, comprised of almost all the psychological processes; they have a very strong and sometimes critical influence on an individual's behaviour and activities. Attitudes that people form and adopt become part of their personalities and influence their behaviour in many ways (Alcock, Carment, & Sadava, 1988; Myers, 1986). Presumably, therefore, newcomer youth who like their new Canadian living environment more than their peers and who are generally more happy and satisfied will have a more positive settlement experience. Conversely, if newcomer youth react to their new environment with dissatisfaction, avoidance, or negative attitudes toward Canadian society, we are likely witnessing the early signs of future obstacles in the process of settlement. FSA's experience with these youth confirms these hypotheses; those whose life histories encompass stress and failures react much more easily and quickly with dissatisfaction, negative feelings, and unhappiness in valuing themselves and many things around them, including social institutions and society as a whole.

From FSA's perspective as well, the very few studies that have been conducted on these issues with respect to newcomer youth have had an overriding focus on self-esteem. There has been a neglect of other aspects of youth's subjective well-being such as satisfaction with oneself, with parents/guardians, with classmates, and with school and teachers as well as general attitudes toward Canadian society; also, there has been no attempt to correlate these factors with eventual outcomes of the settlement process. Our research attempts to fill in some of these gaps.

Our experience with newcomer youth also suggests that more attention should be paid to personality functioning as one of the key features of youth development affecting settlement outcomes. FSA believes very strongly that much can be learned about how individual newcomer youth confront the challenges of their new life by paying attention to the internal and less apparent characteristics and structure of their personalities. Indeed, we consider personality characteristics and dynamic structure as one of the vital and most consistent predictors of both immigrant and refugee youth's success in settlement, adaptation, integration, and well-being in the new Canadian environment.

Identifying the personality dimensions of newcomer youth's behaviour in the process of settlement is necessary in developing more responsive and sensitive settlement services. Indeed, research on this subject is key. We need to know which newcomer youth personality characteristics and dynamic structures are most reliably correlated with positive settlement, adaptation and integration outcomes, and well-being. We also need to review how personality interacts with newcomer youth life circumstances in the new Canadian environment to influence the stability of these outcomes, in order to develop appropriate services that will improve them. This whole area has been generally neglected, and we hope that our modest contribution will begin to fill in some gaps as well as stimulate further studies on this topic.

FSA considers the analysis of the above-mentioned psychological factors as essential in settlement work with newcomer youth. We must grasp the important role of newcomer youth's external and internal psychic structure in strengthening the process of moving toward a new self-identity and ensuring more successful settlement outcomes. Effectively dealing with these factors requires one to recognize their causes and dynamics and the situations they occur in, and identify positive behaviours to overcome negative influences.

The settlement, adaptation, and integration process of newcomer youth is not simple. It has multiple facets, including psychological dimensions, that require investigation. As well as revealing much about the variables affecting successful settlement, the results of the research can provide an important resource for newcomer youth in their new environment as a source of guidance in the development of socio-cultural competence, social values, roles, and rules in their interpersonal relationships and their adaptation to their new environment.

By analyzing the above-mentioned factors in this study, FSA hopes to provide valid data and relevant interpretations that will help inform the policy debates relevant to settlement service providers with respect to immigrant and refugee youth's settlement, adaptation, integration, mental health, and academic success in Canadian society. As professionals working in the field of immigrant and refugee settlement, we want to develop more scientific, empirically based, and effective interventions and programming with newcomer youth. We hope as well that by sharing this knowledge, we will encourage others to do the same. We feel that increased attention to the psychological dimensions of the settlement experience for newcomer youth will lead to new and original forms of intervention that will overcome some of the serious challenges that these youth face in their adaptation to a new life. Hopefully others will share our belief that this study points to new, practical, and acceptable directions.

At the same time, FSA considers that further research into the psychological dimensions of the settlement of newcomer youth, while difficult and challenging, is absolutely essential. Our work with these youth is in many ways difficult, as we share with them their pain, confusion, anxiety, depression, anxiety, isolation, marginalization, racism, discrimination, impaired social-emotional adjustment, minority status-related stress, school-related stress, transitional conflicts, loss and uprooting, and identity crises. We are, however, resolved and indeed very pleased to help search for solutions that will facilitate their settlement through the design and implementation of appropriate interventions and programs to ensure the growth, happiness, satisfaction, and resilience of immigrant and refugee youth throughout their new life in Canada.

Qualitative Methodology

The research included a total of fourteen focus groups, twelve with newcomer youth, and two with parents. The youth groups were organized with the following ethno-linguistic groups: Somalia, the former USSR, Afghanistan, Bosnian/Croatian, Serbian, Chinese, Vietnamese, Chinese (Hong Kong), Finnish, Hungarian, Cambodian, and Spanish. The two parent focus groups were organized with Chinese and Serbian parents.

Approximately eighty different community service and educational organizations and institutions were contacted to recruit focus group participants and secure appropriate spaces to conduct the session. The total number of participants in the focus groups was ninety-seven (eighty-one newcomer youth and sixteen parents). Each participant was paid $25 at the end of the focus group as a token of appreciation for his or her interest, help, and time.

The focus group methodology was used to probe the settlement and adaptation perceptions and experiences of Canadian immigrant youth sixteen to nineteen years of age, as well as their parents, in Canada. Participants were encouraged to report their significant experiences in relation to their settlement, adaptation, and integration and to address their current needs. There was a maximum of eight participants in each group. After participants completed a consent form, the participants and the facilitator introduced themselves, and a general introduction was provided. We explained that the groups would share personal thoughts and experiences for about one and one-half to two hours. We also emphasized that the discussions were completely confidential.

Quantitative Methodology

For the study's quantitative analysis the target population was made up of 300 newcomer immigrant and refugee youth, both male and female. It included Canadian citizens, permanent residents, and those whose application for permanent residence was in progress. Their ages ranged from sixteen to nineteen. The sample consisted of 130 boys (43.3 per cent) and 170 girls (56.7 per cent), with 17.29 (SD'-1.18) years as the mean age of the participants.

To be selected for the study, each participant must have been at least seven years old on arrival and had to have lived in Canada for at least one year. We assumed that during this first year they would need to deal with many functional problems related to settlement including immediate adjustment, orientation to a new life, securing housing, school registration, and functioning in a new language, and begin to develop their own opinions on Canadian society.

The total sample in our study was divided into six different groups, each consisting of fifty participants. The groups were selected to reflect the trends in recent immigration to Canada in general and Toronto in particular, with increasing numbers from areas of the world that were previously largely excluded including Asia, South and Central America, the Caribbean, and Africa. We organized the groups as follows: African, Caribbean, Central and South American, Chinese, Eastern European, and South East Asian.

This study was located within the geographical boundaries of the City of Toronto. After receiving training on recruitment techniques, administration of the instruments, and data collection, the research assistants selected the participants. Before we began the data collection, we conducted pilot tests to assess the instruments for ease of administration, clarity and conciseness of the questions, and general appropriateness. We were particularly concerned that a sixteen-year-old youth might not respond with the same type of understanding based on life experience as a nineteen-year-old, and therefore provided the research assistants with instructions for more detailed explanations of the questions if required.

Data collection took place from November 1999 until the middle of March 2000. Before beginning the interviews, the research assistants explained the purpose of the study and the research instruments. They also emphasized each participant's right to withdraw from the interview process at any time, and obtained consent forms. For participants younger than eighteen, a separate parental consent form was required, while those eighteen or older signed their own consent form. The ethical standards of research were reviewed with the participants, who were informed that all the information collected was strictly confidential, and that no one would be identified individually in the published results. All of the interviews were conducted outside of school hours (evenings, week-ends, school holidays); on average the process took ninety minutes to complete. Participants were paid $20 as a token of appreciation for their interest, help, and time commitment.

FSA approached this study with the conviction that in order to understand the needs of newcomer youth and to develop more appropriate services for these youth and their families, it is essential to have more information about the range and types of services currently available and the psychological factors that determine their settlement, adaptation, and integration. This perspective poses some new theoretical and methodological challenges, in particular the need to develop new measures of these psychological factors.

In our study, participants were asked to complete the demo-graphic questionnaire, adaptation response scale, personal satis-faction scale, satisfaction with parents/guardians scale, satisfaction with classmates scale, satisfaction with school/teachers scale, atti-tude toward Canadian society scale, settlement and adaptation outcomes scale, youth self-report (YSR) and draw a human figure test (DHFT). We created all of these instruments, except YSR and DHFT. The items for these instruments were derived from a review of relevant psychological and research literature; through consul-tation with immigrant, settlement, mental health, and other serv-ice providers; from our everyday experience with newcomer immigrant and refugee youth; and by reviewing previous needs assessments for this population.[3] After the derivation of items, pilot instruments were created and reviewed with representatives from different service providers, ethno-racial communities, and newcomer youth in order to create the final instruments. Details of these instruments are provided in Appendix One.

RESEARCH RESULTS
Outcomes of the Qualitative Research
Summary and Discussion of Youth Focus Groups Findings
(a) English language difficulties
Almost all participants in all groups emphasized that English language difficulties and associated concerns shortly after their

arrival in Canada was their first and most important problem. With no English language skills, the participants felt withdrawn, fearful, confused, guilty, depressed, isolated, and marginalized. In their schools, they could not speak to other children, express their feelings, or understand their teachers and their instructions.

(b) ESL programs

The opportunity for participants to attend English as a second language (ESL) programs at their schools was generally helpful, but also presented certain difficulties. Some stated that they had really responsive ESL teachers who not only provided them with intensive language instruction, but also employed valuable teaching methods and materials. Others reported that the ESL programs were simply not sensitive to their needs, and that the teachers were inflexible or employed teaching techniques that were both boring and inaccessible.

All of the participants saw ESL programs as something that automatically separates and excludes newcomer students from others in the school, who usually make fun of such programs and regard those who go to ESL as "different." Therefore, it is not "cool" for newcomer students to be assigned to ESL programs, and their attendance at these programs results in their being stereotyped by their peers. Our focus group participants were very conscious of how other students perceived their attendance in ESL programs.

(c) Peer network affiliations, support, and communication within the same ethnic group

Almost all the participants valued affiliations, support, and communication within the same ethnic group as one of the most effective ways of getting help in dealing with issues related to settlement, adaptation, and integration. Most participants indicated that their friends, including those closest to them, were from the same culture and spoke the same language. These friends helped them to feel accepted and valued. Trust, support, intimacy, interactive relationships, mutual understanding, positive self-perceptions, and feelings of spontaneity with friends from the same culture were reported as the most important factors in fulfilling and augmenting the participants' needs regarding social involvement, functioning, personal satisfaction, security, self-esteem, and the development of pride, acceptance, belonging, and attachment.

Communications with mainstream peers were indicated as more functionally based (such as working together in curriculum projects or school sports teams). Most of our participants agreed that they were not members of the most popular groups in their schools, and emphasized that being a member of a popular group is associated with general popularity in the school. Some participants reported establishing their own ethnic groups within their schools.

(d) Teachers and the challenges posed by newcomer youth

More than half of the participants positively valued their teachers, explaining that their teachers helped them and provided very valuable support. Some reported that the opportunity to have a teacher from the same culture, who spoke the same language, was very beneficial, even crucial, at the beginning of their life in Canada. Those participants who regarded their teachers positively spoke of open communications with them and received support in terms of understanding, advice, and explanation of the curriculum.

At the same time many of the participants did not regard their teachers as supportive. These participants said their teachers were racist and sexist, ignored the potential of visible minority students, and were insensitive to the children of immigrant and refugee families.

Overall then these students indicated a generally positive assessment of their teachers and schools while simultaneously reporting serious defects in the educational system's capacity to respond to the challenges that they pose. Of particular concern were the divisions between the immigrant and refugee youth and the Canadian-born within the schools, the stereotyping of immigrant and visible minority youth, and the inadequacy of the classroom curriculum in responding to the changing demographics within the student body. These negative factors can make an immigrant or refugee student feel helpless and less intelligent than the other students in the class.

(e) Sense of belonging to (or fitting in with) the mainstream society

Two-thirds of the participants strongly agreed that young people like themselves should have a strong sense of belonging to or fitting in with the mainstream society. They described "belonging" as feeling part of the society and community where they live, and regarded this as a promising start toward their future personal achievement and progress.

Those who did not think that a sense of belonging was important explained that in Canadian society, power and money open all doors, so whether or not people feel they fit in does not matter. These participants stressed that without power and money, feelings of belonging have no practical significance. Some of the youth took an even more radical position, saying that no one in Canadian society cared about them or paid any attention to their needs, so there was no reason for them to feel a part of Canadian society. Naturally, they had no sense of belonging, nor had they developed any social support.

Some of these youth felt bitterly disappointed that Canada took part in dropping bombs on their homeland, and expressed their confusion with double standards that professed to promote human welfare while simultaneously dropping bombs and killing innocent civilians, including children.

Youth from various cultural backgrounds approach the different aspects of life in their new Canadian environment with attitudes ranging from an accepting or "integrationist" approach to a separatist or "monocultural" position. The danger, of course, is that those who reject completely the values and behaviours of mainstream society, who refuse to "fit in," will experience alienation and emotional and other psychological difficulties because they are angry and feel that society is not offering support, acceptance, and hope of progress. Those who are open toward Canadian culture and adopt its beliefs, values, and behaviours, on the other hand, are likely to have positive feelings of personal worth and social success because they are more comfortable in their adopted culture and less at risk of isolation-related stresses.

(f) Traumatic pre-migration conditions and experiences

Traumatic pre-migration conditions and experiences were significant in the settlement and adaptation of participants who had been exposed to war in their home countries (Afghanistan, the former Yugoslavia, and Somalia). These participants explained that they had not only witnessed casualties and injuries to members of their own families or neighbours, but also lived through ethnic cleansing, extremely threatening and dangerous situations, cruelty, combat, killing, pain, constant gunfire and artillery bombardment, and forced separation and isolation from family and friends. The traumas they suffered were the result of deadly hatred between ethnic groups in their home countries. We can conclude that these newcomer youth have been deeply psychologically affected by the war experience, which presents ongoing difficulties in their settlement, adaptation, and integration.

(g) Prejudice and discrimination

The participants also emphasized that their peers' prejudice and discrimination toward them was one of the most significant and painful barriers to settlement. Examples provided included expressions of hate; teasing; experiences of rejection, shunning, and exclusion; harassment; bullying; provocation; vulgar name-calling; and verbal aggression. In the focus groups the researchers observed that some participants made fun of other ethnic groups and their cultures and disparaged their values.

We can assume that the youth who carry out these kinds of behaviours, as well as those who are the victims, are at increased risk for depression, violence, other behaviour problems, and possible incarceration. Combating prejudice and discrimination should be a high priority for the school system and other mainstream institutions in their work with newcomer youth in general and the most vulnerable groups in particular.

(h) Age of the participants when they came to Canada

The age of the participants upon arrival in Canada was considered one of the most important factors in settlement and adaptation. The participants reported that it was much harder to adapt to a new life in Canada for those who arrived as teenagers, because they had already started school in their home countries and established strong friendships with peers there.

In their new Canadian environment these teenage youth felt isolated, shy, uncertain, and passive, and experienced various problems of adaptation. Some of them still feel they are strangers and are uncomfortable in communicating and interacting with peers in their schools and neighbourhoods. Communication and the development of relationships with their peers, especially their mainstream peers, are minimal and difficult, and lacking in understanding, attentiveness, and mutual support. For these youth the experience of separation from extended family members, friends, and places they had to leave behind is still affecting their current relationships and compromising their opportunities for a healthy process of settlement and adaptation.

(i) Participants' lifestyles inside and outside their families

Participants reported strongly contrasting lifestyles inside and outside their family life. Within their families they were required to adhere to tradition with respect to their first language, cultural origins, and religious traditions, and their parents wanted to ensure that they would not become alienated from their cultural roots, beliefs, and values. Outside their family life—at school and in their social life—participants were required to learn a new language and culture and to incorporate Canadian beliefs and values. The discrepancies and conflicts between these two environments affect their identity as well as their cognitive, emotional, and social development.

Within the family, their parents resist adaptation and change with respect to Canadian culture, beliefs, and values. Some participants reported that their parents were rigid and did not understand or accept the mainstream culture. Furthermore, the more these newcomer youth adapted to the new Canadian culture, the more the tensions with their parents increased.

It is evident that newcomer youth form their self-concept (a person's self-perceptions formed through experience with interpretations of one's environment) on the basis of parental influences and the influences of relevant members of mainstream society such as peers, school, teachers, and the media. During their settlement, adaptation, and integration, newcomer youth seek increased opportunities not only for better understanding and more positive interactions with their parents, but also for emotional stability, encouragement, and support. The optimal family atmosphere for these newcomer youth would be one in which their parents encourage them to engage in age-appropriate autonomous activities and

to take up selected mainstream beliefs and behaviours, while maintaining strong ties to their families and original values.

(j) Parents regard academic success as the only way to get ahead

children are pressured

Many of the participants explained that in Canada their parents put
their hopes for the future in their children, and saw their children's
success in school and academic achievement as the only way for
them to get ahead. They also reported that it was common for their
parents to object if they spend time in non-academic activities.

The parents' approach toward their children's academic success
may therefore be problematic in at least some cases. The participants' standards for success in school and academic work differ
from those of their parents.

(k) Parents were not regarded as strong role models

Youth did not regard their parents as strong role models. More than half
the participants reported that their family environment had changed
on arrival in Canada and was less stable than in their country of origin.

These youth said their parents were stressed and in some ways
confused. Some participants reported that their parents were
depressed, wrapped up in their own concerns, and overwhelmed
with problems of underemployment and unemployment and relationships with their spouses and children. In their new environment
in Canada their parents were experiencing mounting disappoint-
ments, frustrations, and tensions; a sense of lack of control over the
changes in their lives; and a deterioration in their sense of well-
being. Some participants reported that for their parents, life in their
new environment made no sense; they felt helpless, confused,
isolated, and marginalized; and their identity as parents was deeply
shaken by their experience of being uprooted from their life in the
home country and feeling lost here in Canada.

We can assume that their parents' experiences have an important
impact on their children's personality development in general and
their identity formation in particular. The discipline of psychology
recognizes that the development of self-identity is essential to socialization and personality development. Adolescents in general need to
use their relationships with their parents to test and evaluate their

new experiences, approaches, and roles. Newcomer youth in particular need warm and accepting relations with their parents and strong
parental figures as positive role models to help them acquire many of
the specific identity characteristic and socialization skills required in
their new environment. As these youth do not regard their parents as
strong and positive role models, they may not only experience a sense
of personal disappointment but also be at risk of developing negative
and destructive values by identifying with alternate role models from
within their peer group or the media (e.g., movie stars).

(l) Participants were not well informed about existing settlement and other social services

Our participants were not well informed about existing settlement
services and other support programs for newcomers. The majority
reported that their only support in the settlement process that they or
their parents had received had come from members of their family (for
those who had family in Canada). A few participants mentioned
getting support from churches and ethno-specific settlement agencies; this support mainly involved ESL instruction for their parents.
⚹ A few also reported that their parents were experiencing problems and needed support, but were too busy working long hours,
including overtime, to pay the rent and put food on the table.
Overall the majority reported that they had never used any kind of
settlement services and that their parents did not access mainstream family support and mental health services. ⚹

During the focus group discussions, however, it was clear that
these newcomer youth were experiencing a variety of personal
problems with potentially serious consequences for their well-
being, and that their parents also had serious mental health problems. Nevertheless, the participants reported that it would be
strange and unusual if they or their parents sought assistance or
counselling for these problems.

(m) English language proficiency, the importance of friends, and views of improved support

All the participants in all of our focus groups mentioned English
language proficiency as one of the fundamental factors in successful

settlement. They felt that newcomer youth's ability to speak English when they arrive in Canada facilitated success in interactions with peers and in school, and also prevented or reduced isolation and marginalization. Our focus group participants also emphasized that it was important for newcomer youth to have friends.

Apart from these two observations, however, the participants had very few suggestions concerning improved assistance for newcomer youth. While we cannot be certain as to the reasons for this, one possible explanation may be that these youth are simply not sufficiently aware of the complex changes and challenges they face in the process of settlement, adaptation, and integration. Another factor could be that they are not currently receiving any assistance, so they cannot imagine and articulate improved supports. A third possible answer might be that many professionals involved with these youth (teachers, health professionals, settlement workers, counsellors), due to inexperience and/or ignorance of the psychological distress and changes that newcomer youth experience, seriously underestimate their difficult conditions and suffering and behavioural problems. Consequently, without proper professional support for and validation of their difficulties, these youth may deny their problems. Finally, another possible reason why these youth cannot envision an improved support system might be because cultural attitudes stigmatize the articulation of emotional needs and mental health problems.

(n) Newcomer youth like Canada's entertainment life
Many of our participants mentioned that they enjoy Canadian entertainment life, and that there are more opportunities for entertainment in Canada than in their countries of origin.

Summary and Discussion of Parental Focus Group Findings
(a) At the beginning of their life in Canada the parents felt
    excited; later they felt uncertain
Almost all participants reported that during the few first months of their life in Canada, they felt very positive, enthusiastic, and excited, and had great expectations for their future. Later, however, due to the changes they experienced in acculturation and integration, they became preoccupied and frustrated with problems that included

searching for work and facing unemployment or underemployment, acquiring a new language, being unsure of their social and professional status, changing their perceptions of personal identity, experiencing difficulties in family life including their relationships with their children, and feeling confused about their relationships with mainstream society.

In elaborating on their experiences of separation from their home country and friends, the parents reported feeling uncertain, guilty, ashamed, confused, and depressed. They also emphasized their need to adapt to new roles and search for new strength and resources in order to survive. The parental experience of the move to Canada, including both pre- and post-migration experiences, is therefore complex and multifaceted. The process disassembles the individual's psychic structure and previously formed self-images and provokes much personal questioning. The result is confusion and emotional disorganization, which in many cases severely tests the individual's sense of personal identity and stability.

(b) Parents would like to see their children retain their cultural values, beliefs, and norms

*The majority of parents felt that their children should retain their cultural heritage. While accepting that the Canadian environment was a new reality, they believed that a strong connection with their culture and values of origin would protect their children from many uncertainties in Canada. Some of the parents explained that they would like to allow their children to decide what they want to learn about their original culture.

It is clear from the focus groups that these parents want to see their children keep their traditional cultural values and heritage. While they recognized that their children were facing life in a new and different environment, they were not really aware of the issues their children confronted in trying to balance their families' lifestyles with the demands of adaptation to their new home.

(c) Parents were concerned about their children's education

Some parents were concerned about their children's education. They thought their children should have lots of homework, and were worried because there was very little or none that they saw. As well they believed that the school curriculum and programs were better articulated in their countries of origin, and that children there learned more than they did in Canada.

From these reports of the parents in focus groups we could conclude that immigrant parents should be more engaged with their children's schools. School boards and immigrant parents have to learn from each other. Parents need to learn more about the Canadian school system and find ways to promote improvements. At the same time, the school system should help parents understand and value the positive aspects of the Canadian education system so they can see how their expectations for their children will be realized.

(d) Parents were concerned about communicating with and disciplining their children

Parents reported difficulties in communicating with their children and in trying to maintain household rules. Some reported that their children were incommunicative and that they did not know what was on their offspring's minds. They felt that these problems were the result of their children being influenced by Western society's encouragement of independence and individual decision making. In some cases the problems in the relationships between parents and their children were rooted in differences in English language facility; if the children facilitated their parents' communication with the larger society, they felt a sense of control over their parents. In other cases parents stated that their children were too young to make many decisions for themselves and still needed strong parental guidance and support.

As an example of their difficulties in controlling and disciplining their children to maintain responsible behaviour, parents cited the example of the "sleepover." Some accepted the "sleepover" as part of Canadian culture, while others absolutely prohibited their children from participating because of concerns about their safety. Some parents allowed only their sons to go to a "sleepover." Others mentioned that their children tended to defy their authority, and worried that in Canada they had become less consistent in their use of discipline and/or less effective in monitoring their children's activities and whereabouts. Parents also were concerned about their children coming home late. Some established a curfew for their children, and others hoped their children would learn to be frank with them.

Many of the parents also emphasized that mainstream Canadian culture emphasized individualism while they wanted to impress on their children a spirit of interdependence, mutual understanding, co-operation, sharing, and reciprocity.

All these parental concerns have had a significant effect on family cohesion and created uncertainty about the future of parents and children alike. It is clear from the focus groups' reports that the issues of communication and discipline are complex. In some cases communications may be diminished if either or both parties feel there is nothing left to talk about. As well, as the children learn more about Canadian society, they may object to the forms of discipline their parents use, such as physical punishment, which was regarded as useful and acceptable in the country of origin but not in Canada. Mainstream service representatives might perceive parents as abusive, or parents may fear that children, as they learn about their rights, may report them to the authorities. These kinds of issues can provoke much confusion and great difficulties in communication, with parents feeling that their children have betrayed them. Furthermore, when parents do not acquire English language skills and their children become interpreters of the outside world for them, children can acquire power over their parents. Communication problems between immigrant children and their parents can also arise when children do not improve their use of their first language or even lose it, while their parents do not develop their ability in the English language.

Results of the Quantitative Research

The Demographic Questionnaire

The findings from the demographic questionnaire provide many useful descriptive statistics for the youth sampled. For example, of the participants in the sample, 9.9 per cent were in Grade 10, 29.7 per cent in Grade 11, 30.0 per cent in Grade 12, and 30.4 per cent in Grade 13. There were 34.1 per cent landed immigrants, 2.0 per cent refugees, and 63.7 per cent Canadian citizens (data missing for one participant).

Mp

* Participants selected as the three main parental reasons for coming to Canada: (a) a better way of life/improved standard of living; (b) more security and better overall life for their children; and (c) better or more suitable jobs. With respect to the parents' control over the decision to come to Canada, 9.0 per cent of our participants stated that their parents did not have control, while 31.0 per cent indicated some degree of parental control, and 43.0 per cent reported total parental control over the decision (16.0 per cent data missing).

At the time of arrival in Canada, 31.3 per cent of the participants had no skills in speaking one of the official languages. Another 21.0 per cent had poor language skills, 17.3 per cent had fair skills, 16.7 per cent had good skills, and 13.0 per cent had excellent language skills (0.70 per cent data missing).

As for the marital status of the parents, 72.7 per cent of participants were married, 13.3 per cent divorced, 5.7 0 per cent separated, and 3.70 per cent widowed (4.70 per cent data missing). With respect to their mothers' level of education, 11.7 per cent had either no education or only elementary school; 41.7 per cent had completed some or all of high school; 27.3 per cent had some university or a bachelor degree; and 7.0 per cent had a master's degree or higher level of education (12.3 per cent data missing). The fathers' level of education was reported as follows: 5.3 per cent had no education or only elementary school; 34.7 per cent had some or completed high school; 26.3 per cent had some university or a bachelor degree; and 12.7 per cent had a master's degree or higher level of education (21.0 per cent data missing).

With respect to the mothers' employment status, 25.3 per cent were unemployed and 68.0 per cent employed (6.7 per cent data missing). For the fathers, the employment status was 11.7 per cent unemployed and 69.3 per cent employed (19.0 per cent data missing). When asked whether their mothers had appropriate jobs in Canada (considering their level of education and the types of jobs they performed in their countries of origin), 66.0 per cent replied that they did not, while 34.0 felt that they did. When the same question was asked with respect to their fathers, the figures were very similar: 65.3 per cent reported that they did not and 34.7 per cent indicated they did.

For the youth sampled, 46.0 per cent of our participants had been employed in Canada and 54.0 per cent had no work experience in this country.

The reported perceptions of the economic status of the participants' families were as follows: 6.7 per cent participants classified their families as "poor"; 21.0 per cent as "low middle"; 48.3 per cent as "middle"; and 7.0 per cent as "high middle." Another 15.0 per cent picked the response "do not know" (2.0 per cent data missing).

When asked if they had experienced some stress at the beginning of their life in Canada, all the participants who answered the question responded in the affirmative (93.3 per cent, 6.7 per cent data missing). Similarly, when asked if their mothers or fathers had experienced some stress when starting out in this country, the responses were uniformly affirmative (89.0 per cent for their mothers, with 11.0 per cent data missing; 78.7 per cent for their fathers, with 21.3 per cent data missing).

Of the youth sampled, 89.7 per cent reported that they had never sought professional help for their problems, while 10.30 per cent indicated that they had sought such assistance. Our participants also informed us that 94.0 per cent of their mothers never asked for any kind of professional help for their problems, while only 6.0 did so. The figures reported for their fathers were very similar, with 96.7 per cent never seeking such help and 3.3 per cent having done so.

Most of the participants (86.7 per cent) informed us that they never spoke with anyone about their problems. Of those who did discuss their problems with others, 39.0 per cent spoke with their parents, 14.0 per cent with siblings, 39.3 per cent with friends, 2.0 per cent with teachers, and 1.3 per cent with professionals.

Participants reported experiencing the following emotional experiences in their new Canadian life: 48.3 per cent felt homesick; 10.0 per cent were withdrawn; 18.7 per cent had stereotypes about Canadians; 6.70 per cent felt aggressive toward Canadians; 18.0 per cent felt that they lost the ability to function effectively in school; 7.0 per cent experienced inexplicable fits of weeping; and 12.3 per cent felt irritable.

Results of the Statistical Analysis

A number of significant findings emerged from our statistical analysis of the data from the various quantitative instruments used in this project. Details of the tests and the results including the various tables are provided in Appendix Two.

According to the mean measures as calculated from the data gathered for the adaptation response scale (Table One, Appendix Two), the emotional response to new life situations was the dominant response followed by passive responses, cognitive responses, and physical responses. Our findings indicate that emotional responses were the dominant response to the problems and challenges that newcomer youth encountered in the settlement process. Perhaps it is because newcomer youth believe that these problems and challenges are outside their control, that the consequences are predetermined.

These results also shed new light on youth's settlement, adaptation, and integration. Contemporary medical and psychological theory and practice suggest that emotional responses are associated with a higher risk of symptoms such as stress and mood change. These and related disturbances may provoke more persistent disorders of internalizing (e.g., depression, withdrawal, anxiety) and externalizing (e.g., aggressiveness, conduct, attention-deficit hyperactivity, oppositional/defiant behaviour). The participants' dominant emotional approach therefore may well be associated with a greater risk of tension, frustration, pressure, and conflict, which may in turn compromise their ability to develop successful and positive outcomes by taking control of the situations they experience.

We also found that there is a significant correlation between all of the measures for the four scales of response to the new life situations offered (outside life, family life, social life, and personal life). The strongest positive correlation (Table Two, Appendix Two) was between physical response and emotional response; there was also a strong positive correlation between physical response and cognitive response, and a weaker but still significant positive correlation between emotional response and cognitive response. The strongest negative correlation was between emotional response and passive response, with weaker but still significant negative correlations between physical response and passive response and between cognitive response and passive response.

Comparison of the measures for the response scales for the different sample groups (African, Caribbean, Central and South American,

Chinese, Eastern European, and South East Asian) revealed that the only significant differences were in the measures for the emotional response scale. For example, the Eastern European group was less likely to have an emotional response than the Central and South American group. Further details of the differences are provided in Table Three, Appendix Two.

As discussed earlier, FSA believes that the assessment of successful settlement for newcomer youth must include a measure of their level of satisfaction with different aspects of their new life in Canada. Too often the "success" of settlement is evaluated in purely economic terms. Our perspective in this study, however, emphasized as more relevant and sensitive the dimensions of satisfaction in terms of happiness, comfort, security, and contentment.

The mean measures of satisfaction with the six different aspects of the participants' new life in Canada (Table Four, Appendix Two) indicate that their satisfaction is generally high. The highest satisfaction level was indicated for the settlement and adaptation outcomes measure, followed by satisfaction with classmates. Next came personal life, then parents/guardians, then school/teachers and finally attitudes toward Canadian life.

We also found that all the correlations (associations) between the satisfaction measures are significant and positive (Table Five, Appendix Two). This validates our belief that these different kinds of satisfaction play very important roles in the lives of newcomer youth in Canada. As well, the correlation coefficients as calculated indicate that the associations between the different types of satisfaction measured are positive, and that when newcomer youth's satisfaction with one part of their lives increases, all the other measures of satisfaction also increase. The highest correlations were between satisfaction with classmates and the settlement and adaptation outcomes; personal satisfaction and satisfaction with classmates; and personal satisfaction and satisfaction with parents/guardians. The lowest correlation was between attitudes toward Canadian society and the settlement and adaptation outcomes measure.

We also measured the correlations (associations) between the six different measures of satisfaction with different aspects of life in Canada and the stress levels reported for the beginning of the participants' life in Canada as recorded in the demographic questionnaire (Table Six, Appendix Two). The results suggest that participants were slightly more likely to be more satisfied with their new life if they were less stressed during the early stages of settlement.

With respect to the measures of different types of satisfaction with the participants' new lives in Canada, we found significant differences between the sample groups in the areas of satisfaction with classmates and settlement and adaptation outcomes. For example, the participants from the Central and South American group are more likely to be satisfied with their classmates than those in the Chinese, South East Asian, and African groups (Table Seven, Appendix Two). As well, those from the Central and South American group are more likely to be satisfied with their settlement and adaptation outcomes than those in the Chinese and African groups (Table Eight, Appendix Two).

The findings from the youth self-report (YSR) data revealed about sixty participants who might be experiencing behavioural difficulties such as social, thought, and attention problems, which can compromise their success in interpersonal relations. About fifty participants had difficulties with internalizing problems, and would likely be depressed, anxious, or withdrawn. About thirty participants had problems of externalizing or "acting out" their feelings and were likely to be aggressive, hostile, or impulsive.

Generally, based on the YSR data, the participants' personality characteristics and behaviour problems related to internalizing and externalizing behaviours mean an elevated risk for psychological maladjustment during their settlement process. With respect to behaviour problems, this risk was also statistically significant for boys and girls combined together, but not for boys or girls separately. The data must be interpreted with caution, because our comparisons were made with randomly selected peers (standardization sample), but not with matched controls.

RECOMMENDATIONS FROM THE RESEARCH PROJECT

There are a number of policy recommendations that result from the findings of this study. We feel very strongly that these recommendations are relevant in increasing mainstream Canadian society's sensitivity to the particular needs of newcomer youth and to the development of effective programs responding to these needs.

From our research we learned that the newcomer youth who participated in the project neither have mainstream youth as close friends nor turn to them for help in developing their capabilities and potential. These newcomer youth usually become accustomed to and comfortable with a more solitary social and community life at the beginning of their life in Canada, and tend to continue this way without developing broader or deeper social networks with their mainstream peers. The research revealed that the first stage of their life in Canada has significantly influenced the later stages of their settlement, adaptation, and integration. At the beginning, because of language problems and feelings of isolation, the newcomer youth are relatively passive in their social life, and therefore have limited ideas about how improve their social status and social competence.

Support from within the existing structures and mechanisms for settlement service delivery is therefore very important for newcomer youth not only for their settlement, adaptation, and integration process but also for their psychological well-being. This could be achieved through the creation of new youth-oriented policies and practices that would foster coherent and integrated service and program initiatives. For example, within the CIC-funded newcomer support HOST program, more could be done to bring together immigrant and refugee youth and their mainstream peers. The planning and implementation of such initiatives, which would facilitate the acceptance of newcomer youth, could be realized within both school- and community-based programs. The focus should be on a variety of opportunities that foster mutual understanding and support, the sharing of experiences, and the promotion of the general welfare of Canadian youth. We therefore recommend that:

> The existing structures and mechanisms for settlement service delivery should be reassessed to provide more opportunities for mutual involvement of newcomer immigrant and refugee youth with their Canadian peers.

Our research also revealed that the youth participants' families have been significantly affected during the settlement, adaptation, and integration process. This process involves many changes in dynamics for both individuals and their families. We learned about many different migration-related stresses and their various negative outcomes. We also observed that almost all our participants and their family members thought it was unusual to seek help from relevant existing services or professionals of any kind. Many of the parents were confused by their own and their children's experiences, about the nature of the problems and issues their children faced, and about how to respond and help their children in an appropriate manner.

This research showed as well that many parents of newcomer youth are very preoccupied with their own burdens and struggles. In addition, they tend to focus on the traditional methods of parenting with which they are familiar, and are confident that such methods are the best and indeed the only ways to secure a better future for their children. From the children's perspective, their parents' confusion and personal struggles leave the children without sufficient parental support for crucial needs, which in turn places these youth at greater risk of negative outcomes with respect to developmental, academic, and settlement issues. This risk, of course, is further intensified by the newcomer youth's serious personal problems, which require appropriate help and intervention. One very notable finding from our research is that emotional reactions were dominant for the participants when reacting to the various problems they encountered in their everyday life in Canada. These reactions were distress, impulsivity, guilt, sorrow, anger, and aggression. If continued, they could pose serious mental health problems in the form of a cumulative and self-fulfilling cycle of deviance.

It is clear that newcomer youth and their families in Canada need specific support to maximize their potential for successful outcomes in settlement, adaptation, and integration. It was also evident from the research that those who had stresses and traumas in the pre-migration process continued to suffer after their arrival. Furthermore, our research confirmed what is common knowledge among those involved in settlement services—that the process of settlement creates new problems and poses new challenges. We believe, therefore, that the federal government should give more support to community-based agencies providing family support services to respond to the many urgent needs of newcomer youth and their families.

Such support could take the form of either increased funding or transfers in funding. For example, language instruction, which currently takes the largest share of federal dollars, is certainly a vital component of settlement services, but in FSA's opinion, it needs to be reassessed with respect to other priorities. FSA considers it essential to provide sufficient funding for family-centred, needs-based, flexible, well-managed, and multifaceted community-based initiatives and programs for newcomer youth and their families. Our basic assumption regarding these initiatives and programs is that the improvement of early assistance for newcomer families would produce more positive relationships and a better climate within these families.

Such an approach would differ from the traditional approach to the provision of individual and/or family counselling services. It would be a community-based approach, engaging newcomer youth and their families to reduce the duration and extremity of their confusion, problems, and crises. Local community-based agencies involved in family services should play a crucial part in settlement, adaptation, and integration, and in order to do so they need the funding to develop programs and initiatives that encourage, support, and facilitate newcomers' engagement and participation in order to positively and optimistically embrace the challenges of a new life. We therefore recommend that:

> As a more integrated and holistic approach to settlement for newcomer immigrant and refugee youth and their families, the federal government should allocate/transfer funds and authority for specific settlement-related needs of newcomer youth to local community-based agencies involved in family services.

For many years, schools and school boards have played a very important role in ensuring the successful settlement, adaptation, and integration of newcomer youth. Schools play a crucial role in fostering the intellectual, emotional, social, and moral development of children and youth, including immigrant and refugees as well as the Canadian-born. The school system also contributes the talents of numerous newcomer children and youth to mainstream Canadian life.

Our research indicates that school boards, schools, and teachers generally provide enjoyable, supportive, and meaningful opportunities for language instruction and general learning opportunities for immigrant and refugee youth. Furthermore, the school boards have demonstrated their commitment and professionalism in contributing to positive settlement outcomes. However, the door still remains open for many practical improvements.

In order to help parents better deal with this collision of cultures and values, school boards should take more active measures in developing strong and functional relationships with the parents of newcomer youth. There is a great need for parents to be more familiar with the methods and philosophy of schooling in Canada. Parents need help in resolving their confusion around the school's expectations of them and their children, and what they themselves should expect from their children. They need to know more about the curriculum, the role of teachers, the relationships between teachers and students, and the relationships among the students themselves. Schools need to acknowledge the potential benefits of such initiatives, and also seek out opportunities to make their curriculum more reflective of the experiences of newcomer youth and their families. Furthermore, teachers need to learn more about the experiences and curriculum preferences of newcomer students. They could stimulate more discussion on various experiences relevant to newcomer youth, and thereby encourage them to see the connections between their own experiences and the curriculum, the teachers, and the school system.

Furthermore, the value of English as a second language instruction needs to be acknowledged throughout the whole school. This would help all students, but particularly the Canadian-born, to reexamine their stereotypes concerning ESL learners. ESL instruction is the first step in helping newcomer students to make progress as equal participants in their schools, and to be more effective and achieve their full potential.

We recognize that implementing these measures requires instrumental help from the settlement workers within school boards. These workers can be active catalysts in building bridges between newcomer and Canadian-born youth, and between parents and their children's schools and teachers. We recommend, therefore, that:

> In order to target priority needs and provide more effective and sensitive settlement service delivery for newcomer youth, more flexible program initiatives should be launched to help school boards (whose involvement and expertise are essential in providing opportunities for positive settlement, academic, and developmental outcomes) to become a crucial member of community players.

We also learned from the research that immigrant and refugee youth experience many specific problems at the beginning of their life in Canada and at the same time have very limited access to many relevant services available within the mainstream society. It is clear that newcomer youth need more help and support in becoming involved in the community, which, along with their families and their schools, is an important pathway for socialization.

These youth and their parents desperately need more information not only about available services but also about how and why they should use them. Relevant programs and initiatives are needed to improve their access to available services, in order to meet a diversity of needs and produce better settlement outcomes. Such an approach would be a more proactive one, one that empowers newcomer youth and their families by enabling them to access resources within mainstream society, to get a good start in the settlement process, and to improve the quality of their life in Canada.

We believe, therefore, that funding initiatives are required to attract and mobilize different mainstream organizations in answering the following questions: What cultural and social factors are needed to maximize a sense of belonging in newcomers? How can these organizations help achieve positive images of diversity in the community and celebrate this diversity? How can they contribute to newcomer employment needs? How can they help in reducing feelings of isolation and marginalization and all the social ills that they entail? We therefore recommend that:

> More funding opportunities should be available for programs and initiatives that not only increase and facilitate information, orientation, community involvement, and newcomer youth access to mainstream services, but also assist mainstream service providers to develop culturally appropriate services for newcomer youth.

In any discipline, its area of practice, its body of knowledge, and its scientific basis need to be developed. Our research has demonstrated that newcomer youth's settlement, adaptation, and integration process has to be viewed from the perspective of their socialization and development. Further research, preferably longitudinal and action-oriented, is therefore needed to explore the specific elements of the settlement of newcomer youth.

We need a greater knowledge of structural and functional factors related to the settlement experience of newcomer youth and their families. These factors influence the basic adaptation capacities of immigrant and refugee youth as well as their perceptions of their new environment. A more scientific understanding of these elements is essential to improve the provision of appropriate settlement services. We therefore recommend that:

> More funding should be available to further investigate the dynamics of personal change that newcomer youth face in the settlement process, and the appropriate settlement services they require. The services must be considered from the perspective of accountability, responsiveness to identified needs, and demonstrated results in accelerating the process of settlement, adaptation, and integration for immigrant and refugee youth.

CONCLUSION

Both the qualitative and the quantitative findings from this study provide clear evidence that the components of the settlement, adaptation, and integration process for newcomer youth are both

multidimensional and multidirectional. These components constitute the basic process of newcomer youth development in their new
living environment, and highlight both positive and negative settlement and developmental outcomes. The study's findings also
clearly indicate that in order to grasp the full magnitude of the problems facing today's newcomer immigrant and refugee youth in
Canada, and of the challenges the mainstream society faces in
addressing and responding to these problems, it is necessary to
probe in detail these youth's experiences in confronting complex
and interrelated problems, and to include a psychological perspective in such analysis. We trust that our recommendations for
improved services will receive serious attention, and we look
forward to collaborating with other researchers and service
providers in discussing the results of this project and in developing
further scientific investigation of this vital topic.

NOTES

[1] In this study "psychological factors" are related to an individual's internal capacities, and self-consistent patterns of cognitive, emotional, and social functioning.

[2] Elkin and Handel (1972) define socialization as the process by which someone
learns the ways of a given society or social group so that she or he can function
within it.

[3] We used the definitions of adaptation provided by Helson (1947) and Matarazzo
(1972). Helson defined adaptation as the diminished responsiveness to repeated
or continued stimuli. Matarazzo provided the following definition: Adaptive
behaviour refers primarily to the effectiveness with which the individual copes
and adjusts to the natural and social demands of his environment. It has two
principal facets: (1) the degree to which the individual is able to function and
maintain herself or himself independently, and (2) the degree to which he or she
satisfactorily meets the culturally imposed demands of personal and social
responsibility. We define settlement "as a long-term dynamic, two-way process
through which, ideally, immigrants would achieve full equity and freedom of
participation in society, and society would gain access to the full human resource
potential in its immigrant communities."

CHAPTER 6

The Needs of Newcomer Youth and Emerging "Best Practices" to Meet Those Needs

PAUL ANISEF, KENISE MURPHY KILBRIDE, AND
RHANDA KHATTAR
*Joint Centre of Excellence for Research on Immigration and
Settlement, Toronto*

INTRODUCTION

The Joint Centre of Excellence for Research on Immigration and Settlement, Toronto (CERIS) has had, from its inception, a focus on the needs of youth who immigrate to Canada, and on the needs of the children of immigrants. Reviews of research in the field, however, consistently find very little on the problems and concerns of "newcomer youth," those who are no longer properly called children, but who, as immigrant teenagers, face special challenges that compound the difficulties encountered by most adolescents. Hence the needs of sixteen to twenty year old newcomers, and various sectors of society's attempts to meet those needs, deserve particular attention.

The purpose of this study was, therefore, to identify the needs of immigrant youth, and to survey organizations that provide educational, employment, health and social services to newcomer youth in order to identify "best practices" for supporting the integration of youth from diverse cultural and racial groups into Canadian society. Information about effective programs and gaps in existing programs and service delivery infrastructure was seen as useful for strengthening programs throughout the Greater Toronto area (GTA). In particular, it could assist service providers and funders in understanding the benefits of the programs and their best practices from the perspective of the service delivery organizations, youth who use the services, and their parents.

RESEARCH NEEDS AND PREVIOUS WORK

In 1996, 52.4 per cent of all immigrants resided in the three largest metropolitan areas in Canada: Toronto, Montreal, and Vancouver. Among those who have arrived since 1991, 74 per cent reside in these three metropolises, with the largest proportion (43 per cent) living in Toronto. In 1997 approximately 80,000 immigrants arrived in Toronto with the largest numbers from China, India, Pakistan, Hong Kong, Iran, Sri Lanka, the Philippines, the Caribbean, Taiwan, and Russia.

The spatial concentration of immigrants in Canada's urban centres has resulted in an increase in social differentiation and further fragmentation in urban Canada (Bourne, 1999) and an increase in the importance of social and settlement services that support the effective integration of these diverse newcomers into Canada. This is especially significant when we consider the cutbacks in social supports and programs by all levels and most departments of government. These cutbacks have far-reaching implications for the funding and delivery of immigrant services, particularly in the capacity of community-based organizations to deliver essential services to immigrants and other disadvantaged groups (Mwarigha, 1997). The Greater Toronto area is now one of the most ethnoculturally diverse metropolises in North America and has secured an increased proportion of the country's recent immigrants, most of whom come from non-traditional source countries in South and East Asia and the Caribbean. Also of key importance to the effective delivery of settlement services is the shift of immigrant populations to the suburbs and, most recently, to the newer suburbs within the GTA where jobs and less expensive housing are available. Suburbanization is important because it may, for example, affect immigrant youth's ability to use centralized services. Degrees of suburbanization vary considerably among immigrant groups: Somalis, Sri Lankans, Vietnamese, Filipinos, and Iranians are the least suburbanized, and those from Hong Kong and India are the most likely to settle in the suburbs (Bourne, 1999).

Issues of immigration and integration are the core of Canadian public policies and have become the focus of much public concern and debate. Integration can be viewed as the extent to which immigrants become full participants in Canadian life, capable of achieving their aspirations and potential. Thus, the goal of settlement policies and of the agencies/organizations that have been developed is to facilitate such integration, and to avoid the marginalization, isolation, and segregation of immigrant groups within Canadian society. While, theoretically, integration can be measured by a variety of economic, social, and cultural indicators, the diversity of cultural groups in the GTA may signify, at least to some newcomers, that cultural change is either unattainable or, perhaps more importantly, undesirable. Thus, the integration measures employed in examining settlement must remain culturally sensitive and responsive to the diverse needs and aspirations of immigrant groups.

Weinfeld (1998), who developed a synthesis of immigrant research in Canada, notes an absence of research focused on the urban setting and immigrant integration in Canada (p. 1). Usually the process of immigrant integration, especially if immigrants are adults, is completed only in the second and third generation, by children or grandchildren of the immigrants (Vanier Institute of the Family, 1998, p. 8). By "completion" we mean a fully representative integration into all the institutions, organizations, associations, and societies of the receiving nation. Recent immigrants, visible minorities, refugees, and family-class immigrants face immense integration challenges. By way of illustration, immigrant minorities often face the devaluation of their credentials when seeking employment in Canada. They may also encounter other forms of systemic discrimination in the Canadian labour markets (Vanier Institute of the Family, 1998, p. 9).

Immigrants' entry status may also affect integration. Some may be sponsored or nominated by close relatives; some may be involuntary immigrants or refugees; while others may come as independents or be sponsored by employers and have prior contracts for employment. Thus, families who immigrate alone or immigrate from the independent class have a greater need to adapt to new situations. They may find that no one can speak their native language or share their customs and rituals. In contrast, when a number of families migrate together, they bring their networks with them and may find it easier to adapt to a new way of life (Vanier Institute of the Family, 1998, p. 9).

Settlement programs funded by various levels and departments of government, including Citizenship and Immigration Canada (CIC), as well as community charities and private foundations, provide employment, education, health, and social services to newcomer youth. These newcomers appear to go through three main stages in the settlement process in the use of these services (Mwarigha, 1997). In the *initial* stage, newcomers require a range of services such as shelter, food, clothing, information, and orientation. In the *intermediate* stage, immigrants learn more about how to gain access to a number of Canadian systems, starting with language (e.g., ESL classes), upgrading training and education, health, housing, and legal systems. The *final* stage refers to newcomers' long-term participation and involves diverse and much more differentiated elements. Many social services direct their attention to the first two stages of the settlement process.

Three basic *levels of services* can be singled out. They include: (1) the public and general mainstream community service agencies; (2) the specific ethno-racial/racial community agencies; and (3) independent professionals. The *first* of these levels includes government agencies, community-based organizations that include service to immigrants in their programs, and community-based agencies formally organized for the purpose of providing services to immigrants and ethnic groups.

The *second* level of agencies includes specific ethnic community-based agencies organized for the purpose of serving immigrants. They may have a particular ethno-racial/racial identity and mandate or be formally mandated to serve immigrants and to include such services in their activities. Examples of the *third* level include immigration lawyers, therapists, physicians, and nurses providing counselling and health care services to refugees and other immigrants.

Many agencies and organizations are challenged to sustain services to immigrants in an era of dramatic cutbacks. Richmond (1996) indicates that funding to immigrant service agencies peaked in 1994 at $70 million and that cutbacks, privatization, and devolution led to net program losses that were greatest for immigrants and refugees. George and Michalski (1996, p. 38) found that 84.9 per cent of 106 agencies surveyed were affected by funding cuts and, as a result, cut services and intake levels. These changes have brought pressure to bear on community-based organizations serving immigrant newcomers; there is some evidence that such organizations are examining a variety of new strategies for survival, including cost-recovery, partnerships, new funding sources, and improved use of volunteers in an attempt to sustain the effective delivery of services (Go, Inksater, & Lee, 1996).

OBJECTIVES AND METHODS

The *first* task of the research was the completion of a *comprehensive literature review* of published and unpublished studies in Canada and the United States pertaining to the settlement and integration of newcomer youth and the provision of services that facilitate settlement and integration. It was important to the research team that, since this area is so seriously under-researched, the review not be limited to the usual scholarly journals on the subject, but also include the published (or at least printed) community sources on the needs of youth and service providers' various attempts to meet those needs. This, then, is not a typical review of the literature but a much more inclusive one, with, it is hoped, the result of a broader and deeper view of this issue than has previously been obtained.

The *second* task was the *identification of a sample of fifteen organizations* reflective of a cross-section of agencies in the education, employment, mental health, social, and health services areas providing services to newcomer youth from diverse cultural and racial backgrounds, using expert referencing and "snowball" sampling techniques (asking individuals identified by an expert reference group to identify other individuals for interviews).

Individual interviews were conducted with management and program staff from these agencies to identify key settlement and integration issues addressed by agencies providing services to newcomer youth. These interviews were designed and conducted in collaboration with the Centre for Evaluation Research in Human Services at Ryerson University, under the supervision of their representative, Dr. David Day. The results of these interviews were analyzed to highlight program themes and issues for these organizations including:

- descriptions of current educational, employment, health,

and social service programs in the sample
- identification of perceived needs, issues, and gaps these organizations faced in serving newcomer youth
- identification of similarities and differences in the program and intervention approaches used in each program area
- identification of services perceived to be "emergent best practices" and key indicators among these service providers
- identification of changes needed to improve service delivery outcomes
- assessment of evaluation approaches and methods used in participating programs
- identification of interorganizational strategies and partnerships used to enhance service provision

Out of this work came the development of the survey questionnaire for a broader array of service providers, the next task.

This *third* task was *interviewing 145 service providers.* The research issue envisioned by CERIS focused on the medium- and longer-term benefits of programs offered by Level 1 and Level 2 agencies[1] in the Greater Toronto area, serving youth aged sixteen to twenty, with a focus on education, employment, mental health, social, and health services. Level 1 and Level 2 agencies were researched, using qualitative and quantitative research techniques, to identify: issues, needs, and problems that the organizations confront when serving the newcomer youth population; the programs and types of interventions that they provide; anticipated outcomes of these interventions; and partnerships and other interorganizational strategies used to support the immigrant youth population. The research included identifying examples and key indicators of "emergent best practices" as well as gaps in interventions and service delivery methods. This was a sizable task, and one for which we were happy to have the services of York University's Institute for Social Research (ISR).

Based on the information gathered during the literature review and the interview of key informants, a questionnaire was developed in collaboration with ISR and administered through a telephone survey by ISR staff to 145 organizations and groups serving newcomer youth in the Greater Toronto area. The questionnaire requested a full program description, a description of populations served, needs addressed, intervention approaches, goals, expected outcomes, key indicators of success, methods used to evaluate the programs, difficulties encountered in program delivery, and funding sources. It asked the organizations to identify the programs in the community that they believe provide examples of "emergent best practices," and to describe what they thought led them to label these "best practices."

A stratified sampling method was employed to identify approximately thirty organizations from each of the health care sectors (hospitals, community health programs) and education sectors (schools from across the GTA in both the public and separate school systems), and from approximately ninety social service organizations providing support for employment, education, and health problems under Language Instruction for Newcomers in Canada (LINC), Immigrant Settlement and Adaptation Program (ISAP), and other funding streams. The Institute of Social Research employed "snowball" strategies for including in its sample service provider agencies that offered what was considered "emergent best practices." The draft questionnaire was subsequently pilot-tested and reviewed with some of the earlier key informants to ensure that it worked effectively. Based on the results of this survey we:

- developed an analysis of services considered to be "emergent best practices," and identified evaluation methods used by these programs and key indicators of the "best practices"
- assessed the commonalities and differences in the provision of services across the GTA and program leaders' views of "best practices" in the field
- assessed the similarities and differences both within and across the range of cultural and racial groups surveyed
- described the gaps identified by survey participants
- determined whether "emergent best practices" can be generalized across different groups of newcomers or whether emergent best practices must be contextualized so that the needs of each newcomer youth group can be met

The *fourth* task was to seek the same information on the needs of newcomer youth and the services that attempt to meet those needs from the youth themselves and from their mothers by conducting *focus groups*. In our original proposal we indicated that we would hold forty focus groups with seven to ten newcomer youth reflecting culturally distinct newcomer groups, half of whom had participated in integration and settlement programs and half who had not. In addition, we would also hold ten focus groups with parents of youth in the sixteen to twenty year age group. The participants in the focus groups would be selected to reflect gender, ethnicity, culture, and racial diversity and to provide views from people who have and who have not participated in programs.

Prior to awarding its contracts, however, CIC had noted the similar interests of a number of applicants for projects researching newcomer youth, so applicants were asked to divide the work among themselves in a collaborative way. CERIS was asked to coordinate this division of labour among the six service provider agencies who had also been awarded research contracts in the youth theme area. This work involved joint discussions on the development of focus group design, protocols for conducting interviews, and strategies for analyzing the information collected within the focus groups. While the data collected by each participant would be owned separately, all participants could share the data that were collected. Two meetings were held to:

- develop a focus group protocol
- identify how information could be shared and analyzed so all could take advantage of the wealth of data available
- develop an understanding of "best practices" and what makes them "best" (or not) for each group
- explore the possibility of making wider comparisons (e.g., geographically, ethnically)
- discuss features of each proposal and design ways to ensure that all major immigrant groups were covered among the partners

It was decided after considerable discussion that all participants shared an interest in the needs, experiences, and concerns that newcomer youth voiced and that this should serve as the major theme of the focus group research conducted by the different participants in the collaborative effort. Some newcomer groups were most appropriately targeted by partners with ties to specific communities. Partners without such ties divided the remaining major immigrant groups among themselves, according to their research interests and budget.

In this new design, sixteen focus groups were separately conducted by CERIS with male and female youth from each of these eight specific ethnic groups: Portuguese, Filipino, Somali, Iranian, Russian, African, Jamaican, and Korean. In addition, CERIS conducted two ethnically mixed Northeast African groups, one male and one female, comprising youth who were Eritrean, Ethiopian, or Ugandan of Somali ancestry. Seven focus groups were also conducted with mothers from the same ethnic groups as those of the youth, with the exception of the Northeast African group.

FINDINGS
1. Review of the Literature

The review of the literature confirmed the the researchers' prior experience: there is no real attention being paid to this age group. Their needs, whether they came as very young children or as adolescents, have not been systematically documented, nor have services for them been systematically identified anywhere. What the review did contribute was a sense of the major issues confronting this age group:

- identity development confounded by dual sources of identity when home and peer groups come from different cultures
- language issues that arise particularly in school
- lack of recognition, for older youth, of prior learning experience
- conflicts in values beyond those characteristic of many adolescents, namely those between home and peer group, as these conflicts are between values of institutions: those of the family and those of the school as representative of the larger community
- differences in issues for male and female youth that are not necessarily found in all youth's experiences but are characteristic of some cultures in particular

Findings on these and other issues will be discussed under four headings: Health and Mental Health, Educational Attainment, Access to Employment and Economic Mobility, and Social Services.

Health and Mental Health

The literature review found a number of significant sources in this area. A federal-provincial study, *Toward a Healthy Future*, reports that "Canadians are among the healthiest people in the world; however, this good health is not enjoyed equally by everyone."[2] The country's youth population is suffering from stress, which is evident in the increased rates of unhealthy practices, such as heavy smoking, having unprotected sex, and dropping out of school, as well as feeling depressed and suicidal. It is argued that stress-related problems among young people are linked to high unemployment and pressure to perform well in school.

In addition, studies reveal that a stable family income improves the likelihood of living in safe neighbourhoods and attending good schools. The absence of some or all of these elements in newcomer households often makes it difficult for parents to create a supportive environment that enhances their children's future well-being.

A recent analysis of data obtained from a longitudinal study of children and youth indicates that "30 per cent of all immigrant children live in families whose total income falls below the official poverty line" (Beiser, Shik, & Curyk, 1999). The researchers note that immigrant children with unstable families are "less likely to prosper scholastically and are more likely to become delinquent" (Beiser, Shik, & Curyk, 1999). Data obtained from community-based samples, according to Beiser, suggest that some newcomer children experience greater risk for alcohol abuse, drug addiction, delinquency, depression, and post-traumatic stress disorder.

It is important to develop course work and in-service training programs to equip counsellors, nurses, teachers, and health educators with the knowledge and experience to deal with children suffering from psychosocial problems. James (1997) suggests that culturally appropriate counselling and social services in schools be developed and made widely accessible. She also proposes that suitable diagnostic and assessment tools be tailored to immigrant children and their families, and that a preventative or early intervention program be created to identify initial "culture shock."

Educational Attainment

The literature confirms that social, economic, and demographic changes in Canadian society have put tremendous pressure on educational systems to respond to the accompanying growth in the diversity of student enrolment. The public school system in Toronto serves an extraordinarily diverse student body (Cheng & Yau, 1997), creating great demand for services from the local board of education, as well as settlement and ethnocultural organizations. Some of the needs identified by researchers include academic support, parental involvement in the education of children, the recognition of the unique circumstances and experiences of newcomer youth, as well as training for teachers, school staff, and settlement workers.

Other research (Anisef & Bunch, 1994) indicates that visible minority youth encounter significant challenges coping with the school system. They have academic problems in the classroom, suffer from behavioural problems, or drop out of school altogether. Some of the principal factors underlying these problems include school policies, teachers' discriminatory attitudes, and schools' organizational structure in which achievement or success among minority youth is not encouraged (Anisef & Bunch, 1994, pp. 8–10). Lam (1994, p. 124) believes that immigrant parents' marginalized labour force status may contribute to their children's decision to leave the school system, with the youth feeling it is more important to enter the labour market and contribute to the family income than to continue studying. As well, Johnson and Peters (1994) report that Ontario students' diverse needs are often overlooked. Accordingly, they are convinced that there is a need for a more student-based, participatory educational program aimed at accommodating diversity and change.

It is essential that more research be conducted on the relation between educational attainment and the positive adaptation experiences of newcomer youth. Researchers' conclusions and recommendations clearly point to the school system's important role in promoting settlement and integration. It is apparent that a collaborative and

THE NEEDS OF NEWCOMER YOUTH

integrative effort must be made to meet the needs of newcomer youth more effectively.

Access to Employment and Economic Mobility

The literature indicates that the youth unemployment rate in Canada is reaching critical proportions and the greatest casualties appear to be newcomer youth. Their ability to obtain gainful employment is hampered by their aptitude for learning in the host society. There are numerous factors inhibiting the academic progress of newcomer children. Their socio-economic experiences and ethnocultural background make them particularly susceptible to negative influences and discrimination. This has made it increasingly difficult for children and adolescents to acquire the level of skills and training needed to compete in the labour market.

The Canadian Council on Social Development (CCSD) reports that there are about 2 million youth between the ages of fifteen and nineteen living in Canada. The high unemployment rate affects all youth living in Canada, but an analysis of statistical data reveals that newcomer youth face greater obstacles to employment and are far less likely than Canadian-born youth to have had any kind of work experience. In 1996, there were twice as many immigrants between the ages of seventeen and nineteen with no previous work-related experience. A correlation was found between socio-economic background and access to employment opportunities. Youth from low-income families face greater challenges in acquiring job experience than do those living in high- or middle-income families. The same pattern holds true for immigrant youth compared to Canadian-born youth. "Immigrant youth may be at a disadvantage in finding work due to their lack of family contacts in business, their efforts to learn one of Canada's official languages, their responsibilities at home or their families' expectations that they focus solely on school work" (CCSD, 1998b, p. 8).

Most researchers accept the positive relation between educational attainment and access to employment. Johnson and Peters (1994) suggest that schools need to be flexible and adaptable in order to accommodate the unique needs of immigrant youth. Researchers examining the economic opportunities for immigrant youth clearly point to the need for more flexibility in the system in order to respond to the needs, concerns, and experiences specific to newcomer youth.

It is evident from this review of the literature that newcomer youth need assistance with the transition from school to work. There was a strong correlation between socio-economic background and access to employment opportunities. The research revealed that immigrant youth may be at a disadvantage in finding work as a result of their ethnic background, family responsibilities, economic insecurity, and difficulties with school. It is essential that more research be conducted to find ways to facilitate newcomer youth in their transition to adulthood and the search for suitable employment.

Social Services

With regard to social services, the dramatic social, economic, and demographic changes in Canada have created serious challenges to the delivery of social services. The process of acclimatization, adaptation, and integration requires a significant commitment to assistance from the various organizations serving immigrants and newcomers. The early stages of acclimatization and adaptation can also be referred to as the period of settlement when newcomers make initial adjustments to life in a new country as they find suitable and affordable housing, learn the language, and search for employment. Integration is the longer-term process that newcomers experience as they endeavour to become full and equal participants in all the various dimensions of society (CCR, 1998, p. 14). A greater proportion of the programs offered by service providers has tended to focus on adult newcomers; however, it has become increasingly important for these organizations to respond to the needs and concerns of newcomer children and youth as well. Younger immigrants need assistance in order to adjust successfully and to participate fully in Canadian economic, social, and political life.

There have been very few research studies or needs assessments targeted specifically at newcomer youth, but those that have been conducted recognize the value of refugee- and immigrant-serving organizations. The strength of these organizations lies in the potential they carry for the adoption of a diversity of approaches to program development and their roots in the community. They are committed to cost-effective programs that work, are accountable to the community they serve, and take a holistic approach in meeting the needs of their clients (CCR, 1998, p. 33). The Canadian Council for Refugees (CCR) identifies four spheres of settlement and integration where service providers should focus their efforts:

- economic integration includes acquiring skills, entering the job market, and achieving financial independence
- social integration includes establishing social networks and accessing institutions
- cultural integration includes adapting various aspects of lifestyle and engaging in efforts to redefine cultural identity
- political integration includes citizenship, voting, and civic participation (CCR, 1998, p. 18)

Research also shows how essential it is to develop services to help newcomer youth acquire the skills and knowledge they need to participate in society. Some of researchers' recommendations include orientation sessions, providing information and referrals, language assessment, family counselling and support groups, and mental health services and health programs (CCR, 1998, p. 37).

There must also be services, such as public education and cross-cultural and anti-racism training, to help the host community adapt to newcomers (CCR, 1998, p. 40).

The CCR identifies several best practices for offering services to newcomer youth. The researchers stress that accessibility must be assured by offering culturally appropriate services in the client's language and undertaking outreach in the community. It is evident that collaboration and flexibility in program development is needed in order to best facilitate the integration of newcomer youth. A holistic approach would recognize the diversity of needs of ethno-cultural groups, provide a range of social services, and build linkages between the community, family, youth, and mainstream institutions (CCR, 1998, p. 45).

2. In-Depth Interviews with Fifteen Key Informants (Conducted by the Centre for Evaluative Research in Human Services at Ryerson University)

Analysis of the issue must start with a recognition that youth have specific needs within this age group (sixteen to twenty years) as well as additional specific needs as immigrants, said key informants. Youth need to develop their cultural as well as personal identity. Specifically, the interviews provided pointed information under some of the target areas of interest.

For *education*, the informants claimed that education is the greatest concern for youth sixteen to twenty years of age and that they badly need services to foster their successful integration within the school system: English language training programs, such as ESL classes genuinely tailored to their level and oriented toward academic learning, and curricula that reflect the experiences of immigrants and refugees and which are responsive to their cultural needs. Those close to these youth believe it is critical to have a greater number of teachers from different racial, ethnic, and cultural backgrounds. Providing services in school-based programs is the most important design component for these youth, since this is the place of greatest contact; these services include counselling and support services, welcoming and reception centres, mentoring and tutoring programs, and assessment services to determine appropriate school placement. Schools need to recognize their role in orienting parents and students to the school system to better prepare newcomer youth for success; and educators should be sufficiently sensitive and experienced so they can offer programs to serve as a bridge between the school and family, and support rather than disrupt the relationship between parents and youth. *Missing* services abound. School-based ESL courses should be available to both non-English-speaking newcomer youth and youth who speak English with a foreign dialect (such as those from the West Indies), and these should be designed to bring youth up to their own age level (so that youth are not singled out or harassed because of language barriers). Language Instruction for Newcomers in Canada (LINC) programs are much more widely available to adults than youth, and these programs should be matched by programs for immigrant youth. Integrated International Language Programs ("heritage language" programs) are available only at the elementary school level, but should be available at the secondary level as well.

For their *health* needs, the key informants reported that immigrant youth require better health information about a range of issues (from smoking to AIDS), and health officials who come in contact with newcomer youth need improved training. Also important is a good and genuinely accessible referral service.

For *mental health* they identified as basic needs: adequate housing for youth with mental health problems, assistance in coping with adjustment as a newcomer, resolving personal identity issues, and balancing pressure from family to maintain old values as well as pressure from peers to adopt new ones. There is a lack of services to help youth form their cultural identity, as well as a lack of services to help youth form their personal identity. Some youth have serious challenges, and need professional and culturally appropriate help in dealing with psychiatric problems. Preventive measures are even more important, in a way, beginning with those dealing with issues as basic as low self-esteem. There must also be a recognition that youth are at risk for violence as a result of a number of factors including alienation, lack of integration, peer pressure, response to harassment, vulnerability from being at high risk for school dropout, racism and discrimination, culture-specific gangs, and limited English language skills. Other important prevention measures are family-oriented support and youth counselling to address the stress on families who undergo a decrease in living standards and other migration-linked stressors.

Regarding the *social services* needs of youth, the key informants specified the need for services that address issues arising from family violence and the stresses that families who sponsor their children to join them in Canada undergo. Support for them is needed, including a better understanding of the role of families in supporting newcomer youth, and the adjustments resulting from this type of family reunification. Difficulties arise in meeting basic needs like accessible and affordable housing, adequate clothing (for example, winter coats and boots), and appropriate and accessible recreational programs, all of which could be eased by appropriate and sensitive social services.

These should be available and accessible to all newcomer youth and their families, regardless of racial, ethnic, or cultural group, location, or other restrictions. There is also a clear need to develop services that are flexible and sensitive to the specific needs of certain often-neglected groups, notably women. The informants repeatedly requested better training for those who come into contact with newcomer youth (for example, teachers, mental health professionals, and immigration officials). There is a lack of positive role model programs to raise youth's expectations for education and employment opportunities, as well as a lack of culture-specific services available to youth in their first language, offered by a professional of the same racial, ethnic, or cultural background (for example, there is a lack of self-help programs for Muslims with substance abuse problems like Alcoholics Anonymous, which is inappropriate because it assumes a Christian philosophy). At the same time, there is a need to balance the existing but sparsely available services, the majority of which are currently geared toward the needs of adult male immigrants, with services for unserved or underserved groups in general. A good evaluation of the current services is needed, which is important before planning funding services on a "best practices" approach. There is also a need, informants stated, for immigration officials to be aware of the existing services for newcomer youth so that they may facilitate appropriate and timely referrals for youth upon entry to Canada.

Finally, under needs related to *employment* (the least mentioned by key informants), there is a need for services to educate youth about labour market standards in Canada, in order to reduce culture shock. There is also a need for programs to provide job-related language assistance to overcome the barriers to employment.

3. Telephone Survey of 145 Agencies Providing Services to Newcomers (Conducted by the Institute for Social Research at York University)

The Institute for Social Research at York University (ISR) asked service providers about the programs and practices that meet the needs of newcomer youth exceptionally well and about problems that organizations face when they serve newcomers between the ages of sixteen and twenty. In total, ISR selected 287 agencies and drew a sample from five distinct sources, including SEPT schools, the Ontario Council of Agencies Serving Immigrants (OCASI) membership directory, immigration services and youth services listed in the *Blue Book Directory of Community Services* in Toronto, and referrals from agencies selected from these listings. The overall response rate was 64.2 per cent or 145 completions.

The agencies are drawn from five broad service sectors (education, employment, health, mental health, and social services) and multi-service or umbrella organizations. They vary in size and length of time they have provided services.

Most (94 per cent) have programs and services available to newcomer youth, although neither an exclusive focus on youth nor an exclusive focus on newcomer youth is the norm. About one-quarter have less than 5 per cent of their newcomer clientele between the ages of sixteen to twenty. For slightly over one-quarter of the agencies, newcomer youth make up more than 20 per cent of their newcomer clientele.

The newcomer youth served by these agencies are culturally and racially diverse. Around three-quarters of the agencies assist newcomer youth from five or more cultural and/or racial backgrounds. About one in ten agencies serve youth from one specific ethnic group. The newcomer youth served have difficulty communicating in English. Only 7 per cent of the agencies report no English language difficulty among their newcomer youth clientele; 27 per cent report English language difficulty for three-quarters of their newcomer youth clientele. Newcomer youth must overcome a variety of barriers in order to adapt to Canadian society. The most serious barriers the agencies identified in the survey are: lack of fluency in English, culture shock (differences between native and Canadian culture and values), intergenerational conflict, and poor school integration.

ISR summarized important aspects of service delivery reported by the agencies as follows:

- *Meeting multiple needs.* Referrals for assistance elsewhere, health information, counselling for social adjustment, and family counselling for intergenerational issues are each provided by over half of the agencies. Counselling for cultural and/or personal identity, employment services, recreational and social opportunities, assistance for basic needs, English language instruction, school level and school readiness assessments, and counselling for religious identity are addressed by smaller proportions. Around 88 per cent offer four or more of these fourteen types of assistance to newcomer youth.

- *Matching the language and cultural background of staff with those of the newcomer youth served.* Eighty-five per cent report having some staff or volunteers from the same cultural/racial background as the youth served. Eighty-two per cent offer some services in the language(s) spoken by their newcomer youth clientele.
- *Evaluation of services.* A majority report that they evaluate their programs to assess how newcomer youth respond to their services. The actual evaluation methods vary.
- *Serious barriers to effective service delivery.* The most challenging service delivery issues are inadequate funding, the varied needs of different cultural and/or racial backgrounds, the varied needs of each gender, and the lack of interagency coordination. Other barriers include eligibility criteria, lack of awareness of available services, and inadequate staffing.

Programs and practices described as meeting the needs of newcomer youth especially well are varied; survey respondents reported to ISR on program content and implementation procedures. With respect to *content*, practical aids to assist integration into the institutional life of Canadian society, aids to social and psychological integration, referrals, and programs specifically for newcomer youth seem to be the dominant themes. Three aspects of *process* stand out: staffing, individualized attention, and newcomer youth involvement in program planning and delivery. The provision of ethnically specific programs and community-based services reference both content and process and seem directly related to issues of access and outreach. The agencies surveyed made suggestions for improving services for newcomer youth. The most prevalent recommendations were for increased funding, more programs for newcomer youth, better interagency coordination, better access to services, and greater outreach and marketing to increase awareness of available services.

Elements of Best Practice in Different Service Sectors

Patterns that appear quite definitely in the overall data are less visible in a sector by sector examination of education, employment, health and mental health, and social services. There are likely several reasons for this, but two factors are especially important in this regard. One concerns how a sector is defined; the other relates to the nature of the data.

Sector has been defined as the service sector of the respondent. This means that the data for each sector consist of the comments made by respondents whose agency falls into that sector even though those comments may refer to a program or service in quite a different sector. This difficulty is compounded because many of the organizations surveyed offered more than one kind of service and because respondents sometimes spoke about specific programs and sometimes about organizations.

ISR described their data as "wide ranging and layered," but also "thin," since answers may reflect a sense that a practice is good because it is ethno-specific, while other answers may identify as excellent the single focus of the program rather than its specific clientele. They encourage us, therefore, to read their sector analysis in the light of concerns about the thinness of the data, the multi-service nature of some organizations, and the willingness of respondents to speak of many needs and services of youth, rather than just those in their sector. They suggest their interpretations should be thought of as merely pointing at directions for further research rather than as offering definitive identifications of sectoral "best practices."

Education

References to content-oriented best practices were diverse and included proper contacts for good referrals, reliable referrals, holding workshops, sustaining interest, and combining educational components with socializing and recreational components of programs. Programs tailored specifically for youth, providing language instruction, health care, a drop-in centre, goal-oriented language and employment services, and practical job training were also described as outstanding because of their content.

Employment

Twenty-five respondents from the employment sector identified programs and practices they believed were outstanding. Those identified are interesting in two respects. First, the majority are social, with housing and shelter referenced more often than by respondents from other sectors. Employment-related programs/services are the next most prevalent, but programs directed at education, health, and mental health are also named.

The second interesting aspect of employment sector respondents' comments is that four specific agencies are identified by more than one respondent. It may be informative to summarize the comments made about these four agencies.

Health

Half of the programs and/or services identified as outstanding by the eight respondents from the health sector focused on health issues (such as planned parenthood, teenage sex information, women's health, or mental health). Three of these were specific to a particular ethnic community, but respondents did not know what made them outstanding.

Location in schools and local community centres was important for the delivery of planned parenthood and community health programs, as well as the dissemination of information targeted particularly at youth.

Mental Health

The diversity of the services provided by the social workers of a local school board and several neighbourhood community centres was singled out as exemplary. Art therapy programs were seen as effective since youth express themselves without having to use words and diagnosis does not need to rely on verbal communication. A program dealing with intergenerational conflict was described as outstanding because of parental involvement. The quality and commitment of staff, individualized life skills programs, and youth involvement in service delivery were also characteristics of these programs. One program was ethnically specific.

Social Services

Twenty-seven respondents from the social services sector (including settlement and referral agencies) identified around fifty programs as outstanding. While the majority seemed to provide social services, programs directed at education, employment, health, and mental health were also identified. Thirteen ethnically specific programs were referred to; three organizations were mentioned more than once.

Umbrella or Multi-service Organizations

Respondents from umbrella or multi-service organizations made fewer comments about implementation aspects of best practices. Included are: program evaluation by newcomer youth, assistance to and coordination with other agencies, working in small groups, staff professionalism, and staff leadership.

4. Focus Groups with Newcomer Youth and Mothers

Major findings from this phase, the lengthiest portion of the work, are rich in their potential for elucidating the needs and concerns of immigrant youth. They also shed light on the perspectives regarding the services offered and those not available in the five sectors of education, health, mental health, social services, and employment, although this was not the focus of their discussions. Education was, as we shall see.

Findings differ according to the ethnicity and gender of the participants; some are corroborated by the mothers, but some findings are exclusively the mothers' insights. Some key findings are:

- Difficulties upon arrival differ depending on whether the family immigrates as a unit or whether parents arrived first; the length of separation in multi-staged migration added significantly to adjustment problems, but there is very little understanding of this.

- Difficulties in the educational system were experienced differently by males and females: females seemed to have less trouble being accepted by teachers and have less trouble in succeeding academically; males had far more trouble with violence, bullying, and racial incidents.
- Males reported experiences of racism in general more frequently than did females; Portuguese, as well as official "visible minority" youth, reported such experiences; and racist behaviour occurred between different visible minority groups, including those of Northeast African heritage like the Somalis and those of Southern African heritage, like most Canadian Blacks.
- Language difficulties were enormous upon arrival, even for those with non-standard English, and the help provided was inadequate and inappropriate (not raising them to the academic level they wanted).
- Females commonly experienced more difficulty within the home as a result of the clash between old and new cultural values; males commonly experienced more difficulties outside the home: in school, job-seeking, and with other institutions like the police.
- Females, except for Somalis, found support structures more available to them; this may be in part because those who are Christian cite support from churches more often; only Korean males cited the churches as a source of support.
- Youths who are Black, both males and females, believed it is difficult to be Black in Canada.
- While the school is the key site for integrating newcomer youth into Canada, it has few if any trained personnel who are responsible for this, and rarely any programs to facilitate their success.

The findings from the focus groups cannot fairly be fitted into the five major categories, although their recommendations can. The young people and their mothers raised very clear topics in their discussions, and these emerged independently of any questions designed to identify needs, services, and emerging "best practices" under the headings of education, employment, health and mental health, and social services. Instead, it became clear that for the youth, school-related issues were the overarching concern, with other social issues (never health, except indirectly) secondary to what goes on in school. Across all groups, youth and mothers reported a variety of agencies and individuals who aided them in Canada. These agencies and individuals included ethnic-based community organizations, recreation centres, schools, friends, relatives, guidance counsellors, teachers, religious organizations, and sports teams/clubs. They tended to be mentioned in passing, rather than as a topic of prolonged reflection. This discussion will therefore follow the headings that arose in these focus groups.

Education and the Challenge of Language

Across all groups, language was a primary source of tension, crisis, and struggle. For Iranian, Russian, Somali, Korean, African, and Filipino immigrant groups—whose first languages were not English—learning a new language produced heightened stress. Participants discussed struggles with language most often in relation to academic and social hardships in school. Most youth regardless of gender cited learning English as a tremendous difficulty, although a few girls showed greater optimism with language learning than boys. Mothers of all immigrant groups identified language acquisition as a major source of struggle in their own lives and those of their children. Specifically, many of the mothers across the groups remarked that their lack of English language skills contributed to the hardships they faced in Canada and their loss of respect and self-esteem.

Some of the Russian mothers did not feel that their children experienced many problems with learning English, and in fact these woman expressed optimism with regard to their children's progress with language acquisition. The Russian youth, however, identified language as a problem that they faced when they first came to Canada. Mothers debated whether their children were using enough English outside the classroom.

Across many groups, debates ensued regarding the pros and cons, in relation to second language acquisition, of living and attending school in areas with high concentrations of students speaking other languages. It was debated whether going to a school with many other ESL students increased or decreased opportunities to learn English. The Korean and Russian mothers spoke about basing their residential and subsequent home buying choices on their selection of schools and fostering optimal conditions for the second language acquisition skills of their children.

The issue of language for Jamaican youth was played out differently, but nonetheless was seen as a source of struggle and tension, as noted by mothers and both male and female youth. Many Jamaican youth and their mothers spoke about discrimination against Jamaican accents and noted that they were routinely placed into ESL classes, even though English is their first language.[3]

Education and the Difficulty of Accurate Grade and Level Placements

All immigrant youth's and mothers' groups expressed concern about the placement of youth into academically appropriate grades and levels of course work at the secondary level (basic, general, or advanced). Most immigrant groups felt general frustration and disillusionment with schools placing students into levels lower than they felt they were capable of. Youth and parents identified language difficulties, racism, and discrimination against immigrants as frequently linked to placements into lower level classes or grades. Only very few students and parents noted guidance counsellors as helpful. In fact, many youth noted guidance counsellors as implicated in the many problems these youth faced. The current findings suggest that other immigrant, non-English-speaking students (as well as African-Canadians) are also experiencing systemic and structural streaming into low levels of study and manifesting poor academic achievement.[4]

Marked gender differences were observed in the Portuguese and Jamaican groups in this regard. In the Portuguese youth groups, males reported more problems in school than did females. In the Jamaican youth groups, males expressed greater desire for basic level courses, whereas Jamaican girls were eager to be placed in an advanced level.

The Jamaican male group also differed with regard to other Black groups such as African-born and Somali youth groups in that the Jamaicans preferred basic levels and college education, while the latter groups wanted advanced level courses and university education. This calls attention to important intragroup differences within the broad pan-African category of "Black" or "African-Canadian" and validates the current study's focus on differing countries of origin as implicated in post-immigration and settlement issues, including schooling.

Education and School Violence

Several groups identified school violence, bullying, and extortion as problems they faced. Many Somali males and one Filipino male talked about experiencing violence first-hand, bullying, and/or extortion. The Somali youth pointed to Jamaican-Canadian youth as the perpetrators, and the Filipino youth spoke about being severely beaten by a gang of Chinese youth. This points to a dynamic of youth violence that involves two "minority" groups. During the Korean male focus group, several of the youth articulated much aggressive racism toward African-Canadians.

In terms of gender differences, none of the young women across the groups mentioned violence as a problem, although many females talked about being teased by other girls because they were immigrants, did not speak English, or were new to schools. Many of the males across all the various youth groups identified the prevalence of physical fights in the younger grades of schooling. Many noted that these fights were initiated by other students who usually teased the youth for their inability to speak English. These playground altercations, however, did not progress to physical violence in the older grades for groups other than the Somali and Filipino groups. The Jamaican male youth group did not speak about school violence as a problem or issue of concern. However, many alluded to tensions within the category of "Black." Violence between Somali and Jamaican youth was at least alluded to in such remarks.

Education and Religious Tension within Schools

Several male Somali youth, but none of their female counterparts, spoke about their problems with prayer time in schools. These males remarked that many teachers did not support their desire to pray during school time. These youth were not permitted a prayer room in the school and were penalized by some teachers for leaving class for prayer. This gave rise to tension between some Somali male youth and the schools.

Education and the Lack of Respect for Teachers

Many youth across groups reported being surprised at the lack of respect given to teachers in Canada. They also mentioned that there was considerable peer pressure to be disrespectful and talk back to teachers. Filipino males and Jamaican, Korean, and Iranian females reported that in their own countries, teachers are treated with the utmost respect, so they were surprised to discover that teachers were not held in high esteem in Canada. In fact, one Filipino youth remarked that Filipino immigrant youth, who have been raised to respect teachers, feel intense peer pressure to talk back to their teachers in order to gain the respect of their peers.

The Devaluation of Foreign Credentials

Many youth and mothers' groups identified Canadian authorities' depreciation of their foreign education and professional credentials as a source of problems within the family. Male and female Iranian and Jamaican youth, in particular, decried the depreciation of their parents' credentials. Several Iranian and Russian males were very articulate in describing how, in addition to economic hardship, the disillusionment stemming from devalued credentials ultimately led to tensions within the family as members worried about the possibility of future career security.

Social Services and Poverty

Many youth were concerned with the poverty they faced in Canada. The Jamaican, Russian, and Iranian youth linked their struggles with poverty to the devaluation of their parents' credentials in Canada. The Portuguese male youth associated much of their poverty with racism against Portuguese people and their restriction to low-paying cleaning occupations. Some youth identified the high cost of post-secondary education as exacerbating problems arising from poverty and discrimination against immigrants in the workforce.

Policing

Two groups spoke at length about frustrations with the police in the GTA. These were the Jamaican male group and the Portuguese male group, who reported problems with police harassment. Jamaican mothers reported difficulties with children staying out all night and getting into trouble with the law. Jamaican youth criticized the widespread stereotype of Jamaicans as drug dealers as contributing to the problems of over-policing.

Intergenerational Tensions and Conflicts

Across many groups youth identified tension with their parents regarding curfew, fashion, lengthy separation, gender discrimination and sexism, and loss of mother's power.

Curfew:

Somali girls were quite outspoken about tension with their parents. Some of these girls explained that in following Islamic tradition, parents were very strict with their daughters. According to one girl, this meant that she had to go home right after school instead of meeting her friends. Similarly, some of the Portuguese girls observed that while their younger brothers were permitted to go out late at night, they were not allowed to do so. Portuguese males did not report as much tension between themselves and their parents as did their female counterparts. The Jamaican mothers remarked that their attempt to prevent their children from staying out late so that they would not get into trouble with the law created friction in their homes.

Several youth commented that in their opinion, their parents became stricter after coming to Canada. For instance, some Korean female and male youth noted that, after moving to Canada, their parents wanted them to focus solely on studying and did not permit them to engage in extracurricular activities. A Korean female youth remarked that the intense pressure to succeed academically caused her tremendous frustration, which created tension between her and her parents. Similarly, most of the Iranian male youth also noted that intense parental pressure for academic success created tension between them and their parents.

Fashion:

Both male and female youth across several groups mentioned that the intense pressure to dress fashionably as defined by their Canadian peers was a source of stress for them. Several noted that the repercussions of not dressing well included teasing, ostracism, and loneliness. Several male Russian youth noted that the clothes they brought from Russia were not fashionable in Canada and in order to fit in, they felt the need to dress like other students in their schools. This caused considerable tension between the youth who wanted to buy their own apparel and their parents who disliked the way Canadian youth dressed and wanted to purchase clothing for their children.

Lengthy separations:

The Jamaican and Filipino groups stand out in terms of noting lengthy family separations as a source of difficulty between them and their parents. In both groups, the mothers came to Canada to work as domestics or babysitters and their families or, in some instances just the children, followed. Several Filipino and Jamaican youth noted that having spent several years apart from their mothers and/or fathers led to tension when they were reunited. These tensions resulted in a lack of trust between youth and their parents and the children's difficulties in adjusting to new rules and sources of authority.

Gender discrimination and sexism:

Many female youth across groups reported a double standard in the way parents treated sons and daughters; girls were expected to maintain traditional roles such as cooking and cleaning, while males had more freedom. While some males across groups admitted to such differences, other males did not acknowledge any gender differences. For example, several Jamaican male youth remarked that Canada was a "woman's" country where women had more power than men. Other youth, such as the Somali males, acknowledged that because of their Muslim faith, Somali girls faced stricter regulation from their parents. As adults, Filipino mothers expressed the most blatant experiences of sexism and racism in comparison to other mothers' groups. One woman who works as domestic worker described being exploited by her employer, who took her passport from her.

Loss of mothers' power:

Many mothers noted that in moving to Canada, they experienced a considerable reduction in their power vis-à-vis their children. This loss of power was often linked to their inability to speak English and their subsequent dependence on their children (many of whom were also just learning English) to translate for them. This role reversal often contributed to a loss of respect and confidence.

Several mothers also spoke of how their children often expressed anger and disillusionment toward their parents for having immigrated to Canada. The youth blamed their parents' decision to move to Canada for the severe decline in the family's comfort, socioeconomic status, and satisfaction levels. The children's sentiments caused much suffering for their mothers.

RECOMMENDATIONS

Recommendations were found in the reports from all four types of sources: the review of the literature, the report on the key informants, the report on service providers, and the focus groups with youth (male and female groups) and mothers. What follows is a synthesis of these recommendations, organized first by the five major sectors the research set out to address, and then by other types of recommendations that emerged.

Education

School-based programs are the most important, since school is the place of greatest contact. Repeatedly requested are counselling and support services, welcoming and reception centres, mentoring and peer tutoring programs to prevent isolation and dropping out, and assessment services to determine appropriate school placement. Schools should actively educate to promote anti-discrimination and the breakdown of racist stereotypes. (Newcomer youth want assistance in order to understand Canadian culture, and also need this culture to understand them—not just with tolerance but with a real openmindedness by community members. These young people stated a strong need to live without prejudice or discrimination in any form, whether based on race, culture, religion, or gender.) ESL classes need to be of a high quality to integrate students into their subject areas at the level of sophistication they need for academic work at their level; they should welcome students whose English represents another dialect, and language level should be distinguished from mastery of other subjects in another language; placement should be determined by subject mastery, with language training provided to support that level.

The government should provide education for immigrants regarding the available resources in Canada. The government needs a fair and efficient system to evaluate and recognize foreign degrees and work experience at all levels. Similarly, schools need more accurate ways of determining where a student should be placed in terms of grade and levels of study. Greater partnerships must be formed between community organizations and schools to which community educators and other members would be invited to talk with youth. Schools need to make a dedicated effort to link parents with the work of the school, especially with what their children are doing in school; every school should have a place where family members are genuinely welcomed and assisted to fit in; just as newcomer youth need to be taught about Canadian culture and Canadian youth, so do their parents, which will ease the school's task of assisting their children's integration.

Designated prayer areas are needed for Muslim students in schools. Services provided in schools, such as the services of guidance counsellors and others, should be culturally sensitive and insightful as to the lived experiences of immigrant and refugee youth and their families. Immigrant students should be able to find themselves both in what they are taught (multicultural curriculum) and by whom (teachers representative of all cultures and genders). To prevent further isolation of the newcomers, school boards should hire qualified immigrant teachers who will not only make newcomer students feel more a part of the school, but would also teach those born in Canada about interacting with newcomers.

(This is particularly important in terms of shaping Canadian teachers' expectations of their new students.)

Since youth need to be part of the community in which they live and the school serves as their gatekeeper to society, it should provide genuine opportunities to make friends and enjoy social interaction, whether through sports or other appropriate activities. This may be a way for schools to address the need newcomer youth have for role models who look like them, understand them and (literally) where they are coming from, as well as speak the same language. Policies of zero tolerance for violence should be established and implemented at all schools. (Across groups, more males than females and mothers suggested initiatives for zero tolerance of violence at school; some males recommended giving harsher sentences to young offenders.)

Parents need to know that schools and schoolyards are safe, lest they curtail their children's hours of socializing, causing further isolation and subsequent resentment of the new country. After-school programs should include students of all cultures, while remaining sensitive to the needs of newcomers; there should, for example, be many opportunities for pursuing sports and activities found across the world.

Mentoring programs or buddy programs are needed, in which already integrated (or native to Canada) youth would not only teach the newcomers about the school and its education system, but also help them understand Canadian (youth) culture. Creating homework clubs would benefit those students whose parents cannot help them with assignments (because of a lack of English or education) and those students who are beginning to slack off because of a perceived less strict academic atmosphere in Canadian schools; these clubs would also ease the embarrassment of parents who are unable to help their children with schoolwork, and preserve family harmony.

Cross-cultural education should be provided for all members of the school community who will come in contact with newcomer youth and their parents, not just for teachers. There should be an active recruitment of immigrant parents to the PTA and school council; as focus group subjects pointed out, the children of PTA members get better treatment from the teachers!

Social Services

Citizenship and Immigration Canada should develop a comprehensive settlement package of information, written in a variety of languages, about the agencies and organizations that serve the community.

Courses should be taught to all newcomers when they arrive, and in their own language; they should include information on the rights of newcomers.

Free vacation camps and retreats for youths of all cultures should be set up to facilitate socializing between newcomers and non-newcomers, possibly or especially those who are the "buddies" or "mentors" during the school year. Programs should be characterized by individualized attention, empathetic and qualified staff, appropriate language of service delivery, and involvement of youth in program planning and delivery. Recreation is an important part of integrating into Canada; opportunities to play soccer in Canada, for example, should be expanded.

Youth and their families need access to affordable housing, health care, and medicine, as well as recreational activities and schooling, and this access should be provided in a safe environment. Family counselling programs for parents and their children need to be set up, as this time of settlement is difficult for the whole family. Counsellors are needed to act as mediators among youths, parents, and teachers, as intergenerational issues loom large in the minds of these youth, and they feel keenly the absence of services here. Parental involvement and client evaluation are important for family conflict resolution programs. Services are needed to provide proper contacts for good, reliable referrals to the types of services youth may need. Every community should have drop-in centres for youth, at which there should be programs that actively seek feedback from clients, have good internal organization, a culturally sensitive staff, good supervision, and programs designed to reduce isolation. Services are needed to facilitate communication and understanding between the police and newcomers (of all ages, but especially youth). Police need considerable education and training about diversity and working with newcomers or any groups different from themselves.

Employment

Many male youth and some females requested greater assistance to attain meaningful employment; like other young Canadians, they need jobs they can thrive in, employers who teach them skills, and wages that are fair. Services need to compensate for the fact that employment opportunities are more difficult for males to find than females.

Since the school system is not the primary job preparation instrument of Canadian society, there is a great need for job training programs for youth, especially non-exploitative paid apprenticeships, and co-operative educational placements.

Services should reflect the fact that employment for newcomer youth is often to support the family financially, as opposed to what their peers might be doing with their money. There should be a program to assist employers to recognize work experience from a newcomer's native land and to recognize foreign credentials. Employers of newcomer youth need services to help them acquire insight and sensitivity to youth's needs. Goal-oriented employment and employment-linked language services are needed.

Health

Lack of health services include affordable medicine (i.e., prescription and non-prescription drugs) and well-designed, culturally knowledgeable programs aimed at health issues affecting youth (anti-smoking campaigns, drug awareness, and alcohol abuse).

The location of youth-oriented health services in schools and local community centres is important for the delivery of planned parenthood and community health programs, as well as the dissemination of information targeted at youth.

Mental Health

Government must address youth's need to be with their families, which is impeded by immigration-linked separation and delays in family reunification; this is especially important as not only have they become separated from their parents, they miss their friends and, quite possibly, an entirely different lifestyle. Similarly, the government needs to make a better match between immigrants and the jobs for which they are encouraged to come to Canada to prevent the common instances of parents having to work so many jobs over such long hours that their moral support of their children is severely limited.

Youth need access to free counselling from counsellors who are both genuinely sensitive to and fully aware of their situation, including their culture, and also wholly committed to confidentiality; youth are not only struggling with their own issues but often they bear the weight of their parents' experiences and frustrations with integration. Male youth in particular need genuine access to counsellors who reach out to them; since males are (more often than not) taught to be "tough," they have a more difficult time integrating than females who feel freer to talk about their emotions.

Services need to address emotionally stressful factors for both children and their parents that arise because young newcomers are often ashamed that their parents do not speak English, and because power roles are reversed as parents become dependent on children to translate.

Other Areas for Recommendations

There should be a program providing a realistic portrayal of job opportunities in Canada so that potential immigrants know what to expect. Greater training and education is needed in the media, as newcomer youth feel either underrepresented in the media or discriminated against by misrepresentation.

CONCLUSION

At the outset, we indicated that the purpose of this report was to identify the needs and concerns of newcomer immigrant youth and the "best practices" offered by organizations that provide educational, employment, health, and social services for supporting the integration of youth from diverse cultural and racial groups. To accomplish this task we conducted an extensive review of literature, held in-depth personal interviews with fifteen key informants, surveyed staff at 145 service provider organizations, and conducted focus groups with male and female newcomer youth aged sixteen to twenty and with immigrant mothers of youth in this same age group. The four sources provided lengthy lists of recommendations.

The literature review confirmed our evaluation that very little research has been conducted on the needs and concerns of newcomer youth in this age group. At the same time, we learned from key informants, service providers, newcomer youth, and immigrant mothers that there is actually much to be concerned about. Thus, all sources revealed that newcomer youth face great difficulty communicating in English and these language problems often relate to settlement issues including: adjusting to a new culture; obtaining necessary information to facilitate settlement in key areas such as education, employment, and health; performing well in school; and adapting to the social climate within schools.

Though language acquisition is particularly important for enhancing integration, our study indicates that there are many other factors involved in this process. Newcomer youth arrive in Canada at different stages of their life course development and from cultures that are often quite distinct. Age of arrival, differences in cultural values, societal intolerance in the form of racism, and intergenerational conflicts involving peers and family members are all linked to stresses that these youth experience. All immigrant and refugee youth confront to different degrees the challenge of dual identities, and the majority confront the barriers of poverty or their parents' initial downward class mobility. Most youth, for various reasons, are successful in overcoming these obstacles, while a significant minority require greater support. The stresses that result from these pressures may place them at greater risk of delinquency, dropping out of school, alcohol and drug addiction, or depression.

These findings, already complex, must also incorporate the effects of gender and ethnicity, as our literature review and focus group results illustrate. Male and female newcomer youth experience the challenges of settlement and integration in different ways and these differences may be strongly influenced by whether the family immigrates as a unit or whether parents arrive first in Canada. Females may clash more with their parents within the home than males and experience greater difficulties with adjustment, as parents seek to protect them from a strange environment. Males, on the other hand, may encounter greater strife outside the home as a consequence of the greater freedom their parents give them. This includes trouble with such institutions as the educational system and the police; they also report difficulties with teachers, bullying, violence, and racism. These gender variations are also nuanced by ethnicity. Thus, many Somali males complained of experiencing school violence, bullying, and extortion while Filipino youth spoke about being severely beaten by Chinese youth gangs. Among the Korean male youth, a great deal of aggressive racism was articulated toward African-Canadians. These results indicate that both gender and cultural differences must be examined in understanding processes of settlement and integration across diverse groups of newcomer youth.

These findings, while suggestive, are not conclusive. It must be understood that the use of a focus group methodology provides a rich tapestry of themes, factors, and areas that require further investigation. This study is no exception. By separately examining the needs and concerns of seven different male and female ethnic groups, we have managed to provide a series of insights and hypotheses. These need to be taken up in additional, carefully planned research studies. Such studies would make use of both in-depth qualitative investigation such as interviews and focus groups and quantitative methods such as statistical analysis of survey data. These triangulated research methodologies would produce more reliable findings.

While the survey conducted by the Institute of Social Research at York University confirms that agencies have services and programs available to newcomer youth, exclusive focus on, or even specialization in, this client group is not the norm. At best, for slightly over one-quarter of the agencies, newcomer youth make up merely 20 per cent of their newcomer clientele. Though the agencies surveyed fully recognize that these youth must overcome a variety of obstacles (e.g., lack of fluency in English, culture shock, and intergenerational conflict) in order to adapt to Canadian society—and most have strategies in place for evaluating the response of newcomer youth to programs—they see serious barriers to effective service delivery. Among those mentioned were an insufficient number of programs, a lack of interagency coordination, inadequate funding, and the varied needs of different cultural and racial groups.

Both agencies and key informants agree that school-based programs are most important because school is the place of greatest contact for newcomer youth in late adolescence. An examination of detailed recommendations by sector at the end of this report reveals that the greatest number of recommendations made by all sources relate to school-based programs (e.g., mentoring, peer tutoring, buddy systems, counselling, and support services).

It is our conviction that these recommendations need to be taken seriously as a basis for further discussion and development. For this to happen, the major players—school boards, the Ministry of Education and Training, service provider agencies offering services and programs to newcomer youth, and the Ontario Administration of Settlement and Integration Services (OASIS, since April 2003 known as the Settlement\Port of Entry Directorate) need to convene to discuss these and other recommendations in the collaborating partners' reports. The objective, however, would not be simply to confer over recommendations but to design strategies and mechanisms (including interagency and intergovernmental coordination) that would enhance the delivery of "best practices" for adolescents in this age group, practices that respect the complex factors and themes identified in this report. And while the delivery of such service is clearly linked to the schools, it cannot end there. Given the late age of entry into Canada of so many youth, there is a vital need for service providers to link youth to the assistance that must be provided when they enter the post-secondary sector or the workforce, lest they not make that transition successfully and fail to move on to full participation in and contribution to Canadian society.

NOTES

[1] By Level 1 agencies are meant those government and community-based agencies that provide service to the general population, including immigrants. By Level 2 agencies are meant those agencies, many of them ethno-specific, that are formed to provide services especially to immigrants.

[2] The results of the federal-provincial study were reported in William Walker, "Canadians healthier but stress hits young," *Toronto Star* (September 17, 1999), 1.

3   Could societal forms of anti-Black racism use discrimination based on accent to marginalize these students? Lippi-Green (1998) has provocatively explored discrimination based upon accent in her book entitled *English with an Accent*. She contends that in North American societies such as the United States, people who speak with an accent are subjected to discrimination.

4   Scholars (Brathwaite & James, 1996; Dei, 1996; Dei, Mazzuca, McIsaac, & Zine, 1997) have written about the systemic streaming of African-Canadian students into basic levels of education. These writers identify structural and systemic racism endemic in the school system and larger society as contributing to the high levels of dropout and low achievement of Black students.

CONCLUSION

Overview and Implications
of the Research

PAUL ANISEF AND KENISE MURPHY KILBRIDE
Joint Centre of Excellence for Research on Immigration and Settlement, Toronto

PRINCIPAL FINDINGS FROM THE RESEARCH

Adolescence, a challenging period in the identity formation of most individuals, is often compounded by settlement difficulties that immigrants generally encounter. When newcomer youth leave what is familiar, including their old schools and friends, family members who remain in the home country, and their cultural surroundings, they must learn to cope with and adapt to life in an unfamiliar country. As newcomer youth negotiate with the new society and culture they now call home, they are confronted with a number of tensions that play themselves out in different spheres—school, family, friends and peers, and the labour market. These tensions are a reflection of the process all adolescents face as they mature from childhood to adulthood, and of the unique experiences newcomer youth undergo as immigrants, particularly when they have difficulty making themselves understood. For newcomer youth, problems associated with English language proficiency, for example, can play a major role in their adaptation.

At other times, the tensions reflect what youth often feel when they are pulled in opposite directions between seemingly irreconcilable cultural standards or value systems and a desire to fit in. Exacerbating these issues is the discrimination that newcomer youth often perceive is being directed toward them, which can further complicate and challenge their integration into Canada. The issues of settlement and adaptation become even more complex when one considers that newcomer youth from different ethnic

235

groups, religions, genders, and cultural background have diverse experiences and, hence, different concerns and needs. As a result, already complex difficulties facing adolescents—such as doing well in school, forging healthy relationships with family members and friends, developing a sense of belonging, and acquiring rewarding employment opportunities—become even more difficult when coupled with the challenges of settlement.

In order to understand the complexity of the youth settlement process, the researchers involved in this immigrant youth needs project have attempted to identify and explore the multifaceted dimensions of the issues facing immigrant youth and their families. As mentioned earlier, the project's holistic approach involved youth as active participants and included in the research the voices of family members, service providers, community members, and other concerned parties. This chapter presents a dialogue among all the organizations' research data. The findings have been organized under four headings or themes. Section one generally deals with settlement issues arising from language proficiency; section two addresses issues of acculturation or fitting in; section three deals with factors that support or exacerbate the settlement process; and section four explores some of the maturation-related transitions that adolescents undergo in the immigration experience.

Three observations must be made about the theme headings. First, they are not mutually exclusive and cannot be treated as such. Second, the themes therefore overlap. Third, while some aspects of the themes are consistently reported by all six organizations, others do not receive unanimous support and these will be noted. Since each organization focused on particular ethnic groups and research contexts, the issues that emerged from each study sometimes illuminated concerns and issues that were particular and unique to the ethnic groups studied (and possibly to the particular individuals interviewed), while at other times the concerns raised were more universal. We have then a synthesis of all the findings, which reflects the work from all sources employed by the six research partners.

1. Language Proficiency Difficulties Comprise One of the Major Struggles Newcomer Youth Face in Adapting and Integrating into Canadian Society

The ability to communicate, to express one's intentions, and to be understood are all integral components of forging new meaning. In order to negotiate the complex territory of a new language, one must be able not only to understand its many nuances and variations, but also to make oneself understood by others. Since language itself tends to be embedded in the traditions, values, and cultural understandings of a society, it is therefore not sufficient merely to know the language's syntax. Learning a new language involves the ability to comprehend and engage in both the formal syntax and pragmatic usage of language. Newcomer families from areas that use standard English may have adequate language proficiency, but they may experience difficulties in understanding jargon and dialect. Those who originate from countries with first languages other than English must begin language training anew in order to function comfortably in English. The findings of all the organizations unanimously identified problems associated with language proficiency as playing a significant role in the settlement process of immigrant youth. Language barriers can, among other things, exacerbate educational difficulties, create family difficulties, reduce employment opportunities, produce low self-esteem, and increase discrimination. To ameliorate these problems, newcomer youth are generally placed in ESL programs, which help them learn the intricacies of English and provide them with ways to cope with settlement issues. While the intentions of these programs are admirable and the results generally positive, the fact remains that placement in ESL classes is often resented by newcomer youth and leads to stereotyping by their Canadian-born peers.

Language Proficiency Difficulties

In the studies conducted, language proficiency difficulties were often voiced as the major reason for youth's struggles in adapting and integrating into Canadian society. In the educational endeavour, the Centre for Research and Education in Health Services, Kitchener/Waterloo (CREHS) highlighted language barriers as one of the key reasons why youth feel lost, stupid, and judged in the classroom. Family Services Association (FSA) also noted that the lack of language competency plays a large role in causing youth to become withdrawn, confused, alienated, and fearful. Moreover, they pointed out that youth's perceptions about their own language incompetence may prevent them from approaching and forming friendships outside their ethnic groups. According to the Coalition of Visible Minority Women (CVMW), which focused on identifying the nature of the language barriers that Caribbean and African youth in Canada face, language barriers are erected because of the youth's unfamiliarity with standard Canadian English and also because of their accents. While some African youth speak English well, they often encounter difficulties in the use of jargon and collo-quialisms. When they do pick up the jargon and use it in their homes, they are often not understood by their parents, who find this foreign use of language disrespectful. Many Caribbean youth, on the other hand, face difficulties in their non-standard use of English.

Both the Joint Centre of Excellence for Research on Immigration and Settlement, Toronto (CERIS) and the CREHS studies support these findings. Most of the interviewed youth reported language barriers (because of poor English skills, non-standard English, or English spoken with an accent) as playing a detrimental role in their settlement process, causing both stress and social/academic diffi-culties. Furthermore, CREHS added that communication barriers in the classroom can cause students to have comprehension diffi-culties in both class and homework material, so they do poorly, and the report by the Council of Agencies Serving South Asians (CASSA) and the South Asian Women's Centre (SAWC) suggested that apti-tude and skills tests are often inappropriate because they do not reflect the knowledge base acquired by youth who have previously attended school under different educational systems.

ESL and Language Proficiency

Youth with English language difficulties, whether they are unfamil-iar with the English language or have accents other than standard Canadian English, are often placed in ESL classes for extra help. Intended as a supportive, acculturative, and basic language learn-ing system, ESL can affect the youth settlement process both positively and negatively. While youth sometimes appreciate this assistance, it often functions as a sorting mechanism that isolates and alienates them. CASSA/SAWC noted that often youth who have language competency problems are not only put into ESL for English subjects, but for other subjects as well. Both Pinecrest-Queensway Health and Community Services, Ottawa/Carlton (PQHCS) and CVMW agreed that the complexity of this issue is not being adequately dealt with through ESL programs. PQHCS reported that youth often feel they are held back by such school programs. According to the research the organization conducted through its Diverse Youth Growing Project, many newcomer youth feel isolated from the rest of their peers and disparaged by the general student population. CVMW observed that while some African and Caribbean youth view ESL classes as beneficial, many want classes that will help them work on their accents.

FSA reported that while ESL classes may function in positive ways, they usually separate those who take them from the rest of the student population. FSA further commented that "It is possible to assume that when newcomer students are relegated to ESL programs, it is not cool to go there." Moreover, FSA suggested that there is inadequate and insufficient help offered to newcomer students in ESL programs. "Often, many teachers, health professionals, settlement workers, counsellors, and other relevant persons, [through] inexperience or/and ignorance of psychological distress and changes experienced by newcomer youth, grossly underestimate or minimize suffering, conditions and the personal and behavioural problems of these youth."

CREHS also noted that while immigrant youth generally view ESL classes in positive terms, they often find the teaching approaches are not supportive of integration. In the in-depth interviews that CERIS conducted, several young people mentioned that ESL classes should be available to both non-English speakers and youth speaking English with a foreign dialect, and that these classes should be set up in ways that reflect the abilities of youth taking them to avoid harassment based on stereotyping according to language.

The Family and Language Proficiency

Language barriers often create problems within the family setting. As CREHS noted, parents often become frustrated because their inability to speak English limits their employment opportunities. Their subsequent reduced ability to provide for their children can strain familial relations. According to the CERIS study, tensions can also arise because parents often do not grasp language intricacies as quickly as their children and may be forced to depend on them to act as translators. CASSA/SAWC added that without the youth's assistance in negotiating on behalf of their parents, parents often are at risk of becoming isolated. The shifting of familial roles can create overwhelming tensions between parents and their children. On the one hand, as CERIS and CASSA/SAWC observed, parents often perceive a loss of control and power in relation to their children, while youth, on the other hand, are encumbered with the burden of becoming translators and cultural brokers, responsibilities that may further complicate their already challenging settlement process.

Employment and Language Proficiency

Language proficiency plays a significant role in accessibility to employment. According to CVMW, most of the youth and parents interviewed alluded to a vicious cycle that prevents them and their parents from seeking social services and attaining good employment. First, many cannot speak English well enough to know how to look for social services that could assist them. Second, while some recognize that they need to speak standard English in order to obtain a better education, employment opportunities, and social mobility, many are discouraged from even aspiring to such goals because of their limited English. PQHCS also explored the relationship between language competency and employment. It found that youth in the Ottawa area often encounter limited employment opportunities because many of the available jobs require bilingual speakers. Youth who speak only French, for example, are unable to procure employment. Others who have difficulty writing in English face barriers to employment as well. CREHS mentioned that language barriers cause parents to become frustrated and disappointed because they are unable to provide for their children.

Discrimination, Self-Esteem, and Language Proficiency

Language difficulties can be exacerbated by perceived discrimination and may lead immigrant youth to develop low self-esteem. It is especially difficult when young people consider themselves to be native English speakers, as Caribbean youth do. CVMW identified teacher stereotypes, based on youth language usage, as a major factor that affects how the youth perceive themselves. Teachers convey perceptions that can often lead to demoralization and low self-esteem among youth. In many cases, youth are put back a few grades or placed in special education or ESL classes because they are assumed to have a minimal or basic understanding of English. These experiences can be demeaning and traumatic, especially for Caribbean youth, who define themselves as unilingual English speakers.

The CERIS findings also identified practices that often resulted in placing many newcomer youth in lower grade levels than what they consider themselves capable of, even when their first language is English. CASSA/SAWC pointed out that often newcomer youth are prevented from taking advanced level courses even when they do well on aptitude tests. The partnering agencies suggested that this failure may be due either to the ways in which ESL programs work or because of stereotyped practices. As CREHS suggested, teachers often base their expectations of newcomer youth's abilities on predetermined assumptions about immigrants and thus relay the message that immigrant youth should be satisfied with lower marks. These discriminatory practices tend to perpetuate a self-fulfilling cycle that begins with placing newcomer students in inappropriate levels or expecting less of them, which can often lead them to perform poorly because of factors such as minimal stimulus, low self-esteem, and embarrassment at being demoted. The youth's poor performance then justifies their being placed in lower grades or being treated unfairly.

2. Struggling to Fit in

Issues of acculturation or fitting in occupy a large portion of the youth settlement process. Immigration to a new country is sufficiently difficult in terms of finding a home and proper schooling for children, learning about the rules and regulations, and establishing a network of support. When immigrants come to a country that espouses very different customs, values, religious practices, and traditions, they often encounter difficulties coping with and understanding their new experiences. Language proficiency problems are by no means the only issues that complicate the settlement process. Some of these issues result from individual factors, such as the age of arrival in Canada and personal characteristics. Others can be identified as environmental issues, including pre-immigration experiences, culture shock, and familial expectations. The magnitude of these issues is reflected both generally in how newcomer youth negotiate with a new culture in terms of school, peers, and family dynamics, and particularly: how youth from different ethnic backgrounds, religions, and genders experience integration.

Age and Integration

The age of arrival in Canada plays a major role in how easily immigrant youth learn to adapt and are integrated into Canadian society. When they arrive in Canada at a young age, they generally have more opportunities to learn about the Canadian system. They have a longer time in the school system to adjust to cultural differences and are less entrenched in their original culture. Many of those who arrive in Canada during their adolescence must learn to cope with immigration struggles as well as with the expectations and pressures associated with this phase of life. As FSA noted, adolescents who have recently immigrated to Canada often feel more isolated, passive, and uncertain. Because they enter the school system at an age when most of their peers are already in well-established friendship circles, their relationships with Canadian-born peers tend to be uncomfortable. Moreover, they find it difficult to adapt to the new curriculum because they are accustomed to a different educational system. In short, the FSA findings suggest that younger children tend to acculturate faster than those who migrate at an older age. CREHS added that, in general, immigrant youth who have resided in Canada for a number of years feel less disillusioned and isolated, not only because they have become accustomed to Canadian life, but also because their earlier arrival has given them the opportunity to develop long-term friendships.

Personal Factors and Integration

Personal factors also play a role in the integration of newcomer youth. While for some youth, coming to a new country may be exciting and a source of adventure, for others it may be a source of ambivalence or even resentment. FSA found that factors such as personal satisfaction and attitudes toward Canadian society can play a major role in youth's adaptation because it informs their identity development. In order to learn about a society's values and traditions and reduce feelings of isolation, it is helpful to form friendships and good relationships with indigenous members of society. Conversely, lack of satisfaction and negative societal attitudes can seriously prevent youth from reaching out to forge bonds with peers and others in the community. If newcomer youth feel isolated in Canada, and their lack of satisfaction and negative societal attitudes prevent them from seeking friendships, they may then experience Canadian life as isolating and alienating. The key informants whom CERIS interviewed said that youth's mental health can also significantly affect their adaptation to Canada. They observed that low self-esteem and potentially more dangerous behaviour such as self-inflicted violence and violence toward others must be dealt with adequately in order to help immigrant youth adapt. Accessibility to adequate housing, counselling services for youth and their families, and specialized psychiatric facilities can help address youth's feelings of isolation and alienation.

Pre-immigration Situations

From the many discussions with youth, parents, and community and service providers, the researchers found that newcomer youth must also learn to cope with the lingering effects of pre-immigration experiences. Settlement issues become even more complicated when coupled with traumatic pre-immigration situations and refugee issues. Many youth arrive in Canada from war-torn countries with economic, social, and political turmoil. Often these youth have experienced horrific events and incidents that can traumatize the fragile identity of the developing adolescent and that often cannot be adequately met by services designed to cater to ordinary settlement needs. According to the FSA study, which explored the issues faced by youth coming from Afghanistan, the former Yugoslavia, and Somalia, many of those interviewed experienced "consequences of ethnic cleansing, extremely dangerous situations, cruelty, combat, killing, pain, extreme threat, constant artillery and gunfire, separation [and] forced isolation." As a result of such experiences, FSA identified in some immigrant youth post-traumatic stress disorder (PTSD) symptoms, including concentration problems, sleep disturbances, and nightmares.

Many youth (and their parents) who come to Canada from countries of war and turmoil arrive as refugees. Feeling as if they do not fit in anywhere and are persecuted wherever they go, refugees encounter several additional settlement problems, including those concerning identity papers. Refugees must await a hearing to be admitted as convention refugees. As convention refugees, however, they do not automatically receive work papers. While it is possible to apply for these papers, employers can discern their refugee status from their social insurance numbers, and they often hesitate to hire individuals who may soon be forced to leave the country. Another factor PQHCS identified is refugees' low socio-economic status arising from lack of employment opportunities. Often refugee families must rely on public housing because they lack the funds to reside elsewhere. Sometimes refugee youth who seek employment are rejected because of the neighbourhood they live in. As one participant commented, "because the neighbourhood has a bad name, all the individuals living there automatically have a bad name." The difficulties refugees face are sometimes compounded by racial and systemic discrimination, which can have tremendous adverse effects on refugee youth's sense of self-worth. Thus, many youth attempt to distance themselves from being labelled as refugees. CASSA/SAWC, who interviewed Tamil youth in their study, found that many of these adolescents did not discuss their pre-immigration situations. The researchers surmised that, although it is possible to assume that these Tamil youth do not perceive themselves as convention refugees because they arrived in Canada directly from Sri Lanka, it is also conceivable that they may want to distance themselves from the stereotypes of refugees.

Cultural Tensions and Integration

As youth negotiate their way within a new society, struggling to cope with the many acculturative challenges they confront, they often experience a number of settlement problems that arise in large part because of cultural differences among themselves, their families, their peer groups, and the host society. Two forces appear to be at work: one directing newcomer youth to form an attachment to the mainstream culture and the other to resist it. This tension between the old and new cultures places newcomer youth in a difficult tug-of-war, as they are pulled in one direction by the desire to fit in with their peer group, while simultaneously being urged to behave in other ways because of parental expectations. Newcomer youth are often torn between adhering to their families' values and expectations and those of their peer group, especially their Canadian-born peer groups. CASSA/SAWC described newcomer youth as straddling two cultures. They often behave in ways that stem from a desire to conform to the mainstream society, while simultaneously rejecting its values, norms, and cultural practices.

Both CASSA/SAWC and FSA noted that many aspects of the newcomer youth experience can be identified as a form of resistance to conforming to the culture, values, and established norms of the mainstream society. This resistance can be viewed as a way to cope with settlement challenges, including the racism they encounter. According to the study conducted by CREHS, youth often feel caught between two cultures—old and new. In both the major spheres of their experience—school and family life—they confront a cultural schism that may lead to confusion and disillusionment. For example, it reported that youth are often confused about how they should treat elders. CVMW pointed out that many youth are astonished and disappointed with the lack of respect given to elders, such as teachers, in Canada in comparison to how they are treated in their home countries. CERIS also noted that immigrant youth are often encouraged to be disrespectful and talk back to school authorities, a form of behaviour that newcomer youth and parents of more traditional backgrounds generally deem inappropriate.

Family Tensions and Integration

To compound the difficulties of negotiating between two cultures, newcomer youth often find themselves in a difficult position because of their families' expectations of them. These expectations can confuse newcomer youth and disrupt traditional family dynamics. Unlike family dynamics in some home countries, which tend to be characterized by more time spent with family members (including extended family) and community members, in Canada parents who have to work longer hours and for less pay often have little time to give their children moral support. CERIS pointed out that when parents, who are already frustrated because of their decreased socio-economic status, are forced to work under unfavourable conditions because their foreign work credentials are devalued, they may have new expectations of their children. Children who have been used to having more parental supervision and guidance are often expected to stay home alone, look after younger siblings, do grocery shopping and cooking, and find a job. Such changes in the family dynamic can create a burden on newcomer youth for which they are unprepared. According to the community members interviewed by PQHCS, parents are an essential component in the acculturation of their children. Yet when parents are confronted with such difficulties as not finding employment, a devalued education, limited financial resources, and a large family to provide for, youth are often left to fend for themselves.

While giving their children more responsibilities, parents often expect to retain the same degree of authority over them. Newcomer youth sometimes have to negotiate situations that in their former country they may not have had to deal with until they are older, and they may begin to resent their parents' exercise of authority. As CASSA/SAWC observed, youth tend to adapt and learn English more quickly than their parents and consequently often act as brokers or liaisons between their parents and the host society. CREHS and CERIS also noted that this sometimes results in a role reversal between parents and their children as youth become the interpreters, problem-solvers, and source of financial resources in the family. While acquiring such added responsibilities can be stressful for youth, parents may experience a consequent loss of authority as children look to other individuals as role models. This loss of authority is often exacerbated by lengthy family separations. As CERIS observed, long family separations, such as when youth come to Canada before or after one or both of their parents, are another cause of adjustment tension in families. Tension results because of a developing lack of trust among family members, and because youth must adjust to new household rules and discipline when they are reunited with their parents. Another source of tension arises from intergenerational conflict. PQHCS found in its Diverse Youth Growing Project that youth and their families are often torn between conflicting desires to assimilate the mainstream values and norms and maintain traditional beliefs. Parents, especially older ones, tend to want to maintain their culture, while youth often see assimilation as a way of integration into Canadian society. All these issues can lead to tense or broken relations among family members.

Experiences of Newcomer Youth That Differ by Ethnicity, Religious Affiliation, and Gender

While some integrative struggles arise because of the process of immigration itself, other tensions result from factors specific to ethnicity, gender, and religious affiliations.

(a) Ethnicity and Religious Affiliation:

Ethnicity and religious background play a larger acculturative role for some groups than for others. Westernization is a source of ethnic tension among newcomer family members. While many immigrant parents encourage their children to understand and adopt modern ways of doing things because these skills may help them acquire a good education and employment opportunities, they are often concerned that their children will become too Western in their thinking and practices. According to CASSA/SAWC, South Asian parents view their children's westernization as a threat to their established cultural beliefs and values. These beliefs and expectations often cause conflict between children and their parents regarding dating, curfews, dress styles, discipline measures, and choice of friendships.

Discipline is a common source of friction among newcomer youth and their parents, especially in families whose discipline measures in the home country differ greatly from those in Canada.

For example, according to CVMW, corporal punishment is an accepted way of disciplining children in many African and Caribbean families. Once in Canada, however, parents and youth learn that such forms of discipline are negatively regarded by the mainstream culture. Unaccustomed to other forms of discipline, parents feel a loss of control and power. Youth, on the other hand, are sometimes confused by their parents' change of behaviour.

Religious factors can also affect the settlement process, especially in families whose cultural background differs significantly from mainstream cultural values. CASSA/SAWC discussed cultural tension in terms of its effects on family relationships. According to the partner organizations, youth from Muslim families tend to confront more stringent parental expectations in terms of dress and the types of friends with whom they are permitted to associate.

(b) Gender-Related Issues:

While some issues are relevant to both male and female newcomer youth, others are more gender specific. For example, although issues of dating and fraternizing with peers come into play for both females and males, parents tend to be more strict with their daughters. However, parents generally have difficulty accepting dating practices for both their sons and daughters. CASSA/SAWC observed that parents can feel threatened by their children's growing sexuality or view such fraternizing as representing all that is "bad and wild" about the West, including "drinking, smoking, drugs, sex, and rock n' roll." However, both CERIS and CASSA/SAWC reported that females commonly encounter more difficulties than males within the home because of the clash between old and new cultures. Girls are generally seen as custodians of family values and are expected to behave in ways that reflect this role. This double standard means that females face more restrictions in dress styles, socializing with males, and going out with peers. Often, females experience restrictions that cause them to react in adverse ways. As CASSA/SAWC noted, "One of the coping mechanisms that girls seem to develop to survive this schizophrenic kind of existence is to start leading dual lives." For this they pay a high price in terms of stress and conflict in identity development.

3. Successful Integration Facilitated by Supportive Friends, Family, and Institutions/Isolation and Alienation Linked to Cultural Differences and Discrimination

When immigrant families and their children arrive in Canada with few financial resources, language barriers, and different cultural backgrounds, they need to develop ways to cope with their surroundings. While access to services and networks of support are important for parents, they are especially crucial for adolescents, who are often torn between the two cultures. Parents usually begin their settlement process in Canada by relying more heavily on traditional ways of negotiating with their surroundings, but immigrant youth, because of their age, are often less grounded in their culture. They are particularly susceptible to confusion and frustration as they straddle two cultures on a daily basis. Consequently, they are in acute need of helpful friends and institutions to assist them in developing coping strategies to meet their settlement needs.

As newcomer youth and their families struggle to understand and cope with the many immigration challenges they confront, several forces can facilitate their settlement process, while others may obstruct or hinder it. Some of the positive factors include: a network of supportive friends, extended family, community members, and institutions that can help newcomer youth and their families deal with the difficulties they confront. Other factors such as unresolved cultural differences and discrimination intensify newcomers' feeling of isolation and alienation and exacerbate the settlement process.

Supportive Friends and Institutions Can Facilitate Integration

The need to belong manifests itself strongly in the desire to form friendships. Youth who leave behind old friends need to form new friendships that can help them learn about the Canadian system, understand the codes of appropriate behaviour, and develop coping strategies. In the study conducted by PQHCS, youth reported that friends often are a major source of information about services, jobs, and activities. CERIS observed that across all groups, youth and mothers mentioned that friends and family are a major source of support in their struggle to adjust to life in Canada. Many of those interviewed also noted that extended family already settled in Canada helped them find accommodation and employment, connected them to appropriate mainstream and community organizations, and provided all the necessary translation for them in the early years in Canada. Most of the youth identified friends they met at school as most helpful to them in adjusting. These school friends told them what to do in school and after school, what to watch on TV, how to dress, and what subjects to choose at school.

CREHS noted that while some newcomer youth try to become integrated into the host culture by making friends with youth who are born in Canada or who have been here for a long time, many turn to those from their country of origin or those who share their ethnic background. As PQHCS stated, "Knowing that a person has the same culture or religion automatically creates a bond of trust for the youth." FSA's findings also showed that the interviewed youth preferred associating with peers from their own racial and ethnic background because they shared a common heritage, they could sympathize with newcomer situations, and they helped them feel valued and accepted. According to CASSA/SAWC, some schools recognize the need for youth to engage with other youth from similar backgrounds and have therefore initiated buddy systems, which pair newcomer youth with other students who act as cultural brokers. CVMW added that by pairing up newcomer youth with more established immigrant youth, the buddy system can also reduce the gap between the needs of newcomer youth and the services currently available.

The research from all the organizations confirmed that when newcomer youth and their families have a network of support composed of friends and institutions, they can more easily adapt to life in Canada. Often, however, newcomer youth do not turn to formal services and facilities for help; instead, they turn to informal sources of support. One reason is that although there are agencies that cater to the needs of youth, many do not focus exclusively on particular immigrant needs, nor do they adequately meet the settlement needs of newcomer youth. Among the barriers to effective service provision are the varied needs of different ethnic groups, the lack of necessary interagency coordination, and the inadequacy of funding.

CREHS identified the lack of resources as one of the major problems in the provision of services, particularly school services. Many of these services existed in the past, but recently lost their funding (e.g., ESL summer school programs). PQHCS, which explored the nature of services and support in terms of employment programs, reported that while immigrant youth know that services are available, they often do not seem to respond to their needs. Most of these services are designed for mainstream youth or youth who are job-ready, while many newcomers need services that can train them for employment. In the case of migrants to the Kitchener/Waterloo region, CREHS observed that this area is significantly populated by immigrant families who landed in other parts of Canada (mainly Quebec) and then migrated to the region. These families were attracted to the increased employment opportunities available in the area, the attractive and affordable housing, and the diverse educational opportunities provided in English in the area.

However, there are insufficient formal services to help these migrants. According to the research that CREHS conducted, ESL registration increased from 1,437 in 1994 to 3,107 in 1998, indicating a significant increase in the number of immigrant children in the Kitchener/Waterloo region. But the diverse needs of such groups are often not met because their arrival through secondary migration (relocating to a different destination than that indicated at the time of arrival) is not recorded in official government statistics. The settlement needs of these groups, therefore, while generally similar to those of other immigrant children and youth, simply do not receive enough support from government, and many in need must resort to using informal sources of support for help. CVMW pointed out that it is not sufficient that formal services exist; they also must become known and accessible to youth who need them. The organization found that many youth do not know what services are available to them, and others may know about the availability of services, but feel they are not accessible because of language barriers and cultural differences.

Among the more informal sources of support for settlement, CERIS's study identified a number of helpful religious institutions that have alleviated some of the difficulties that newcomer youth and their families encounter. Korean, Jamaican, Filipino, and Portuguese mothers mentioned that they received the greatest help and comfort from their church. Their church also gave them an opportunity to meet and make friends with other people of similar backgrounds and offered a variety of programs, including social events for adults and youth. These youth also said their church offered them assistance and support in their settlement process. Jamaican youth mentioned a youth support group in their church where they were able to talk about daily experiences and ways of dealing with difficulties. Somali and Iranian mothers and youth discussed the religious meetings they attended and the spiritual and moral support they derived from these meetings, and Russian-Jewish youth stated that their rabbi helped their families adjust to life in Canada.

CVMW discussed the role of institutions in assisting Caribbean youth. It stated that as in many other cultures, people from the Caribbean often feel that their problems are private and cannot adequately be dealt with by strangers. As a result, many turn to an informal support network of friends, family members, and sometimes the church to help them solve problems. FSA also noted that while youth often reported that their parents had problems, the parents did not take advantage of counselling services partly because both they were overworked and had no free time, and partly because they viewed the idea of counselling as "strange and unusual." Instead, many youth and their families turned to family members or to churches and, when available, culturally sensitive settlement service providers.

Discrimination Impedes Integration

Prejudice and discrimination are detrimental to the successful settlement of immigrants. Stereotypes of any kind tend to label individuals as a sort or a type without allowing them an opportunity to be themselves. Negative stereotypes are especially injurious because they can be demeaning and hurtful. Discrimination can occur on many levels and in many ways. Often it results from the intentional exclusion and singling out of certain groups from the mainstream society; at other times it can be caused by a lack of understanding and ignorance on the part of those who are prejudiced. All forms of discrimination, intentional or otherwise, can negatively affect the process of settlement and integration of youth into Canadian society.

(a) Discrimination in Schools:

One of the first places youth may encounter discrimination is in school. There, immigrant youth perceive they are discriminated against because of language limitations, the colour of their skin, racial origins, ethnic background, or cultural practices. According to the CERIS findings, females tend to experience fewer incidents of discrimination in school than males do. They are often more easily accepted by teachers and perform better academically. Males, on the other hand, report more racial incidents in terms of bullying and violence. In the study conducted by CASSA/SAWC, issues of prejudice were identified as highly significant in the youth settlement process. The report noted that, "Any attempt at understanding the adaptation and settlement challenges and concerns of South Asian youth must be contextualized within the realities of their everyday experiences in Canada where cultural imperialism and White supremacy are exercised through Eurocentric institutions that reinforce a racialized society."

Discrimination in the form of ethnic jokes, racial slurs, threats, harassment, and physical assault are often encountered by youth. CASSA/SAWC also pointed out that the curriculum is often set up in ways that exclude the lived realities of immigrant youth. For example, schools do not usually offer sports options such cricket or soccer, which South Asian youth are familiar with and in which many may excel. They also perpetuate stereotypes of Muslims as terrorists and violent and evil, which are demeaning and insulting. In turn, many immigrant youth lose faith in the school system's ability to help them combat discrimination. As a result, many learn to cope by seeking peer groups from their own cultural background as a way to create a sense of belonging and cultural identity.

(b) Teachers/Counsellors and Discrimination:

In the school setting, which occupies a significant portion of the lives of immigrant youth, teachers are major facilitators of youths' primary socialization to Canada. Thus, a teacher's experiences, attitudes, knowledge, and compassion become crucial to the settlement and adaptation of youth. Many of the interviewed youth, however, expressed ambiguous feelings toward teachers and other school authorities. While they frequently reported that particular teachers had been very helpful, they also were critical of their teachers in general for not understanding their problems. They did not make an effort to engage them as unique individuals on issues that affected their personal experiences, and instead imposed on them already-formed assumptions and expectations. More significantly, they did not have the same expectations of immigrant youth as they did of other students. CASSA/SAWC pointed out that when teachers engage in discriminatory behaviour, intentionally or otherwise, they give the message that such attitudes are acceptable. FSA suggested that educational practices need to become more "flexible and responsive, ensuring the development of innovative and comprehensive programs and interventions which balance the need for settlement, adaptation and integration of newcomer youth with [a] deep respect for a variety of their personal experiences, interests, and personality/identity development."

Guidance counsellors, who represent another major source of support, are in a special position to help immigrant youth in their socialization and adaptation process. Yet they hinder rather than facilitate youth settlement when they engage in discriminatory behaviour. Youth in both the CVMW and the CERIS studies found that counsellors were not generally helpful; rather, they sometimes contributed to the problems they encountered. Most newcomer youth who went to counsellors for help reported that they were discouraged by their counsellors' disparaging attitudes toward their aspirations for post-secondary education. Others were wholly unaware that there were guidance counsellors toward whom they could turn. These sentiments were also echoed by the findings of FSA and CASSA/SAWC.

(c) Peers and Discrimination:
While peers can be a major source of support for newcomer youth, they can also exacerbate settlement challenges. As discussed above, peer groups often have a considerable influence over newcomer

youth and when young people are tormented and rejected by their peer groups, they become depressed and dejected. Prejudicial attitudes and behaviour, which tend to make immigrant youth feel even more isolated, can evoke anti-social behaviour. FSA noted that "It is possible to anticipate that both youth who have demonstrated the hatred and discriminatory acts toward their peers and those who have been targets of various forms of hate and discrimination, are at increased risk, respectively, for incarceration, depression, behaviour problems, violent behaviour and many other negative developmental outcomes." CERIS explored the role of gender as a factor in discrimination, and found that males encountered prejudice more overtly in the form of bullying, extortion, and fights and other modes of violence. Females, on the other hand, reported being teased about being immigrants, about not speaking English well, or being new to a school.

CASSA/SAWC considered the effects of racism on the friendships that immigrant youth make. In many cases, males are drawn to gangs that are respected or feared by Canadian-born students. Immigrant females, however, reported being ostracized not only by members of the dominant race but also by their own ethno-racial group, perhaps because those who have been in Canada longer feel that they cannot afford to support newcomers for fear of also being singled out. Reasons for discriminatory behaviour stem from many factors ranging from ignorance of another individual's situation to an intentional desire to inflict harm on others.

(d) The Media and Its Role:

The media can play both a positive and negative role in the youth settlement process. Sometimes it can be a source of information and present positive role models for youth. Often, however, the media can affect youth settlement in an adverse way. CREHS examined the role of the media in pressuring youth to conform to Canadian cultural expectations. Although this influence is felt by most adolescents, it is often more acutely experienced by newcomer youth who feel that they must fit in. CASSA/SAWC described the media's perpetuation of existing negative stereotypes with respect to minority groups. The researchers noted that "negative stories about the [immigrant] community seem to get a lot more space and coverage in the media as compared to similar events in other communities and positive achievements are either completely ignored or reported as a form of tokenism."

(e) Violence, Police Harassment, and Discrimination:
Violence and police harassment were reported by a number of research partners. Such incidents are seen as discrimination that is often part of the ethnic minority group's lived experience. For example, PQHCS found that youth from visible minorities, especially Black males, often encounter harassment by police who regularly go into their neighbourhoods and routinely check their identity and car registration papers. CERIS found that Portuguese and Jamaican males had similar experiences of "over-policing." These youth also reported the persistence of negative stereotypes— for example, that Jamaican youth are drug dealers—as a major factor behind their experience of harassment.

Violence and police harassment, however, cannot completely be attributed to discrimination by the dominant mainstream society. CVMW acknowledged that discriminatory practices are often at the root of police harassment, but it also pointed to youth behaviour as being partly to blame. As mentioned above, immigrant youth who arrive in Canada from areas where discipline measures are much more strict often become more wayward when the type of discipline they had been accustomed to all their lives is abandoned. Some of the parents CVMW interviewed blamed the lax discipline measures condoned in Canada as one of the major factors causing youth to run into trouble with the police. This type of behaviour can cause police to become more stringent and perhaps lead to a self-perpetuating cycle of more general police discrimination toward certain youth groups. While violence and police harassment ought not to be condoned under any circumstances, it is important to recognize that there are many factors at work in such situations and it is necessary to break the vicious cycle that perpetuates all forms of discrimination.

4. Adolescent Transitions to New Adult Identities, Especially as They Relate to Employment, Can Be Hindered by the Immigration Experience

Employment factors play a major role in the immigrant youth settlement process. Through meaningful employment opportunities, youth learn to understand and cope with a number of adaptation and integration issues. Acquiring a job allows youth to learn about the Canadian economic system, to develop mechanisms for coping with people of different backgrounds, and to gain Canadian employment experience, which is often a prerequisite for better employment. Programs that help youth find employment can facilitate youth settlement by providing information, resources, and linkages between prospective employers and youth. All the organizations noted, however, that there are few services specifically targeted toward helping immigrant youth find employment. Several factors impede newcomer youth from finding employment. These include language barriers, acculturative issues, and discrimination.

Fitting in and Employment

According to PQHCS's study, which engaged specifically in employment issues, immigrant youth have a strong motivation to work. By working, they hope to acquire the same opportunities afforded to Canadian-born adolescents to purchase material goods, go out, and save funds for university or college. In acquiring employment, they also hope to gain Canadian experience, build up their resumé references, and achieve a measure of independence, which, as PQHCS observed, was very important to the participants in its study. CERIS found that the youth settlement process can be further facilitated by information about labour market standards in Canada.

Discrimination and Employment

Employment opportunities, however, are often limited by prejudice. According to CVMW, immigrant youth and parents often attempt not to stand out in order not to draw attention to themselves, and for this reason may have difficulty acquiring a job. The study conducted by PQHCS examined this aspect of the settlement process extensively, and identified several factors at work. First, when youth are not hired because they do not have Canadian experience, they are often uncertain whether they are being discriminated against or whether they lack the required skills. This ambiguity can often lead newcomer youth to lose confidence and doubt their abilities. Second, when they are hired, they often perceive that they are treated differently from other employees or not given the same respect. As PQHCS noted, "These youth are . . . ill equipped to deal with situations of discrimination, which they react to the only way they know how: by lashing out [in] their anger, which then perpetuates the stigma that they are violent and untrustworthy" or by withdrawing, thus fuelling the impression that they are lazy or lackadaisical at work. This behaviour is then used to reinforce and perpetuate many of the negative stereotypes attributed to these youth.

POLICY IMPLICATIONS

The information gathered by all the research teams involved in this project is useful in identifying issues, needs, and problems confronted by a wide range of newcomer youth and their families. Individually and collectively, the six studies will no doubt prove relevant to a variety of settlement-linked institutions and organizations and provide them with information about effective programs and gaps in the existing service delivery infrastructure. The information will, moreover, help funders to understand the benefits of the programs they support, and strengthen their services for immigrant youth and their families. The findings, recommendations, and conclusions also offer practical suggestions and insights to assist government officials and service providers in creating and enhancing programs and facilities to meet the settlement needs of immigrant youth.

A theoretical framework that lends itself well to the task of examining the experiences of children and youth is the human ecological model of Bronfenbrenner (1979). Children and youth are seen as members of families, which are nested in communities with their own institutions, which in turn are part of a larger society, with its world view, ideologies, and the policies that reflect them. This systemic approach does far more to illuminate not only the experiences of children and youth but also the sources of much of the environmental support (and stresses) for them and their families, as it examines surrounding institutions and the ideologies or belief systems that shape them.

In examining the findings and recommendations of the six partners in these research projects, there was a consensus among the youth (and their mothers when they were interviewed) that they be viewed as a part of a larger whole. They and their families wanted to be seen not only as parts of an immigrant community, but also as part of the larger society to which they had immigrated. In other words, the youth whose voices are heard in these interviews were rarely part of the marginalized, to use Berry's (1997) typology. They were not alienated from their own cultural group and those of "mainstream" groups, nor were they assimilationist in their attitudes, wanting merely to blend in with the larger group of Canadian-born peers, or segregationist, wanting to stay aloof from those peers and mix only with their own ethnic groups. Rather, these youth seemed to be identifying with both their home and new cultures or, to continue Berry's terminology, to be integrationist. The needs that emerged from these studies are clearly linked to a desire to succeed in the process of selective integration, as articulated principally by the youth themselves and secondarily by their families as well as concerned service providers. Based on this research, the following summarizes the main policy issues as identified by the participants.

Youth as Individuals

The newcomer youth aged sixteen to twenty experienced challenges in identifying and articulating how they wish to be young men and women in the tradition of their ancestors, and also of Canada, with a mixture of values selected by them. Their freedom to do this without the demeaning pressures of external prejudice or what they see as the expected but difficult pressures of parental expectations is an essential element of the policy recommendations derived from this study.

Youth in the Context of Their Families

Following Bronfenbrenner's framework of seeing youth in the context of their families, we read the testimony of the youth as themselves supporting that analysis. First, they object to the Canadian immigration policies that result in, or seem to make necessary, family separation in the migration process. When children are separated from a parent for years, they experience a deterioration of the trust they had previously enjoyed. Building new relationships with family members at a time when the family members are supposed to be their chief source of support is one of the difficulties they find hardest to overcome, so they need assistance with this.

Another source of alienation of youth from their families stems from the economic hardships that their parents often experience because their prior training and job experience in their home countries are not recognized. Consequently, both parents work long hours and are away from their children just when they most need parental assistance in adjusting to a new and often perplexing society. Policies to provide appropriate recognition for credentials, good training for adjustment to the specifics of Canadian occupations and professions, and job placement would help the youth retain the family life they had been accustomed to, with parents who have time to help them.

The newcomer youth seek to maintain family unity, yet do not want to pay too high a price for it. They believe that there should be programs to assist and support families in integrating into Canadian society, so that their own integration will be smoother as well. They seek these in their community of residence as well as within their ethnic community, and believe both types of programs should be in place. These family-centred programs should offer assistance to help families decide together where adjustments in traditional culture can be made at the request of youth, and where youth can be assisted to bridge the two cultures successfully. Intergenerational or family counselling is a very necessary component, according to the youth interviewed.

They also look for programs that will eliminate the specific causes of their families' poverty. There are few challenges so devastating for them as poverty, which seems utterly unjust, given their parents' educational levels and experience. Addressing this seems to indicate employing an empowering and inclusive community development model, rather than an approach based on assumptions of deficiency in the newcomers. This should also apply to some extent to the schools, which should involve parents in their children's education and introduce them to the workings of the Canadian educational system and its underlying philosophy in general. The study by the Family Service Association, for example, strongly argued for flexible funding for community service providers. FSA called for family-centred, needs-based, flexible, well-managed, and multifaceted community-based initiatives and programs for newcomer youth and their families; the basic assumption of these initiatives and programs is that improving early assistance for newcomer families will result in more positive relationships and a healthy climate within these families.

The early provision of a community-based approach that will engage newcomer youth and their families in a more successful process of settlement will also strengthen the family unit that the youth rightly believe should be there to support them. Their families at this stage of their lives are not the only source of support for newcomer youth, but they should be able to provide a continuing presence in their children's lives when they first arrive in Canada and as they pass through the challenges of adolescence. Ideally, Canada's settlement programs in school and in the broader community will enable families to be that source of support.

Youth in the Community: Peers Groups and Peer Group Memberships

Newcomer youth prized social cohesion among all youth, and asked for opportunities for Canadian-born and newcomer youth to interact in regularly scheduled, well-designed programs in social settings. Yet, to combat the isolation and psychological alienation of being newcomers, they also wanted programs designed to connect them regularly with other youth of their own background, as well as with Canadian-born youth.

The young people spoke of specific programs that addressed the need to help each other to excel. Mentoring programs in which older Canadian youth who have been here much longer or who were born here could partner with newcomers and help them adjust, or buddy programs in which youth of their own age who spoke their language could be paired with them for friendship's sake were seen as particularly useful. Regular and summer recreational programs and camps were praised as opportunities for such structured and unstructured interaction.

They also spoke of the need for programs that would explain their culture to Canadians, and Canadian ways to them. Without this knowledge of each other, without a knowledge of the diversity in their communities, they did not see much prospect of what we would call social cohesion.

Beyond this, they spoke of the need to combat racism among themselves. They encountered incidents of one group bullying another, of one group racializing another, and of violence as the inevitable but inexcusable outcome. Children and youth should be safe at school and on playgrounds, on streets and in malls, they said. But they felt that they often were not safe, and that this lack of safety was linked to the adult world's failure to provide opportunities for young newcomers to become part of an inclusive whole. Instead this exacerbated existing divisions among them, some inherited from parents, some newly acquired as they learned the pecking order of the schoolyard.

They indicated that integrative programs among youth are important, as are traditional ones. Sports such as soccer, as well as football, cricket, baseball, field hockey, and ice hockey, may be a source of increasing interaction among all youth, as will chess, music, and dance. Drop-in centres and other meeting places offering homework clubs and other after-school activities are loci of integration when they are well designed, culturally sensitive, and age appropriate in their programming.

Youth in the Community: Schools and Education

Respectful inclusion begins with a proper assessment of students' level of achievement, independent of their level of expertise in

English. The researchers heard immigrant youth saying that courses in academic subjects are too easily watered down when they are designed for newcomer youth who speak other languages. Schools need to meet the challenge of academically appropriate education for students whose language skills need improvement. Where linguistic differences are those of dialect rather than of language, speakers of other dialects should be welcomed into programs well designed for them. It is not only speakers of other than standard English who need support in the structure of traditional English grammar and syntax: many Canadian-born students would also profit from such instruction. If assignment to specific types of English classes were based on good placement tests, as assignment to particular French classes in universities commonly is, the classes would likely be far more mixed in student background than they are currently.

Further to the issue of language, where numbers warrant it, students' first languages should be taught so that they may continue to increase in their level of analysis, the sophistication of which is linked to their ability to manipulate language. As long as we are a nation of immigrants, heritage language classes are a necessity, not a luxury, if we want to make the most of the brainpower of new Canadian youth.

Inclusion also means assisting all students and staff to value the diversity that newcomers add to Canadian society. This can be done partly through curriculum, but it can also be achieved when interaction takes place on an equal footing among students, staff, and parents. The best schools are the ones that can accomplish this, rather than relegating newcomer services to the fringes, where they are offered "as time, money, and space permit."

While education was just one of the service domains targeted by the researchers, for the youth being interviewed, it was the only real focus. Education is the institution that enables them to integrate successfully into the Canadian mainstream, which is their parents' dream for them. Again and again we heard them argue for ESL as a respected academic approach, with rich content to support students' development and gifted teachers who will expect much of them. The Council of Agencies Serving South Asians (CASSA), for example, concluded that ESL classes need to be flexible, graduated in level, and of a high quality to integrate students into their subject areas at the level of sophistication they need for their academic work rather than the current "same size fits all" structure.

And while the ESL and heritage language teachers are often the ones to be recruited from among newer communities, it is not only these teachers (much less only the maintenance or custodial staff) who should represent the diversity in their schools. Teachers in all disciplines and staff at all levels should together reflect the community, so the newcomers can believe it is their school too.

Boards should have policies requiring schools to offer opportunities for immigrant parents to learn about the educational content and methods of their children's teachers, and to hear explicit discussions of Canadian understandings of the teachers' role, the types of relationships between teachers and students, and the types of relationships that are fostered among students themselves. This will be easier for schools to undertake if they have close working relationships with professionals from the communities they serve, as well as, ideally, teachers recruited from those groups. In addition, every school should have a place where family members are genuinely welcomed and assisted to fit in; just as newcomer youth need to be taught about Canadian culture and Canadian youth, so do their parents, which will then ease the school's task of assisting their children's integration.

The schools and their teachers need to know their students' experiences, including their educational traditions, migration, and educational experiences. Students who have suffered family separation, who have witnessed or experienced traumatic events, or who have had their education interrupted for protracted periods need to be known as youth with unusual challenges. They may have done a superb job of overcoming many of them, but the usefulness of the school to their continued growth may well be linked to the understanding it has of these youth.

The curriculum received special attention far beyond the issues of language instruction and ESL streaming. Students wanted the curriculum to be more broadly inclusive in two ways: First, they want their classmates to learn more about the world beyond Canada, so that they will understand that global diversity is the source of their local community's diversity. In this vein, they want to have their particular countries of origin presented in an accurate and contemporary way to their fellow students, including the ways in which daily life is experienced there. Historical representations that are no longer true or summaries of foreign wars are not what they consider helpful. Second, they want fair inclusion in Canadian historical accounts and their compatriots to be given appropriate places in Canadian history. They would like to have their contributions and those of others from their homelands presented in educational media so that all students may have a better idea of how the nation was built. They are keen to dispel any lingering notions of Canada as the work of only two groups, with others tolerated in later years.

Beyond the curriculum, other services that schools can provide received much attention. The current Settlement Education Partnership in Toronto (the SEPT program) was the envy of many students from other places, as they realized that some newcomers had the advantage of settlement workers in their schools. It seemed to them such a very logical approach that they wondered why the program was not available everywhere and for all newcomers. Settlement workers as catalysts for improvement in their education, as bridges between them and the mainstream youth and teachers, and as integrators of their parents into the school system was a goal for the educational system to consider worth striving for. When high schools, colleges, and universities have foreign exchange students or foreign visa students, they usually have a special program to welcome and assist them throughout their stay. But new students (and their families) arriving from those same countries as immigrants usually have no such welcome or supportive services available to them.

Youth in the Community: Services for Youth

Youth in these studies noted that both schools and community centres serving youth should partner to ensure that no community or neighbourhood is without a place for youth to seek formal and informal assistance. There should be drop-in centres with activities for youth as well as centres with after-school programs that provide homework clubs and recreational opportunities under the guidance of an integrated community family council.

The community centres serve newcomer youth best when they provide information for all family members, particularly about access to all services in the community, plus how and when to utilize them and why. In addition, community centres need to become community action centres, with information and advocacy for housing, health, employment, and legal services, including information (in a variety of languages or with adequate translation) on where these services can be found.

In particular, given the economic stress that so many families new to Canada experience, there is a need to provide youth with information about the services and opportunities available for obtaining appropriate employment. Youth who need to support or supplement the family income need information and assistance in learning how they can continue with their education while they are employed, and how to gauge the best combinations of work and study. As the CERIS report indicated, many male youth and some females requested greater assistance in attaining meaningful employment. Like other young Canadians, they need jobs they can thrive in, employers who will teach them skills, and wages that are fair. As well, given that young newcomer males reported greater difficulty in finding employment than their female cohorts, it seems that males need assistance with training skills and employment opportunities.

Mainstream service providers, like the schools discussed before, need to integrate culturally appropriate practices in their organizations and institutions, and include culturally diverse staff. This needs to occur at many levels, not just the lowest, thus making the health and social service agencies genuinely representative of and more insightful about the communities they serve. Youth argued persuasively for the provision of services such as information on health, family planning, and substance abuse in the community centres where youth hang out.

They also want their own ethno-specific communities to have youth support programs, especially ones that enable them to work on cultural activities and events. Such programs will strengthen their identities, their ties with their own compatriot youth, and their self-confidence in showing the larger society what they can do.

CONCLUSION: OVERVIEW AND IMPLICATIONS OF THE RESEARCH

Youth and Their Ideological Representations: Racism, the Media, and the Police

The newcomer youth were concerned about racism. As many newcomers to Canada now arrive from countries populated by "visible minorities," they find their skin colour an issue, usually for the first time in their lives. Being "seen as a member of a different race" is not a pleasant experience, and they argued strongly for more and better public education at all levels to eliminate such racialization, and for zero tolerance for violence based on skin colour.

To combat hurtful stereotypes, racial and otherwise, the youth discussed the media as institutions of great power. They were well aware of some good efforts made in print and broadcast media and wanted more of them. More precisely, they wanted a focus on youth of all backgrounds in the positive stories being circulated. They were aware of stories and images that seemed to them unfair and likely to perpetuate old stereotypes. A number of groups said the police are likely to "over-police" males of certain ethno-racial groups, thus reinforcing the police's impression that these groups are indeed the troublemakers in the community. While youth regarded this as racist, it is interesting that it was not linked to any one skin colour, as various groups of black-, white-, and brown-skinned youth believed they were victimized by this racism, while other groups of similarly black-, white-, and brown-skinned youth did not. Clearly the link is with a combination of colour and ethnicity, and reinforced by gender.

Efforts to mitigate these problems must include ways to decrease the prejudicial attitudes that confront newcomers. Both policy-making measures and educational strategies are needed to help newcomer youth deal with the various settlement difficulties and the discrimination they often encounter. We must note as well that media representation, discrimination, and racism loom even larger given the shifting climate of public discourse after the tragic events of September 11, 2001, particularly for immigrant and refugee students who follow the Muslim faith or come from Arab or Middle Eastern backgrounds. Basic issues of education on immigrant and refugee rights and ethnic and religious tolerance must now receive even greater attention and a corresponding commitment of material resources within the school system, the media, and the public political sphere.

Principal Policy Themes

In summary, we suggest four principal elements in successful settlement of newcomer youth that were revealed consistently by all the research initiatives in this collective effort:

- the important role of schools and the necessity of strong academic support for both individuals and groups
- the necessity of broad support for family and community involvement in education
- the need for systemic efforts at the societal level to improve the employment opportunities of new Canadians, both adult and youth, and to reduce the risk of poverty for immigrant and refugee families
- the importance of cross-cultural understanding and respect for ethno-racial identities developed in a clear framework of anti-discrimination and anti-racism

PERSPECTIVES FOR FUTURE RESEARCH

There are a variety of theoretical frameworks we can use to conceptualize and synthesize the various factors that encourage or hinder the successful settlement of newcomer youth. The four that are most directly relevant to the research summarized and interpreted in this book are the following.

The human ecology framework, as outlined earlier in this chapter (Bronfenbrenner, 1979), emphasizes that youth live in families, located in communities, which exist in a larger society and act collectively through and with institutions, both their own and those of the larger society.

The notion of social capital emphasizes that newcomer youth's success in settlement and their life opportunities in Canada depend on access to economic, social, and cultural resources through their families and communities, but not all immigrant families and communities possess these resources, or possess them to the same degree.

The concepts of marginalization or exclusion focus on barriers to successful settlement and life opportunities due to lack of access through family or community to larger networks, or access solely to networks of other youth who are marginalized and labelled as deviant.

The status of risk is that resulting from lack of access to social capital and from marginalization and exclusion, reducing the resilience of immigrant youth and their families and increasing their vulnerability to unsuccessful outcomes in education and the labour market. The Organization for Economic Co-operation and Development (OECD) defines children and youth "at risk" as "those failing in school and unsuccessful in making the transition to work and adult life and [who] as a consequence are unlikely to be able to make a full contribution to active society" (OECD, 1995, p. 21). The factors contributing to the development of risk for newcomer youth are multidimensional, interrelated, and dynamic; they are often grounded in socio-economic disadvantage and include such stressors as poverty, discrimination, and unemployment.

Another important concept discussed in the relevant literature is that of ethnic resilience. Researchers have began to examine why some youth, despite the presence of risk factors, remain resilient and develop into healthy adults (Blum, 1998; Garmezy, 1991). Beiser, Shik, and Curyk (1999), for example, suggest that family stability may help foster personal resilience, and Portes (1994) notes that immigrant families and communities have material and moral resources that can benefit their children in the process of successful adaptation or settlement. James (2000) identifies "immigrant drive" or "minority determination" as possible factors in the educational and occupational success of the children of foreign-born parents in Canada, factors that helped to overcome their parents' deficits with regard to finances and social and cultural capital.

The notion of social exclusion or its opposite, social inclusion, have also become increasingly important in research oriented toward social policy. During the last decade the European Economic Community has adopted the social exclusion framework as a major element of a pan-European policy perspective. More recently, the concepts of social exclusion and social inclusion have begun to receive attention from policy-makers in the Canadian federal government as well as concerned academics and progressive foundations. The notion of social inclusion (or cohesion) can be interpreted as a broadening of the concept of "social capital," and as a means of identifying the factors that mitigate risk, marginalization, and social exclusion. Freiler (2000), for example, identifies social inclusion as a process encouraging the development of talents, skills, and capacities necessary for children and youth to participate in the social and economic mainstream of community life.

Other scholars examine the prospect of successful outcomes for youth in terms of life opportunities by linking the notions of social capital or social inclusion with the tension between factors of risk and marginalization in terms of structures on the one hand, and the role of individual choices or agency on the other. Raffo and Reeves (2000), for example, present a theoretical approach in which youth's social capital is individualized within their interactions with peers and significant others; youth's life choices are therefore shaped but not determined by social structures and are mediated by individual agency. Both Anisef (2000) and James (2000) present a similar perspective, concluding from their research on the experiences of first-generation Canadians that the educational and employment outcomes of youth born to families of immigrants in Canada are shaped by social structures (factors of risk, marginalization, or social exclusion) and by how they interpret their choices and shape their aspirations within these structures (individual agency).

Another research issue of enormous importance from a policy perspective is the development of an integrated service framework. The research summarized and interpreted in this book has revealed consistently that the settlement issues for newcomer youth are highly multidimensional and that as a consequence service delivery must be approached holistically and viewed as an integrated system. Such an approach is validated by other scholars investigating the general contemporary situation of youth, such as Shonert-Reichl (2000), who confirms the multidimensional nature of risk factors and concludes that an integrated service approach is therefore essential. Similarly, Wotherspoon and Schissel (2000) conclude that there is a need for an integrated approach to risk prevention in which schools work with parents and communities, and Dryfoos (1998) promotes the notion of full-service community schools integrating quality education with appropriate health and community services. These conclusions from academic research are completely consistent with the perspective of community-based service providers who stress the necessity of a holistic approach to services for immigrants and refugees including children and youth (Canadian Council for Refugees, 1998).

Along with the need for further quantitative and qualitative research on the conditions of newcomer youth, there is ample room for creative dialogue and cross-fertilization on the conceptual level among the proponents of various theoretical approaches to the socio-economic condition and life opportunities of youth in industrial society. The discussion of ethnic resilience, for example, might be developed further by linking it to the elements of risk, marginalization, or exclusion, which weaken resilience; social capital, which strengthens resilience; and social cohesion as an indication of successful outcomes in settlement. As well, the concept of the tension between (individual) agency and (social) structure provides a useful means for examining the unique conditions (based on factors such as ethnicity, race, cultural norms, and expectations of their ethno-racial community, and the socio-economic/cultural capital of their parents and communities) that particular groups of newcomer youth face without denying the importance of the general economic and social structural factors that shape the opportunities of all newcomers to Canada at any given time. Further examination of the concept of integrated services will also provide opportunities for academic researchers to support service providers with scientific validation of their concerns and to focus policy perspectives with appropriate input from practitioners.

As a final note regarding the development of integrated theoretical perspectives, we must keep in mind that newcomer youth face particular challenges as immigrants and refugees while also confronting changing socio-economic conditions and opportunities in Canadian society. Tyyska (2001) demonstrates convincingly that the age status of the young in Canada has become a factor of disadvantage (or risk, or marginalization, or social exclusion) along with related factors such as gender, poverty, and visible minority status. It has been estimated that 20 per cent of all Canadian children and youth are at risk of developing problems that may threaten their transition into a healthy and productive adulthood (Shonert-Reichl, 2000); at the same time, the proportion of immigrant youth among Canadian youth in general has increased to 26 per cent in just five years (Canadian Council on Social Development, 1998). As demonstrated by the research in this book, the social and economic indicators of risk are particularly high for newcomer youth. We must be aware, therefore, of the general barriers faced by newcomer youth as youth as well as the particular contradictions rooted in their status as children of immigrants and refugees. Nor can we forget that in comparison with middle-class and Canadian-born youth, newcomer youth are almost entirely dependent on government agencies or government-subsidized services for the "social capital" necessary for prospects of success in education and employment. Untangling and understanding the specific barriers faced by immigrant and refugee youth versus the generic obstacles faced by Canadian youth is therefore an additional and essential challenge in developing a theoretical understanding of the experiences of newcomer youth in Canada.

AFTERWORD

The success of these research projects in revealing the conditions, prospects, and challenges of the settlement of newcomer youth in Ontario has depended on the collaborative approach of the research partners. For that spirit of collaboration, we must express our most sincere appreciation. The roots of this collaboration lie in the commitment of all the research partners to listening to and valuing the voices of immigrant youth as well as those of their families and service providers. It is our most sincere hope that future research in the settlement of newcomer youth will continue to listen to these voices, and that analysis of their expressions will result in policies promoting the rapid and successful settlement and integration of newcomer youth and their families into a genuinely multicultural Canadian society.

REFERENCES

Abella, R.S. (1984). *Report of the Royal Commission on Equality in Employment*. Ottawa: Supply and Services Canada.

Abt, L.E., & Bellak, L. (1950). *Projective psychology*. New York: Alfred A. Knopf.

Achenbach, T.M. (1979). The child behavior profile: An empirically based system for assessing childrens' behavioral problems and competences. *International Journal of Mental Health*, 7, 24–42.

Achenbach, T.M, & Edelbrock, C. (1991). *Manual for the YSR*. Burlington: University of Vermont, Department of Psychiatry.

Adams, G.R., & Looft, W.R. (1977). Cultural change: Education and youth. *Adolescence*, 12, 137–150.

Advisory Committee on Immigrant and Refugee Issues. (1997). *Who Is Listening? The Impact of Immigration and Refugee Settlement on Toronto*. Toronto: Advisory Committee on Immigrant and Refugee Issues.

Agnew, V. (1993). Feminism and South Asian immigrant women in Canada. In M. Israel & N.K. Wagle (Eds.), *Ethnicity, Identity, Migration: The South Asian Context*. Toronto: University of Toronto Press.

Ainsah-Mensah, S.K. (1996). *In the web of racism: The African experience*. Toronto: Canadian Ghanaian Organization.

Alcock, J.E., Carment, D.W., & Sadava, S.W. (1988). *Textbook of social psychology*. Scarborough: Prentice-Hall Canada Inc.

Ali, M.N. (1995). *Needs assessment of high risk Somali youth in the west end of Ottawa.* Ottawa: Pinecrest-Queensway Health and Community Services.

Anderson, W.W., & Grant, R.W. (1987). *The new newcomers: Patterns of adjustment of West Indian children in Metropolitan Toronto schools.* Toronto: Canadian Scholars' Press.

Anisef, P. (1994). *Learning and sociological profiles of canadian high school students.* Lewiston, NY: Edwin Mellen Press.

————. (1998). Making the transition from school to employment. In National Forum on Health (Ed.), *Canada health action: Building on the legacy,* 1, 275–310, Determinants of Health: Children and youth. Sainte-Foy: Editions MultiMondes.

Anisef, P. (2000). Navigating the life course: school-to-work transitions in the 1990s. In P. Anisef, P. Axelrod, E. Baichman-Anisef, C. James & A.H.Turrittin (Eds.), *Opportunity and uncertainty: The life course experiences of the class of '73.* Toronto: University of Toronto Press.

Anisef, P., & Bunch, M. (1994). *Learning and sociological profiles of Canadian high school students, an overview of 15 to 18 year olds and the educational policy implications for dropouts, exceptional students, employed students and Native youth.* Lewiston, NY: The Edwin Mellen Press.

Anisef, P., & Kilbride, K.M. (2001). *The needs of newcomer youth and emerging best practices to meet those needs.* Toronto: Joint Centre of Excellence for Research on Immigration and Settlement, Toronto (CERIS).

Anisef, P., & Okihiro, N. (1982). *Winners and losers.* Toronto: Butterworths.

Arora, A., & Mutta, B. (1997). *Health project for South Asian seniors.* Toronto: CASSA, Punjabi Community Health Centre, and South Asian Women's Centre.

Atkinson, D.R., Morten, G., & Sue, D.W. (1993). *Counseling American minorities: A cross cultural perspective.* Dubuque: Brown and Benchmark.

Bannerji, H. (Ed.). (1993). *Returning the gaze: Essays on racism, feminism and politics.* Toronto: Sister Vision Press.

Barankin, T., Konstantareas, M., & deBosset, F. (1989). Adaptation of recent Soviet Jewish immigrants and their children to Toronto. *Canadian Journal of Psychiatry*, 34, 512–518.

Basran, G.S. (1993). Indo-Canadian families historical constraints and contemporary contradictions. *Journal of Comparative Family Studies*, 24(3) (Autumn 1993), 339–352.

Basran, G. S., & Zong, L. (1998). Devaluation of foreign credentials as perceived by visible minority professional immigrants. *Canadian Ethnic Studies*, 30(3), 7–23.

Beiser, M. (1999). *Strangers at the gate: The "boat people's" first ten years in Canada*. Toronto: University of Toronto Press.

Beiser, M., Shik, A., & Curyk, M. (1999). *New Canadian children and youth study: Literature review*. Toronto: Joint Centre of Excellence for Research on Immigration and Settlement, Toronto (CERIS). <http://ceris.metropolis.net>

Berry, J.W. (1997). Immigration, acculturation, and adaptation. *Applied Psychology Review*, 46, 5–68.

Berry, J.W., Kim, U., Minde, T., & Mok, D. (1987). Comparative studies of acculturation stress. *International Migration Review*, 21, 491–511.

Bertrand, J. (1998). Enriching the preschool experiences of children. In National Forum on Health (Ed.), *Canada health action: Building on the legacy*, 1, 3–46, Determinants of health: Children and youth. Sainte-Foy: Editions MultiMondes.

Beserve, C. (1976). Adjustment problems of West Indian children in Britain and Canada: A perspective and review of some findings. In V. D'Oyley & H. Silverman (Eds.), *Black students in urban Canada*, TESL Talk, Jan. 1976. Toronto: Ontario Ministry of Culture and Recreation.

Blum, R.W. (1998). Healthy youth development as a model for youth health promotion. *Journal of Adolescent Health*, 22, 368–375.

Borkman, T.J., & Schubert, M. (1994). Participatory action research as a strategy for studying self-help groups internationally. *Prevention in Human Services*, 11, 45–68.

Bourne, L.S. (1999). *Migration, immigration and social sustainability: The recent Toronto experience in comparative context*. CERIS Working Paper. Toronto: Joint Centre of Excellence for Research on Immigration and Settlement, Toronto (CERIS).

Brathwaite, K., & James, C.E. (1996). *Educating African Canadians.* Toronto: James Lorimer & Co. Ltd.

Bronfenbrenner, U. (1979). *The ecology of human development.* Cambridge: Harvard University Press.

Buchignani, N. (1987). Research on South Asians in Canada: Retrospect and prospects. In M. Israel (Ed.), *The South Asian diaspora in Canada.* Toronto: Multicultural History Society of Ontario.

Buchignani, N., & Indra, D. (1985). *Continuous journey: A social history of South Asians in Canada.* Toronto: McClelland & Stewart.

Burke, P. (1991). Identity process and social stress. *American Sociological Review,* 56, 836–849.

Canadian Council for Refugees (CCR). (1998). *Best settlement practices: Settlement services for refugees and immigrants in Canada.* Ottawa: CCR.

Canadian Council on Social Development (CCSD). (1998a). *Youth at work in Canada: A research report.* Ottawa: CCSD.

———. (1998b). *The progress of Canada's children: Focus on youth.* Ottawa: CCSD.

———. (2000). *Immigrant youth in Canada: A research report.* Ottawa: CCSD.

Canadian Institute for Advanced Research and Centre for Studies of Children at Risk. (1995). *Healthy children, healthy communities: A compendium of approaches from across Canada.* Toronto: Canadian Institute for Advanced Research and Centre for Studies of Children at Risk.

Canadian Task Force on Mental Health Issues Affecting Immigrants and Refugees. (1988). *Review of the literature on migrant mental health.* Ottawa: Health and Welfare Canada.

Canadian Youth Foundation (CYF). (1995). *Youth employment: Canada's rite of passage.* Ottawa: CYF.

———. (1996). *Towards improved employment practices for youth.* Ottawa: CYF.

———. (1997). *The corporate council on youth in the economy: Backgrounder.* Ottawa: CYF.

————. (1999). *Taking on youth unemployment: Canada's business venture for the new millennium.* Ottawa: CYF.

Caplan N., Whitmore, J.K., & Choy, M.H. (1989). *The boat people and achievement in America: A study of family life, hard work, and cultural values.* Ann Arbor: University of Michigan Press.

Carey, E. (1998). Minorities set to be majority. *Toronto Star* (June 7, 1998), A6.

Cheng, M., & Yau, M. (1997). *The 1997 every secondary student survey, report no. 230.* Toronto: Research and Assessment Department, Toronto Board of Education.

Chesler, M.A. (1991). Participatory action research with self-help groups: An alternative paradigm for inquiry and action. *American Journal of Community Psychology,* 19, 757–768.

Chiu, Y.W., & Ring, J.M. (1998). Chinese and Vietnamese immigrant adolescents under pressure: Identifying stressors and interventions. *Professional Psychology: Research and Practice,* 29, 444–449.

Church, A.T. (1982). Sojourner adjustment. *Psychological Bulletin,* 91, 540–572.

Citizenship and Immigration Canada (CIC). (1998). *Intended destination data (1993–1998).* Ottawa: Citizenship and Immigration Canada.

————. (1999). *Canada commits to a dynamic immigration program in 2000.* Ottawa: Citizenship and Immigration Canada. <http://www.cicnet.ci.gc.ca>

City of Toronto. (1999). *Toronto youth profile,* Vols. 1 and 2. Toronto: Social Development and Administration Division and the Community and Neighbourhood Services Department, City of Toronto.

Clifford, A. (1999). *Food for thought: The state of school breakfast programs.* Newsletter (Spring 1999). Ottawa: Social Planning Council of Ottawa-Carleton.

Coalition of Agencies Serving South Asians. (1994). The Need for Community Services: A study of the South Asian community in Metropolitan Toronto. No. 124. Toronto: Coalition of Agencies serving South Asians.

Coalition of Inquiry on Equity in Employment (1984). Report of the Commission on Equality in Employment. Rosalie Silberman Abella,

Commissioner. Ottawa: Canadian Government Publishing Centre, Supply and Services Canada.

Coelho, E. (1988). *Caribbean students in Canadian schools*. Toronto: Carib-Can Publishers.

Coleman, J. (1988). Social capital in the creation of human capital. *American Journal of Sociology*, 94 (Supplement), 95–120.

Council of Agencies Serving South Asians (CASSA). (1998). Exploring organizational structures of South Asian agencies providing direct services. Toronto: CASSA.

———. (1999). South Asian Community Legal Initiative (SALCI). Toronto: CASSA.

Cummins, J. (1997). Minority status and schooling in Canada. *Anthropology and Education Quarterly*, 28(3), 411–430.

Dei, G.J.S. (1995). Integrative anti-racism: Intersection of race, class and gender. *Race, Gender and Class*, 2(3), 11–30.

———. (1996). *Anti-racism education: Theory and practice*. Halifax: Fernwood Books.

Dei, G.J.S., Holmes, L., Mazzuca, J., McIsaac, E., & Campbell, R. (1995). *Drop out or push out? The dynamics of Black students' disengagement from school*. Final report submitted to the Ontario Ministry of Education. Toronto: Ontario Ministry of Education.

Dei, G.J.S., Mazzuca, J., McIsaac, E., & Zine, J. (1997). *Reconstructing "drop-out": A critical ethnography of the dynamics of Black students' disengagement from school*. Toronto: University of Toronto Press.

Denetto, S. (1994). *West end youth needs assessment*. Ottawa: Pinecrest-Queensway Health and Community Services.

Desai, S. (1998). But you are different: In conversation with a friend. In C. James & A. Shadd (Eds.), *Talking about difference: Encounters in culture, language and identity*, 2nd ed. Toronto: Between the Lines.

Deyhle, D. (1995). Navajo youth and Anglo racism: Cultural integrity and resistance. *Harvard Educational Review*, 65(3), 403–445.

Doucet, M. (1999). *Toronto in transition: Demographic change in the late twentieth century*. CERIS Working Paper Series. Toronto: Joint Centre of Excellence for Research on Immigration and Settlement, Toronto (CERIS).

Dryfoos, J.G. 1998. *Safe passage: Making it through adolescence in a risky society*. New York: Oxford University Press.

Early, M., & Hooper, H. (1989). The Vancouver School Board language and content project. In J.H. Esling, *Multicultural education and policy: ESL in the 1990s*. Toronto: OISE Press.

Edwards, V. (1986). *Language in a Black community*. Clevedon: Multilingual Matters Ltd.

Elkin, F., & Handel, G. (1972). *The child and society: The process of socialization*. New York: Random House.

Erikson, E.H. (1968). *Identity, youth and crisis*. New York: Norton.

Fern, E. (2001). *Advanced focus group research*. Thousand Oaks: Sage.

Foster, C. (1996). *A place called heaven: The meaning of being Black in Canada*. Toronto: HarperCollins Publishers Ltd.

Four-Level Working Group. (1992). *Towards a new beginning, the report and action plan of the Four-Level Government/African Canadian Community Work Group*. Toronto: Four-Level Working Group.

Fralick, P., & Hyndman, B. (1998). Strategies to promote the optimal development of Canada's Youth. In National Forum on Health (Ed.), *Canada Health Action: Building on the Legacy*, 1, 311–356, Determinants of health: Children and youth. Sainte-Foy: Editions MultiMondes.

Freiler, C. (2000). *Social inclusion as a focus of well-being for children and families*. A paper prepared for the Advisory Committee, Children's Agenda Program. Toronto: Laidlaw Foundation.

Furnham, A., & Bochner, S. (1986). *Culture shock: Psychological reactions to unfamiliar environments*. London: Methuen.

Gaetz, S., O'Grady, W., & Vaillancourt, B. (1999). *Making money: The Shout Clinic report on homeless youth and employment*. Toronto: Central Toronto Community Health Centres.

Garmezy, N. (1991). Resiliency and vulnerability to adverse development outcomes associated with poverty. *American Behaviour of Science*, 34, 416–430.

Gaventa, J. (1993). The powerful, the powerless, and the experts: Knowledge struggles in an information age. In P. Park, M. Brydon-Miller, B. Hall, & T. Jackson (Eds.), *Voices of change: Participatory research in the United States and Canada* (pp. 21–40). Westport: Bergen and Garvey.

George, U., & Michalski, J.H. (1996). *A snapshot of service delivery in organizations serving immigrants: Final report.* Toronto: Centre for Applied Social Research, Faculty of Social Work, University of Toronto.

Gibson, M. (1997). Complicating the immigrant/involuntary minority typology. *Anthropology and Education Quarterly*, 28(3), 431–454.

Go, A., Inksater, K., & Lee, P. (1996). *Making the road by walking it: A workbook for re-thinking settlement.* Toronto: CultureLink.

Gold, S.J. (1992). *Refugee communities: A comparative field study.* Newbury Park: Sage Publications.

Goodenow, C., & Espin, O.M. (1993). Identity choices in immigrant adolescent females. *Adolescence*, 28, 173–184.

Gottlieb, B. (1998). Strategies to promote the optimal development of Canada's youth. In National Forum on Health (Ed.), *Canada health action: Building on the legacy*, 1, 235–276, Determinants of health: Children and youth. Sainte-Foy: Editions MultiMondes.

Green, A., & Green, D. (1995). Canadian immigration policy: The effectiveness of the point system and other instruments. *Canadian Journal of Economics*, 28(4b), 1006–1041.

Greenbaun, T. (1999). *Moderating focus groups: A practical guide for group facilitation.* Thousand Oaks: Sage.

Heller, A., Rafman, S., Zvagulis, I., & Pless, I.B. (1985). Birth defects and psychosocial adjustment. *American Journal of Diseases of Children*, 139, 257–263.

Helm, B., & Warren, W. (1998). Teenagers talk about cultural heritage and family life. *Transition*, 28(3), 4–7. Ottawa: The Vanier Institute of the Family.

Helson, H. (1947). Adaptation level as frame of reference for prediction of psychophysical data. *American Journal of Psychology*, Vol. 60, 1–29.

Henry, F. (1983). Some problems of South Asians' adaptation in Toronto. In G. Kurian and R. P. Srivastava (Eds.), *Overseas Indians: A study in adaptation.* Calgary: University of Calgary.

Henry, F., & Ginzberg, E. (1985). *Who gets the work: A test of racial discrimination in Toronto.* Toronto: Urban Alliance on Race Relations and Social Planning Council of Metro Toronto.

Henry, F., Tator, C., Mattis, W., & Rees, T. (2000). *The colour of democracy: Racism in Canadian society.* Toronto: Harcourt Brace.

Hicks, R., Lalonde, R.N., & Pepler, D. (1993). Psychosocial considerations in the mental health of immigrant and refugee children. *The Canadian Journal of Community Mental Health,* 12(3), 70–87.

Hiebert, D. (1998). *Immigrant experiences in Greater Vancouver: Focus group narratives.* Vancouver: Research on Immigration and Integration in the Metropolis (RIIM).

Hill Collins, P. (1990). *Black feminist thought: Knowledge, consciousness, and the politics of empowerment.* Perspectives on gender, Vol. 2. New York: Routledge.

Huang, L.N. (1989). Southeast Asian refugee children and adolescents. In J.T. Gibbs and L.N. Huang (Eds.), *The children of colour.* San Francisco: Jossey-Bass.

Human Resources Development Canada (HRDC). (1995). *High school may not be enough: An analysis of results from the school leavers follow-up survey.* Ottawa: Applied Research Branch, HRDC.

———. (1996). *Growing up in Canada: A detailed portrait of children and young people.* Ottawa: Applied Research Branch, HRDC.

———. (1999). *The Ottawa labour market semi-annual review, January-June 1999.* Ottawa: Applied Research Branch, HRDC.

Ima, K., & Hohm, C. (1991). Child maltreatment among Asian and Pacific Island refugees and immigrants. *Journal of Interpersonal Violence,* 6, 267–285.

Israel, M. & Wagle, N.K. (Eds.), (1993). *Ethnicity, identity, migration: The South Asian context.* Toronto: University of Toronto Press.

James, C. (1990). *Making it: Black youth, racism and career aspirations in a big city.* Oakville: Mosaic Press.

———. (1995a). Multicultural and anti-racism education in the Canadian context. *Race, gender and class,* 2(3), 31–48.

———. (1995b). *Seeing ourselves.* Toronto: Thompson Educational Press.

———. (Ed.). (1996). *Perspectives on racism and the human service sector: A case for change.* Toronto: University of Toronto Press.

————. (2000). The experiences of first generation Canadians. In P. Anisef, P. Axelrod, E. Baichman-Anisef, C. James, & A.H. Turritin (Eds.), *Opportunity and uncertainty: The life course experiences of the class of '73*. Toronto: University of Toronto Press.

James, C.E., & Brathwaite, K. (1996). The education of African Canadians: Issues, contexts, expectations. In K. Brathwaite & C.E. James (Eds.), *Educating African Canadians*. Toronto: James Lorimer & Co. Ltd.

James, D.C. (1997). Coping with a new society: The unique psychosocial problems of immigrant youth. *Journal of School Health*, 67(3), 98–102.

Janzen, R. (1992). *Working for work: A program evaluation*. Unpublished master's thesis. Waterloo, Ontario: Wilfrid Laurier University.

Janzen, R., Ochocka, J., & Sundar, P. (2001). *Study on parenting issues of newcomer families in Ontario: Waterloo Region findings*. Kitchener: Centre for Research and Education in Human Services (CREHS).

Janzen, R., Ochocka, J., & Wing Sang Wong, V. (1998). *Dignity and opportunity: Assessing the economic contribution of foreign-trained newcomers*. Kitchener: Centre for Research and Education in Human Services (CREHS).

Johnson, L., & Peters, S. (1994). Vision of reform and educational policy implications. In P. Anisef (Ed.), *Learning and sociological profiles of Canadian high school students* (pp. 121–130). Lewiston, NY: Edwin Mellen Press.

Kasozi, A.B.K. (1986). *The integration of Black African immigrants in Canadian society: A case study of Toronto CMA*. Toronto: Canadian-African Newcomer Aid Centre of Toronto.

Kilbride, K.M. (1999). *A review of the literature on the human, social and cultural capital of immigrant children and their families with implications for teacher education*. CERIS Working Papers Series. Toronto: Joint Centre of Excellence for Research on Immigration and Settlement, Toronto (CERIS).

Kilbride, K.M., & Anisef, P. (2001). *To build on hope: Overcoming the challenges facing newcomer youth at risk in Ontario*. Toronto: The Ontario Administration of Settlement and Integration Services.

Kilbride, K.M., & D'Arcangelo, L. (2000). *Meeting immigrant community college students' needs: A case study of one GTA college campus*. Paper presented at the Fourth National Metropolis Conference.

Toronto: Joint Centre of Excellence for Research on Immigration and Settlement, Toronto (CERIS).

Kirby, S., & McKenna, K. (1989). *Experience, research, social change: Methods from the margins*. Toronto: Garamond Press.

Kohli, R., Desai, S., & Mukherjee, A. (1995). *A case for an integrated anti-racism framework*. Unpublished paper, Toronto.

Kurian, G. (1983). Socialization of South Asian immigrant youth. In G. Ghosh & R. Kanungo (Eds.) *South Asian Canadians: Current issues in the politics of culture*. New Dehli: Shastri Indo-Canadian Institute.

———. (1991). South Asians in Canada. *International Migration Review*, 29(3) 421–432.

Kurian, G., & Ghosh, R. (1983). Child-rearing in transition in Indian immigrant families in Canada. In G. Kurian & R.P. Srivastava (Eds.), *Overseas Indians: A study in adaptation* (pp. 128–138). New Delhi: Vikas Publishers.

Kurian, G., & Srivastava, R.P. (Eds.). (1983). *Overseas Indians: A study in adaptation*. New Delhi: Vikas Publishers.

Lam, L. (1994). Immigrant Students. In P. Anisef (Ed.), *Learning and sociological profiles of Canadian high school students* (pp. 122–130). Lewiston, NY: Edwin Mellen Press.

Lewin, K. (1946). Action research and minority problems. *Journal of Social Issues*, 2, 34–46

Lewis, S. (1992). *Report on race relations to Premier Bob Rae/The Stephen Lewis report*. Toronto: Government of Ontario.

Li, P. (1999). *Race and ethnic relations in Canada*. Don Mills: Oxford University Press.

Li, P., & Bolaria, B.S. (Eds.). (1983). *Racial minorities in multicultural Canada*. Toronto: Garamond Press.

Lincoln, Y.S., & Guba, E.G. (1985). *Naturalistic inquiry*. Newbury Park: Sage.

Lippi-Green, R. (1998). *English with an accent*. New York: Routledge.

Lipsitz, J.S. (1979). Adolescent development. *Children Today*, 8, 2–29.

London, C. (1990). Educating young new immigrants: How can the United States cope? *International Journal of Adolescence and Youth*, 2, 81–100.

Lord, J., & Hutchison, P. (1993). The process of empowerment: Implications for theory and practice. *Canadian Journal of Community Mental Health*, 12(1), 5–22

Lorde, A. (1984). *Sister outsider*. Freedom: The Crossing Press.

Machover, K. (1949). *Personality projection in the drawing of the human figure: A method of personality investigation.* Springfield: Charles Thomas.

Madriz, E. (2000). Focus groups in feminist research. In N.K.Denzin & Y.S. Lincoln (Eds.), *Handbook of qualitative research*, 2nd ed. (pp. 835–850). Thousand Oaks: Sage.

Marquardt, R. (1998). *Enter at your own risk: Canadian youth and the labour market.* Toronto: Between the Lines.

Matarazzo, J.D. (1972).*Wechsler's Measurement and appraisal of adult intelligence.* Baltimore: Williams & Wilkins.

McCaskell, T. (1993). *Presentation to the community forum sponsored by The Metropolitan Toronto Council Committee to Combat Hate Group Activity.* Toronto: Municipality of Metropolitan Toronto.

McDonnell, M., & Hill, P. (1993). *Newcomers in American schools: Meeting the educational needs of immigrant youth.* Santa Monica: RAND Publications.

McElhaney, M. (1969). *Assessment of the HFDT*. New York: Bruner/Mazel

McIntosh, P. (1989). White privilege: Unpacking the invisible knapsack. *Peace and Freedom* (July–August), 10–12.

Meneses, A. (1999). *Halton Multicultural Council's Settlement Services needs assessment report.* Burlington: Halton Multicultural Services

Ministry of Citizenship. (1989). *Visible minority youth project*. Toronto: Government of Ontario.

Mwarigha, M.S. (1991). *Project on the African communities in Toronto: A demographic profile.* Toronto: Metro Working Group on Ethno-racial Access to Services.

———. (1997). The impact of cutbacks and restructuring on the NGO sector and the delivery of immigrant services. In *Proceedings of the First Metropolis National Conference on Immigration.* Edmonton: Prairie Centre of Excellence for Research on Immigration and Integration (PCERII).

Myers, D.A. (1986). *Psychology.* New York: Worth Publishers.

———. (1987). *Social psychology.* New York: McGraw-Hill.

Naidoo, J.C. (1985). A cultural perspective on the adjustment of South Asian Women in Canada. In I.R. Lacqunes & Y.H. Poortinga (Eds.) *From a different perspective: Studies of behaviour across cultures.* Lisse, The Netherlands: Swets and Zeitlinger.

Naidoo, J.C., & Davis, J.C. (1988). Canadian South Asian women in transition: A dualistic view of life. *Journal of Comparative Family Studies, Special Issue in India and North America,* 19(2) (Summer), 11–27.

Nelson, G., Ochocka, J., Griffin, K., & Lord, J. (1998). "Nothing about me, without me": Participatory action research with self-help/mutual aid organizations for psychiatric consumer/survivors. *American Journal of Community Psychology,* 26, 881–912

North York Board of Education. (1988). *ESL & SESD programs and services: Report on community involvement initiatives* (Record 5974). North York: North York Board of Education.

Ochocka, J., Janzen, R., Anisef, P., & Kilbride, K.M. (2001). *Study on parenting issues of newcomer families in Ontario.* Kitchener: Centre for Research and Education in Human Services (CREHS) and Toronto: Joint Centre of Excellence for Research on Immigration and Settlement (CERIS).

Ochocka, J., Janzen, R., & Nelson, G. (2002). Sharing power and knowledge: Professional and mental health consumer/survivor researchers working together in a participatory action research project. *Psychiatric Rehabilitation Journal* 25(4), 379–387.

OCSSPP Visible Minority Advisory Working Group. (1994). *Report on visible minority equity and access to health and social services in Ottawa-Carleton.* Presented to District Health Council, Ministry of Community and Social Services, Regional Municipality of Ottawa-Carleton, and United Way. Ottawa: Regional Municipality of Ottawa-Carleton.

Ogbu, J.U. (1978). *Minority education and caste.* New York: Academic Press.

Ogbu, J. U. & Matute-Bianchi, M. E. (1986). Understanding Sociocultural Factors: Knowledge, Identity, and School Adjustment. In California State Department of Education (Ed.), *Beyond Language: Social and Cultural Factors in Schooling Language Minority Students.* Los

Angeles: Evaluation, Dissemination and Assessment Center, California state University, Los Angeles.

Ontario Council of Agencies Serving Immigrants (OCASI). (1991). *Immigrant settlement counseling: A training guide.* Toronto: OCASI.

Opoku-Dapaah, E. (1993). *Directory of African community groups in Metro Toronto.* Toronto: York Lanes Press.

Organization for Economic Co-operation and Development (OECD). 1995. *Our children at risk.* London: OECD.

Ornstein, M. (1996). *Ethno-racial inequality in Metropolitan Toronto: Analysis of the 1991 census.* Toronto: Access and Equity Centre, Municipality of Metropolitan Toronto.

Ottawa Economic Development Corporation. (2000). *Ottawa's hidden workforce.* Ottawa: OEDC.

Park, P., Brydon-Miller, M., Hall, B., & Jackson, T. (Eds.). (1993). *Voices of change: Participatory research in the United States and Canada.* Westport: Bergen and Garvey.

Patton, M.Q. (1986). *Utilization-focused evaluation.* Beverly Hills, CA: Sage Publications.

———. (1990). *Qualitative evaluation and research methods,* 2nd ed. Newbury Park: Sage.

Pawiluk, N., Grizenko, N., Chan-Yip, A., Gantous, P., Mathew, J., & Nguyen, D. (1996). Acculturation style and psychological functioning in children of immigrants. *American Journal of Orthopsychiatry,* 66, 111–121.

Perkins, K., Pohlmann, J., & Brutten, S. (1988). A factor analysis of direct and indirect measures of English as a second language writing ability. *Educational and Psychological Measurement,* 48(4), 1111–1121.

Phinley, J.S., Lochner, B.T., & Murphy, R. (1990). Ethnic identity development and psychological adjustment in adolescence. In A.R. Stiffman & L.E. Davis (Eds.), *Ethnic issues in adolescent mental health.* Newbury Park: Sage.

Portes, A. (1994). Introduction: Immigration and its aftermath. *International Migration Review,* 28(4), 632–639.

Portes, A., & Zhou, M. (1993). The new second generation: Segmented assimilation and its variants. *American Academy of Political and Social Science,* 540, 74–96.

Raffo, C., & Reeves, M. (2000). Youth transitions and social exclusion: Developments in social capital theory. *Journal of Youth Studies*, 3(2), 147–166.

Reza-Rashti, G. (1994). Islamic identity and racism. *Orbit*, 25(2), 37–38. Toronto: Ontario Institute for Studies in Education, University of Toronto.

Richmond, T. (1995). *Numbers and needs: Identifying demographics and service needs of ethnoracial communities*. Toronto: CERIS Resource Library.

Richmond, T. (1996). *Effects of cutbacks on immigrant service agencies*. Toronto: City of Toronto Public Health Department.

Rivera-Sinclair, E. (1997). Acculturation/biculturalism and its relationship to adjustment in Cuban-Americans. *International Journal of Intercultural Relations*, 21, 379–391.

Riverdale Immigrant Women's Centre. (1993). *VAWPI focus groups study report*. Toronto: Riverdale Immigrant Women's Centre.

Rogers, D. (1985). *Adolescents and youth*. Englewood Cliffs: Prentice-Hall Inc.

Rosenthal, D.A., Demetriou, A., & Efklides, A. (1989). A cross-national study on the influence of culture on conflict between parents and adolescents. *International Society of the Study of Behavioural Development*, 12, 207–219.

Rousseau, C., Drapeau, A., & Corin, E. (1997). The influence of culture and context on the pre- and post-migration experience of school-aged refugees from Central America and Southeast Asia in Canada. *Social Science and Medicine*, 44, 1115–1127.

Rowe, W., Benett, S., & Atkinson, D.R. (1994). White racial identity models: A critique and Alternative Proposal. *The Counseling Psychologist*, 22, 129–146.

Royal Commission on Learning. (1994). *For the love of learning: Report of the Royal Commission on Learning*. Toronto: Publications Ontario.

Rumbaut, R. (1991). The agony of exile: A study of the migration and adaptation of Indochinese refugee adults and children. In F.L. Ahearn & J.L. Athey (Eds.), *Refugee children : Theory, research, and services* (pp. 53–91). Baltimore: Johns Hopkins University Press.

Runyan, D.K., Hunter, W.M., Socolar, R.R.S., et al. (1996). Children who prosper in unfavourable environments: The relationship to social capital. *Pediatrics*, 101(1), 37–41.

Saidulla, A. (1993). *South Asians: Issues, concerns and recommendations: Moving towards a barrier-free society*. Toronto: Ontario Anti-racism Secretariat, Ministry of Citizenship.

Samuda, R.J., & Kong, S.L. (1989). *Assessment and placement of minority students*. Toronto: C.J. Hogrefe.

Satzewich, V. (1993). *Deconstructing a nation: Immigration, multiculturalism and racism in '90s*. Halifax: Fernwood Publishing.

Seat, R. (1997). *The integration of immigrants into Canadian Society: A new experience from FSA Toronto*. Toronto: International Association for Public Participation—Participation in Turbulent Times.

Seat, R., & Richards, S. (1998). *Children at risk*. Toronto: Ontario Council of Agencies Serving Immigrants (OCASI).

Shakir, U. (1995). *Presenting at the Boundary: Wife assault in the South Asian community*. Toronto: Multicultural Coalition for Access to Family Services.

Shonert-Reichl, K.A., (2000, April 6–7). *Children and youth at risk: Some conceptual considerations*. A paper presented to the Pan-Canadian Education Research Agenda Symposium: "Children and Youth at Risk," Ottawa.

Siddique, M. (1977). Changing Family Patterns: A Comparative Analysis of Immigrant Indian and Pakistani Families of Saskatoon, Canada. *Journal of Comparative Family Studies*, 8(2, Summer), 179-200.

———. (1978). Social Structural Pressures to Change: A Case Study of the Immigrant Indian and Pakistani Community of Saskatoon, Canada. *Asian Profile*, 6 (1978), 231–47.

Smith, D. (1987). *The everyday world as problematic: A feminist sociology*. Toronto: University of Toronto Press.

Social Planning Council of Ottawa-Carleton. (1999). *Environmental scan: Final report, October 1999*. Ottawa: Ottawa-Carleton Training Board.

Social Planning Council of Ottawa-Carleton and United Way/Centraide Ottawa-Carleton. (1999). *A tale of two cities: Socio-demographic and economic trends in Ottawa-Carleton*. Ottawa: Social Planning Council of Ottawa-Carleton and United-Way/Centraide Ottawa-Carleton.

Solomon, P.R. (1992). *Black resistance in high school*. Albany: State University of New York Press.

Spigelblatt, L. (1999). *Between two worlds: Newcomer youth*. Newsletter (Spring 1999). Ottawa: Social Assistance Reform: Consequences and Outcomes in Ottawa-Carleton.

Srivastava, R.P. (1983). The evolution of adaptive strategies: East Indians in Canada. In G. Kurian & R.P. Srivastava (Eds.), *Overseas Indians: A study in adaptation* (pp. 30–40). New Delhi: Vikas Publishers.

Srivastava, A., & Ames, M. (1993). South Asian women's experience of gender, race and class in Canada. In M. Israel & N.K. Wagle (Eds.), *Ethnicity, identity, migration: The South Asian context*. Toronto: University of Toronto Press.

Stasiulius, D. (1990). Theorizing connections: Gender, race, ethnicity and class. In P. Li (Ed.), *Race and ethnic relations in Canada*. Toronto: Oxford University Press.

Statistics Canada. (1996). *Census nation tables*. Ottawa: Statistics Canada.

———. (1999). *Youth and the labour market (1998–99), labour force update*. Ottawa: Statistics Canada.

Steinhauer, P.D. (1998). Developing resiliency in children from disadvantaged populations. In National Forum on Health (Ed.), *Canada health action: Building on the legacy*, 1, 47–102, Determinants of health: Children and youth. Sainte-Foy: Editions MultiMondes.

Strauss, A.L., & Corbin, J. (1990). *Basics of qualitative research: Grounded theory procedures and techniques*. Newbury Park: Sage.

Stringer, E.T. (1996). *Action research: A handbook for practioners*. Thousand Oaks: Sage.

Task Force on Employment. (1999). *Investing in the community: An employment plan, final report*. Ottawa: Partners for Jobs in Ottawa-Carleton.

Tatum, B.D. (1992). Talking about race, learning about racism: The application of racial identity development theory in the classroom. *Harvard Educational Review*, 62(1) (Spring), 10–21.

Tatum, B.D. (1997). *Why are all the Black kids sitting together in the cafeteria? And other conversations about race.* New York: Basic Books.

Taylor, O.L. (1990). *Cross-cultural communication: An essential dimension of effective education.* The Mid-Atlantic Equity Center, The American University, Washington, DC.

Tonks, R., & Paranjpe, A. (1999). *Two sides of acculturation: Attitudes toward multiculturalism and national identity amongst immigrant and Canadian-born youth.* Paper presented at the Third National Metropolis Conference. Vancouver: Research on Immigration and Integration in the Metropolis (RIIM).

Torjman, S. (1999). *A labour force development strategy for Ottawa-Carleton.* Ottawa: The Caledon Institute of Social Policy and Partners for Jobs.

Toronto Board of Education. (1997). *Meeting the special needs of students in the Toronto Board of Education.* Toronto: Research and Assessment Department, Toronto Board of Education.

Trudgill, P. (1974). *Sociolinguistics: An introduction.* Harmondsworth : Penguin Books.

Tyyska, V. (2001). *Long and winding road: Adolescents and youth in Canada today.* Toronto: Canadian Scholars' Press Inc.

Urban Poverty Consortium of Waterloo Region. (2000). *Let's talk about poverty: Facts sheets #1 and #2.* Waterloo: Regional Municipality of Waterloo.

Vanier Institute of the Family. (1998). *Transition: Newcomer immigrant families adapting to life in Canada.* Ottawa: Vanier Institute of the Family.

Wadhwani, Z. (1999). *To be or not to be: Suicidal ideation in South Asian youth.* Master's thesis. Montreal: McGill University.

Wakil, S. Parvez, Siddique, C.M., & Wakil, F.A. (1981). Between Two Cultures: A Study in Socialization of Children of Immigrants. *Journal of Marriage and the Family* 43(4, Nov), 929–940.

Walker, W. (1999). Canadians healthier but stress hits young. *Toronto Star* (September 17, 1999), A1.

Weinfeld, M. (1996). *A preliminary stock-taking on immigration research in Canada: A synthetic overview of state-of-art reviews on immigration and immigrant integration in Canada from six disciplinary perspectives*. Paper prepared for the Metropolis Project. Ottawa: Department of Strategic Policy, Planning and Research and The Metropolis Project, Citizenship and Immigration Canada.

Westermeyer, J., & Her, C. (1996). Predictors of English fluency among Hmong refugees in Minnesota: A longitudinal study. *Cultural Diversity and Mental Health*, 2(2), 125–132.

Winks, R.W. (1997). *The Blacks in Canada: A history*. Montreal: McGill-Queen's University Press.

Wong, K.W. (1999). Acculturation, peer relations and delinquent behavior of Chinese-Canadian youth. *Adolescence*, 34, 107–119.

Wood, J.R. (1983). East Indians and Canada's new immigration policy. In G. Kurian & R.P. Srivastava (Eds.), *Overseas Indians: A study in adaptation* (pp. 30–40). New Delhi: Vikas Publishers.

Wotherspoon, T., and Schissel, B. (2000). *Risky business? "At-risk" designations and culturally diverse schooling*. A paper submitted to The Council of Ministers of Education Canada, Pan-Canadian Education Research Agenda.

Wyn, J., & White, R. (1998). Young people, social problems and Australian youth studies. *Journal of Youth Studies*, 1, 23–38.

Yau, M. (1995). Refugee students in Toronto schools : an exploratory study. Toronto : Research Services, Toronto Board of Education.

Yusuf, Z. (1995). *West-end Somali women need assessment*. Ottawa: Pinecrest-Queensway Health and Community Services.

Zamana Foundation. (1997). *A project to assess the needs of South Asian community in the Greater Toronto area*. Summer project funded by Employment Centre for Students, HRDC. Toronto: Zamana Foundation.

Zhou, M. & Bankston, C.L. (1998). Social capital and the adaptation of the second generation: The case of Vietnamese youth in New Orleans. *International Migration Review*, xxviii(4), 821–845.

———. (1998). *Growing Up American: How Vietnamese Children Adapt to Life in the United States*. New York: Russell Sage Foundation.

Zine, J. (1997). *Muslim students in public school: Education and the politics of religious identity*. Master's thesis. Toronto: Ontario Institute for Studies in Education, University of Toronto.

APPENDIX I

FOCUS GROUP QUESTIONS
AND SURVEY INSTRUMENTS:
Family Service Association Study

The focus groups questions were developed and employed as follows:

For youth focus groups, five key questions were chosen to cover some of the most important aspects of their settlement, adaptation, and integration process:

1. personal experiences and major difficulties on first arrival and current problems
2. differences between their lifestyle inside and outside the family, confusion in values, conflicts over desires to adapt to Canadian values, and friendships
3. types of help needed and asked for or given from different sources (family members, schools, churches, members of the same ethnic groups, community organizations, and institutional service providers)
4. suggestions for improvements in services for newcomer youth based on their personal experiences and perspectives
5. any other areas of the settlement, adaptation, and integration process not covered

For the parental focus groups, we chose seven key questions to cover their own experiences of settlement, as well as their perceptions of the challenges their children faced:

1. personal experiences and major difficulties on first arrival as well as current problems
2. the ways that parents maintain their children's original culture and their view of their children's need to adopt the values, beliefs, and behaviours of the dominant culture
3. how parents adapt (change or remain the same) to their new environment
4. forms of communication with their children
5. the ways that parents control and discipline their children
6. types of help needed and asked for or given from different sources (family members, schools, churches, members of the same ethnic groups, community organizations, and institutional service providers)
7. suggestions for improvements in services to newcomer youth and their families

The *demographic questionnaire*, as a semi-structured instrument, covered questions related to sex, grade, length of stay in Canada, immigration status in Canada, reasons for migration, and official language proficiency. It also covered parental marital status, parental education background, parental employment status in Canada, participants' and parental level of stresses experienced at the time of arrival in Canada, the nature of stresses experienced, possible health changes as a result of stresses experienced, help-seeking behaviours, use of existing settlement services, and suggestions for settlement service improvement.

The *adaptation response scale* consisted of twenty-four hypothetical situations relevant to newcomer youth's everyday life in Canada. The hypothetical situations were created and used in this scale to record the participants' varied experiences and the range of their responses and coping strategies in response to these situations. The situations were divided into four areas: outside life, family life, social life, and personal life.

The following situations are examples of outside life situations: "While waiting at a red light in the car, together with two friends, and listening to songs from your home country, a pedestrian approachs the car and, through an open window, sarcastically comments: 'What a stupid noise. . . . Is something wrong with either that CD or the car's speakers?'" and "You brought old newspapers in your language of origin to your local neighbourhood centre that collects old newspapers, and a collection person says to you: 'Oh, I am sorry, but these newspapers are garbage, not recyclable.'"

The following situations are examples of family life situations: "Your father, who was a well-known professional in his field in your home country, is informed that he got a job in Canada as a security guard" and "Your parents/guardians are refusing to participate in your class project named 'Families together,' which proposes bringing ethnic and mainstream families together to share and discuss parenting issues."

The following situations are examples of social life situations: "Popular Canadian media negatively portrays your original nation" and "You are listening to a call-in radio program in which a few immigrant activists are talking about equity and human rights in Canada, but the telephone responses from many listeners are: 'If immigrants are not satisfied with human rights and democracy in Canada, why don't they go back to their home countries?'"

The following situations are examples of personal life situations: "You just realized that some of your mainstream peers from your school said a lot of untruths about you and that they made fun of you," and "You are preoccupied with the dream, that you had a few days ago, in which you burned the Canadian flag and tried to hide out, but was arrested."

The possible responses/answers were divided into four different categories: physical, emotional, cognitive, and passive. Each consisted of three separate responses/answers, which were marked from A to L. Physical responses included: (A) I start to tremble, (B) I become red/blush, and (C) I feel my heart beats harder. Emotional responses included: (D) I get angry/upset—I swear, (E) I become sad, and (F) I feel a big tension. Cognitive responses included: (G) I will learn a lesson, (H) I am patient/calm, and (I) I can control myself. Passive responses included: (J) I don't care, (K) I will pray, and (L) I will put it off.

The number of responses was not limited, so participants could choose as many responses or answers as they felt necessary to describe their true reaction to the situation.

The *personal satisfaction scale* was a twenty-item measure of personal satisfaction consisting of a ten-item subscale of positively worded elements and a ten-item subscale of negatively worded elements. The following examples are from the positively worded subscale: "In Canada, I am satisfied with how I am doing in school" and "I feel that in my new life in Canada, I make full use of my whole potentials (abilities)." Items from the negatively worded subscale included elements such as "In Canada I feel like a stranger lost in a new city who is in need of a map for help in reaching his/her destinations" and "I ignore my problems and think about other things."

The *satisfaction with parents/guardians scale* was a twenty-item measure of satisfaction with parents/guardians consisting of a ten-item subscale of positively worded elements and a ten-item subscale of negatively worded elements. The following items are examples of the positively worded subscale: "My parents/guardians are open to and allow me to be friends with my peers/classmates from other cultures/nationalities" and "The bond that I have with my parents/guardians has helped to make me a confident, secure, and effective (intelligent) human being." Examples are from the negatively worded subscale included: "I feel that my parents/guardians and I represent two different worlds in Canada. I am changing, but they are remaining the same" and "I am afraid that my parents/guardians could desert me because of changes due to my acculturation and adaptation in Canada."

The *satisfaction with classmates scale* was a twenty-item measure of satisfaction with classmates. Again, it consisted of a ten-item subscale of positively worded elements and a ten-item subscale of negatively worded elements. Examples of positive wording included: "I feel comfortable sharing my interests, values, beliefs, and attitudes with my mainstream classmates" and "My mainstream classmates see me as an interesting individual." Typical negative elements were: "It is only wishful thinking to believe that my mainstream classmates would accept me as a real friend" and "I find talking about smoking, alcohol drinking, my sexual activities, risk-driving, etc., are the easiest ways to seek comfort and affirmation among my mainstream classmates."

The *satisfaction with school/teachers scale* was a twenty-item measure of satisfaction with school/teachers. Once more, it was composed of a ten-item subscale of positively worded elements and a ten-item subscale of negatively worded elements. Positively worded examples included: "I view my school as a safe and welcoming environment" and "My school provides me with both a solid knowledge base and motivation to plan and strive for my continuing education." Negatively worded examples included: "I feel that my teachers do not understand how I feel as an immigrant adolescent experiencing settlement, adaptation, and other relevant changes in my life" and "I experience difficulties in identifying with my school values or following the school discipline rules."

The *attitudes toward Canadian society scale* was a twenty-item measure of attitudes toward Canadian society, again with a ten-point subscale of positively worded items and another ten-point subscale of negatively worded items. Examples of the former included: "There is equity and justice for all in Canadian society, with plenty of opportunities" and "In Canadian society, values of multiculturalism and inclusion are highly recognized and practised." Typical of the latter were: "Canadian environment is a harmful (place) that is unpredictable and full of worry and uncertainty" and "There is a significant gap in Canadian society between governmental policies about immigrants and implementation and realization of these policies in real life (or at the local community level)."

The *settlement and adaptation outcomes scale* was a twenty-item measure of settlement and adaptation outcomes, once more with a positively worded ten-point subscale and a negatively worded ten-point subscale. Typical elements from the former were: "I experience many interesting, rewarding, and pleasant things that are happening to me in my new life in Canada" and "I feel that I am well adapted and integrated, and as a result that I have a positive and satisfying life in Canada." Examples of the latter were: "I am confused about what I, as an adolescent immigrant, am supposed to look like and act like in my new Canadian environment" and "I feel that I will always be considered a stranger in Canada."

For the 5 above 20-point measures of satisfaction, responses were on a 5-point Likert-type scale anchored by (1) strongly disagree,

(2) somewhat disagree, (3) neutral, (4) somewhat agree, and (5) strongly agree. Participants could choose only one of these five answers for each item.

Youth self-report (YSR) is a well-known and well-researched, psychometrically sound scale comprising 112 items developed by Achenbach and Edelbrock (1991). It is used to assess specific youth behaviour and provides information of their functioning within a number of areas. An adolescent rates different items as 0, 1, or 2.

In our study we were concerned with the participants' responses to several items representing three global constructs that generalize from the instrument. The first construct is that of "total behaviour problems" representing an amalgamation of behaviour issues, including social problems, thought problems, and attention problems, all related to the adolescent's ability to handle himself or herself in an interpersonal context. The other two constructs were called "internalizing symptomatology" and "externalizing symptomatology." The former construct was an amalgamation of internal behaviour problems such as withdrawal, somatic complaints, and anxiety/depression. The latter construct represented a cluster of overt behaviour problems such as delinquency and aggression. The YSR appears to have adequate reliability with test-retest reliability coefficients ranging from .82 to .90 (Achenbach & Edelbrock, 1991).

Draw a human figure test (DHFT), developed by Machover (1949), is one of the most popular and commonly used personality measurement instruments. In our research, we used the DHFT only as a screening tool, based on the interpretations of human figure drawings in Machover (1949), Abt and Bellak (1950), and McElhaney (1969) to provide some general information about the participants' personality characteristics that might affect their settlement, adaptation, and integration. We used the DHFT because it is free from cultural bias and easy to administer.

The administration was as follows. A participant was given a blank sheet of paper, pencil, and eraser and asked to draw a human figure. After finishing, the participant was given another blank sheet of paper and asked to draw another human figure of the opposite sex. From the variety of formal scoring systems developed for the DHFT, our research focused on: (1) the size of the figure, which is associated with the person's self-concept and relationship with his or her environment; (2) the location (placement) of the figure, which is associated with subjective feelings that may imply a certain direction to the person's orientation system; (3) distortions and omissions on the drawing, suggestive of conflicts related to the part distorted or missed; and (4) other significant indicators associated with potentially serious personal problems.

APPENDIX II

DETAILS OF THE QUANTITATIVE RESEARCH

THE ADAPTATION RESPONSE SCALE

A reliability analysis was conducted for each of the scales (physical response, emotional response, cognitive response, and passive response) to test the reliability of the measure. Each of the scales resulted in a Cronbach's alpha (α) over .82 (physical response scale: $\alpha=.8858$; emotional response scale: $\alpha=.8337$; cognitive response scale: '.8710; passive response scale: $\alpha=.8289$).

Each scale could range from 0 to 24. Table One shows the mean scores for each of the four response scales.

TABLE ONE: MEANS AND STANDARD DEVIATIONS FOR THE FOUR RESPONSE SCALES

Scale	Mean	Standard Deviation	Min.	Max.	N
Physical response	3.69	4.52	0	24	300
Emotional response	11.70	5.22	0	24	300
Cognitive response	7.05	5.45	0	24	300
Passive response	8.67	5.04	0	24	300

Table Two shows the correlations among ratings of the four responses to the new life situations offered (outside life, family life, social life, and personal life).

TABLE TWO: CORRELATIONS AMONG THE FOUR RESPONSE
SCALES TO THE NEW LIFE SITUATIONS OFFERED
(outside life, family life, social life, and personal life)

	Physical Response	Emotional Response	Cognitive Response	Passive Response
Physical response	1.000	.383**	.245**	-.169**
Emotional response			.114*	-.292**
Cognitive response				-.132*
Passive response				1.000

Notes: * Pearson Correlation is significant at the 0.05 level (2-tailed).
     ** Pearson Correlation is significant at the 0.01 level (2-tailed).

Table Two shows a significant correlation among all of the measures. The coefficient of correlation indicates both the direction and the strengths of linear relationships between the four scale responses. The above calculated correlation coefficients confirm that there is an association (either positive or negative) between the four types of adaptive responses to the new life situations (outside life, family life, social life, and personal life) that the youth experience in their everyday life in their new Canadian environment. Thus, the positive correlations between any two scales indicate that the participants scoring higher on one scale tend to do so on another, while a negative correlation between two scales indicates an inverse association.

To determine if there were any significant differences between the means of the six sample groups and the responses to new life situations offered (outside life, family life, social life, and personal life), a one-way analysis of variance (ANOVA) was conducted. To allow for the analysis of multiple dependent measures, ANOVA was tested at $p<.01$. If a significant relationship resulted from the ANOVA, it was followed by post-hoc tests using the Tukey's HSD (honestly significant difference) test at $p<.05$ to examine the specific nature of the groups' differences and determine the multiple comparisons between the sample groups.

The one-way ANOVA suggests that only the emotional response scale to the new life situations offered (outside life, family life, social life, and personal life) was significantly different for the sample groups (F=8.307; df=5; p<.000). Table Three shows the results of the post-hoc test.

TABLE THREE: POST-HOC TEST: RESPONSES TO THE NEW LIFE SITUATIONS (outside life, family life, social life, and personal life)

		Mean Difference (between groups)
EUR	CSA	-5.24*
	CHI	-1.22
	CAR	-4.48*
	SEA	-3.48*
	AFR	-2.00
CSA	EUR	5.24*
	CHI	4.02*
	CAR	.76
	SEA	1.76
	AFR	3.24*
CHI	EUR	1.22
	CSA	-4.02*
	CAR	-3.25*
	SEA	-2.26
	AFR	-.78
CAR	EUR	4.48*
	CSA	-.76
	CHI	3.26*
	SEA	1.00
	AFR	2.48
SEA	EUR	3.48*
	CSA	-1.76
	CHI	2.26
	CAR	-1.00
	AFR	1.48
AFR	EUR	2.00
	CSA	-3.24*
	CHI	.78
	CAR	-2.48
	SEA	-1.48

Notes: AFR = African, CAR = Caribbean, CSA = Central and South American, CHI = Chinese, EUR = Eastern European, SEA = South East Asian
(* significant difference)

According to Table Three, a follow-up Tukey test shows significant differences among the different groups related to their emotional response to their new life situations. For example, the negative coefficient of the Tukey's test (-5.24), which shows a significant difference between the European and Central and South American groups, indicates that the participants in the European group were less likely to react emotionally to their new life situations (outside life, family life, social life, and personal life) than those from the Central and South American group. Like their peers in the Caribbean group, they were responding differently to their challenges and problems and did not have the same degree of emotional responses.

The results were essentially the same for the post-hoc testing between the European group and the Caribbean and the South East Asian groups. There was no difference between the European group and the Chinese or the African groups. The Central and South American group was more likely to have an emotional response to the new life situations/problems than the Chinese group and the African group. The Chinese group was less likely to have an emotional response than the Caribbean group or African group.

PARTICIPANTS' SATISFACTION WITH DIFFERENT ASPECTS OF THEIR LIVES IN CANADA

The satisfaction measures in our study covered the following six aspects of our participants' new life in Canada: (1) personal, (2) parents/guardians, (3) classmates, (4) school/teachers, (5) attitudes toward Canadian society, and (6) settlement and adaptation outcomes. The participants were asked to provide a rating on a 5-point Likert scale—from "strongly disagree" (1) to "strongly agree" (5)—for twenty statements related to these six aspects. Each series of statements contained positive and negative situations; negative items were recoded for the analysis.

Reliability analysis was conducted for each set of the twenty questions pertaining to the six aspects of satisfaction with life in Canada. The Cronbach's alpha for each aspect suggests that the measures are reliable: Personal scale $\alpha=.7605$; parent/guardian scale $\alpha=.7738$; classmates scale $\alpha=.8332$; school/teachers scale $\alpha=.7941$; attitudes toward Canadian society scale $\alpha = .7251$; and settlement and adaptation outcomes scale $\alpha = .8765$.

Each scale ranged from 0 (total dissatisfaction) to 80 (total satisfaction). Table Four shows the mean and SD scores for each of the six scales.

TABLE FOUR: DESCRIPTIVE STATISTICS FOR SATISFACTION WITH LIFE IN CANADA

Scale	Mean	Standard Deviation	Min.	Max.	N
Personal	52.82	9.49	25	75	300
Parents/guardian	49.25	9.83	15	73	300
Classmates	53.49	11.17	15	79	300
School/teacher	48.78	9.71	5	75	300
Attitude toward Canadian society	42.61	8.13	7	78	300
Settlement outcome	54.01	12.34	15	79	300

Table Five shows the correlations among the measures of satisfaction with life in Canada for newcomer youth.

TABLE FIVE: CORRELATION AMONG THE MEASURES OF SATISFACTION WITH THE NEW LIFE IN CANADA SCALES

	Personal	Parent	Classmates	School/ Teacher	Attitudes	Settlement Outcomes
Personal	1.000	.577**	.625**	.461**	.237**	.568**
Parent/guardians			.537**	.419**	.199**	.483**
Classmates				.520**	.194**	.696**
School/teacher					.331**	.545**
Attitude						.188**
Settlement outcomes						1.000

Note: ** Pearson correlation is significant at the 0.01 level (2-tailed).

We also measured the correlations (associations) between the six different measures of the satisfaction with different aspects of life in Canada and the stress levels reported for the beginning of the participants' life in Canada as recorded in the demographic questionnaire. In this questionnaire participants had rated their stress levels from 0 to 10, with 0 indicating no stress at all and 10 very high stress. Table Six shows the correlations between these reported levels of stress and the indicated measures of satisfaction with various aspects of the participants' new lives.

TABLE SIX: CORRELATIONS OF STRESS LEVELS AT THE BEGINNING OF LIFE IN CANADA AND SATISFACTION WITH LIFE IN CANADA

	Personal	Parent/ Guardian	Classmates	School/ Teacher	Attitudes	Settlement Outcomes
Participants' stress at beginning of life in Canada	-.132*	-.179*	-.089	-.067	-.058	-.093

Notes: * Pearson Correlation is significant at the 0.05 level (2-tailed).
     ** Pearson Correlation is significant at the 0.01 level (2-tailed).

While all of the above calculated correlations are negative, only two of them are significant, indicating weak negative correlations between stresses experienced at the beginning of their new life in Canada and both personal satisfaction and satisfaction with parents/guardians.

To determine if there were any significant differences between the sample groups with respect to the measures of different types of satisfaction with the participants' new lives in Canada, a one-way analysis of variance (ANOVA) was conducted. To allow for the analysis of multiple dependent measures, ANOVA was tested at $p < .01$. If a significant relationship was revealed by the ANOVA testing, we followed up with post-hoc tests using the Tukey's HSD (honestly significant difference) test at $p < .05$ to examine specific differences and determine the multiple comparisons between the sample groups.

The one-way ANOVA suggests that only the satisfaction with classmates ($F = 4.70$; $df = 5$; $p < .000$) and satisfaction with settlement and adaptational outcomes ($F = 3.28$; $df = 5$; $p < .007$) were significantly different for the sample groups. The post-hoc tests were done for both satisfaction with classmates, and settlement and adaptation outcomes. Table Seven shows the results of the post-hoc test calculated for satisfaction with classmates.

TABLE SEVEN: POST-HOC TEST: SATISFACTION WITH CLASSMATES BY SAMPLE GROUPS

		Mean Difference (between groups)
EUR	CSA	-2.14
	CHI	5.80
	CAR	2.48
	SEA	4.72
	AFR	5.98
CSA	EUR	2.14
	CHI	7.94*
	CAR	4.62
	SEA	6.86*
	AFR	8.12*
CHI	EUR	-5.80
	CSA	-7.94*
	CAR	-3.32
	SEA	-1.08
	AFR	.18
CAR	EUR	-2.48
	CSA	-4.62
	CHI	3.32
	SEA	2.24
	AFR	3.50
SEA	EUR	-4.72
	CSA	-6.86*
	CHI	1.08
	CAR	-2.24
	AFR	1.26
AFR	EUR	-5.98
	CSA	-8.12*
	CHI	-.18
	CAR	-3.50
	SEA	-1.26

Notes: AFR = African, CAR = Caribbean, CSA = Central and South American, CHI = Chinese, EUR = Eastern European, SEA = South East Asian
* significant difference

TABLE EIGHT: POST-HOC TEST: SETTLEMENT AND ADAPTATION OUTCOMES BY SAMPLE GROUPS

		Mean Difference (between groups)
EUR	CSA	-4.56
	CHI	2.94
	CAR	-.90
	SEA	.56
	AFR	4.30
CSA	EUR	4.56
	CHI	7.50*
	CAR	3.66
	SEA	5.12
	AFR	8.86*
CHI	EUR	-2.94
	CSA	-7.50*
	CAR	-3.84
	SEA	-2.38
	AFR	1.36
CAR	EUR	.90
	CSA	-3.66
	CHI	3.84
	SEA	1.46
	AFR	5.20
SEA	EUR	-.56
	CSA	-5.12
	CHI	2.38
	CAR	-1.46
	AFR	3.74
AFR	EUR	-4.30
	CSA	-8.86*
	CHI	-1.36
	CAR	-5.20
	SEA	-3.74

Notes: AFR = African, CAR = Caribbean, CSA = Central and South American, CHI = Chinese, EUR = Eastern European, SEA = South East Asian
* significant difference

The results of the follow-up Tukey test outlined in Table Seven show that for the European and Caribbean groups, the reported level of satisfaction with their classmates is not significantly different than that for the other sample groups. They also reveal a significant difference in reported level of satisfaction between the Central and South American group and the other three groups. The positive coefficients indicating significant differences suggest that the participants in the Central and South American group are more likely to be satisfied with their classmates than those in the Chinese, South East Asian, and African groups.

Table Eight shows the results of the post-hoc test calculated for settlement and adaptation outcomes.

Table Eight shows no significant differences with respect to the settlement and adaptation measure for each of the European, Caribbean, or South East Asian groups in comparison with any of the other groups. For the Central and South American group, however, there are significant differences in comparison with two other groups. These positive coefficients indicating significant differences suggest that the participants in the Central and South American group are more likely to be satisfied with their settlement and adaptation outcomes than the participants in the Chinese and African groups.

PERSONALITY CHARACTERISTICS AS FACTORS THAT AFFECT THE SETTLEMENT, ADAPTATION, AND INTEGRATION OF NEWCOMER IMMIGRANT AND REFUGEE YOUTH

Using the youth self-report (YSR) data, we developed a separate comparison for males and females with normative data for randomly selected peers from the youth self-report instrument (standardization sample). YSR provides several subscale scores, but only a total behaviour problem score. For our study we used the internalizing (e.g., anxious, depressed, withdrawal) and externalizing (e.g., delinquent problems, aggression) scores as two indicators/dimensions of dysfunction.

Table Nine illustrates the separate mean scores for boys, for girls, and for boys and girls combined on the three measures (total behaviour problem scale, internalizing scale, and externalizing scale).

TABLE NINE: MEANS AND STANDARD DEVIATIONS FOR BOYS AND GIRLS ON YSR

Total Behaviour	Internalizing	Externalizing	Problem Scale
Boys (N'130)			
Mean	56.74*	57.91***	57.64
SD	11.02	9.54	9.81
Exceeding 90th percentile	28 (21.5%)	27 (20.7%)	14 (10.8%)
Girls (N'170)			
Mean	53.19	54.00	48.93
SD	7.95	9.87	7.71
Exceeding 90th percentile	21 (12.4%)	35 (20.6%)	18 (10.6%)
Boys and Girls (N'300)			
Mean	55.12**	55.69**	50.87
SD	9.87	9.81	8.98
Exceeding 90th percentile	49 (16.3%)	62 (20.1%)	32 (10.7%)

Notes: * p<.10; **p<.05; *** p<.01

On the total behaviour problems scale, significant differences from the randomly selected peers (standardization sample) were found for YSR for boys and girls together (t=2.08; p<.05) and for boys alone (t=1.90; p<.10). No significant differences were found for girls alone. Similarly, on the internalizing scale there were significant differences for boys and girls together (t=2.35; p<.05) and boys alone (t=2.89; p<.01), and none for girls. For the externalizing scale there were no significant differences for boys, or girls, or boys and girls together.

In interpreting this data with respect to the settlement outcomes for newcomer youth, we have to be aware that the (measured) rates of adaptation within a population vary with the criteria of adaptation that is established. For analysis of the data from the YSR instrument, we adapted a criterion employed by Heller et al. (1985). A score above the 90th percentile (score>=63) was set as the criterion or cutoff point for an indication of adaptation difficulties. About one-fifth of the participants exceeded the cutoff point on the total behaviour scale, and about one-sixth on the total internalizing scale. The rate for the externalizing problems scale was considerably lower— only about one-tenth of the participants.

Index